D0107421

STRATEGIC ASIA 2016–17

STRATEGIC ASIA 2016–17

UNDERSTANDING STRATEGIC CULTURES

in the Asia-Pacific

Edited by

Ashley J. Tellis, Alison Szalwinski, and Michael Wills

With contributions from

Jiun Bang, Alexis Dudden, Colin Dueck, Isabelle Facon,
Christopher A. Ford, Ian Hall, David C. Kang,
Yohanes Sulaiman, and Ashley J. Tellis

 NBR THE NATIONAL BUREAU *of* ASIAN RESEARCH
Seattle and Washington, D.C.

THE NATIONAL BUREAU *of* ASIAN RESEARCH

Published in the United States of America by
The National Bureau of Asian Research, Seattle, WA, and Washington, D.C.
www.nbr.org

Copyright © 2016 by The National Bureau of Asian Research

All rights reserved. No part of this publication may be reproduced, stored in a retrieval system, or transmitted in any form or by any means, electronic, mechanical, photocopying, recording, or otherwise, without prior permission of the publisher.

ISBN (print): 978-1-939131-46-1
ISBN (electronic): 978-1-939131-47-8

Cover images

Front: Go Game © fpm/iStock

Back (left to right): Shadow, or wayang, puppets, Ubud, Bali © John W. Banagan/Getty Images; Still image taken from the May 21, 2015, video "U.S. Navy P-8A Poseidon flies over new islands in South China Sea" ⊖ U.S. Navy video/Released; The archer © David Pedre/iStock; Japanese Maritime Self-Defense destroyer Fuyuzuki transits into formation during a photo exercise as a part of Exercise Malabar 2015 ⊖ U.S. Navy photo by Mass Communication Specialist 2nd Class Chris Brown/Released

Design and publishing services by The National Bureau of Asian Research

Cover design by Stefanie Choi

Publisher's Cataloging-In-Publication Data
(Prepared by The Donohue Group, Inc.)

Names: Tellis, Ashley J., editor. | Szalwinski, Alison, editor. | Wills, Michael, 1970- editor. | Bang, Jiun, contributor. | National Bureau of Asian Research (U.S.)

Title: Understanding strategic cultures in the Asia-Pacific / edited by Ashley J. Tellis, Alison Szalwinski, and Michael Wills ; with contributions from Jiun Bang [and 8 others].

Other Titles: Strategic Asia ; 2016-17.

Description: Seattle ; Washington, D.C. : The National Bureau of Asian Research, [2016] | Series: Strategic Asia ; 2016-17 | Includes bibliographical references and index.

Identifiers: ISBN 978-1-939131-46-1 (print) | ISBN 978-1-939131-47-8 (electronic)

Subjects: LCSH: Asia--Military policy--History. | Asia--Defenses--History. | Asia--Foreign relations--United States. | United States--Military policy--History. | United States--Defenses--History. | United States--Foreign relations--Asia.

Classification: LCC UA830 .U54 2016 (print) | LCC UA830 (ebook) | DDC 355.0331095--dc23

Printed in Canada

The paper used in this publication meets the minimum requirement of the American National Standard for Information Sciences—Permanence of Paper for Printed Library Materials, ANSI Z39.48-1992.

Contents

Preface

Richard J. Ellings

Strategic culture comprises the set of factors that influence strategic decisions, helping us understand why leaders make the choices they do. This analytical approach complements assessments of states' sources of power, international distributions of capabilities, and webs of interdependencies. As Ashley Tellis points out in his chapter overviewing this volume, strategic culture is the ideational frame of reference of elites that shapes their countries' ambitions and determines how their countries understand the strategic environment and limitations of power in competitive politics. This edition of *Strategic Asia* is an important one, for it aims to do two things: (1) make an intellectual contribution to the field of international relations by exploring critically the concept of strategic culture and (2) apply this concept to elucidate contemporary affairs at the center of world power.

Every nation has its founding myths, classic texts, unique historical attributes, continuing influences, and other political and social influences that make up its complex and evolving strategic culture. In turn, this culture shapes the behavior of the nation's elites. Some of these cultural influences, even the games people play, can provide striking insights. Chess is about the clash of forces, a decisive battle with the goal of securing total victory over one's opponent. In contrast, the ancient Chinese game of *weiqi*, or Go, portrayed on this volume's front cover, is a game of relative gain and long-range encirclement, which starts with an empty board and ebbs and flows until a winner finally achieves a partial victory. Henry Kissinger believes that understanding the tactics of weiqi is crucial to comprehending Chinese strategy in both warfare and business.[1] In fact, the differences between chess and weiqi constitute one of the many examples

---

[1] Henry Kissinger, *On China* (New York: Penguin Books, 2011).

of the divergence in strategic thinking that has evolved over the centuries between Europe and Asia.

David Lai sees a direct connection between weiqi and Chinese statecraft. He states that "weiqi is a living reflection of China's nuanced culture—its strategy, thought, philosophy, and operational tactics. One can almost read *The Art of War* and then play it on the board."[2] A famous manifestation is Deng Xiaoping's foreign policy directive to "secure our position; cope with affairs calmly; hide our capacities and bide our time; be good at maintaining a low profile"—that is, to position China advantageously over time by focusing on the development of economic and military power before expressing China's ambitions. A more recent example is Beijing's step-by-step approach—moving forward where there is no effective resistance—to asserting Chinese power in the western Pacific by island building and using quasi- or actual military vessels to probe resistance to, or to simply assert, Chinese sovereignty. Two other current examples are the Asian Infrastructure Investment Bank (AIIB) and the One Belt, One Road (OBOR) initiative. Both are long-term programs aimed to integrate smaller surrounding countries more deeply into the Chinese economy by building relevant capacity in those countries, thereby adding to China's economic strength, regional influence in strategic corridors, and reputation for leadership in international affairs. With or without reference to weiqi, of course, one could argue that all these policies were logical things for China to do, but the analogy gives the observer the sense that this ancient game influences the way Chinese strategists think and act.

China's strategic culture is as rich as that of any nation in the world, imbuing Chinese statesmen with lessons learned from hundreds of generations. Important elements of this culture are rooted in the 19th, 20th, and early 21st centuries as well, adding experiences of humiliation at the hands of foreigners and of inevitable national resurgence to the traditional ones of enduring, deserved greatness and careful strategic positioning. The deep grievances from Western and Japanese domination, the "third way" internationalism of the Bandung Conference, the unease with radical ideas inherited from the Cultural Revolution, and the country's astonishing industrialization and the associated rise of Chinese nationalism in recent decades are all aspects of China's changing strategic culture.

There is tension among cultural aspects in part because of the political system. In the absence of democratic elections, and with endemic corruption and the slowdown of China's economic growth, Chinese Communist Party (CCP) leaders face questions of legitimacy. Xi Jinping and his faction have

---

[2] Keith Johnson, "What Kind of Game Is China Playing?" *Wall Street Journal*, June 11, 2011.

answered with relentless efforts to bolster the party's grip on power through actions and words that appeal to patriotism and the desire for justice. The latter is reflected in a wide-reaching anticorruption campaign, purge, and repression of dissidents. Consequently, Xi has become the most powerful leader of China since Deng. In addition, by championing the "China dream" (the re-establishment of China's preeminence internationally), rapidly developing military and space capabilities, asserting Chinese influence abroad, and promoting one historical memory over another, the party is seeking to enhance its and the country's power and in doing so embellish its legacy. This helps explain, for instance, the rapid island- and base-building in the South China Sea, the CCP's ongoing emphasis on the superiority of the party's policies and Chinese accomplishments compared with those of the United States, and the vilification of Japan regardless of the day-to-day ebbs and flows in actual Sino-Japanese relations. A central question for foreign observers concerns the tension between Deng's approach to "bide our time" and the pressures today's leaders feel (and have fed) to move more decisively to attain the "China dream."

Chess fell somewhat out of favor among Russians toward the end of the Soviet Union. Today, however, with a recent boost from the top leadership, Russians are repopularizing the game at home, and, arguably, playing it abroad as one of the game's strongest adherents, Vladimir Putin, engineers bold moves in Eastern Europe, the Middle East, and Asia. In the culture of chess, these moves appear aimed to protect and advance Russian positions and, ultimately, to outmaneuver the opponent (the United States), break its concentration and will, and defeat its positions. "Biding one's time" and "maintaining a low profile" do not describe Putin's grand strategy.

Elements of strategic culture can lie dormant in a nation's collective subconscious for decades before re-emerging. Eurasianism, an early twentieth-century philosophy that originated in the post-revolution Russian émigré society in Paris in the 1920s, albeit with much earlier roots, was the idea that Russia's identity was closer to Asian rather than Western European culture. The ideology seemingly died a natural death in the 1950s, but it re-emerged in the 1990s and found a widespread following among both the Russian intelligentsia and Vladimir Putin's inner circle in the 2000s, much to the chagrin of "westernizers" in Russian policymaking circles. Moscow's relations with the West have been precarious since at least the Georgian war of 2008, but they completely collapsed after Russia annexed Crimea and invaded eastern Ukraine in 2014. Under these conditions, key members of the Russian intellectual elite, already familiar with the major precepts of Eurasianism, vigorously advocated Russia's own "pivot to Asia." Their voices resonated with the top echelons of the Russian leadership, which sought a return to greatness in the wake of the collapse of the Soviet Union.

Initially, the pivot was meant to include all of Asia, but the nature of Japan's and South Korea's alliances with the United States has thus far prevented Moscow from developing a closer relationship with either Tokyo or Seoul (although there have been indications that this may be changing). Consequently, the Russian pivot to Asia has been largely confined to China and, to a lesser extent, Vietnam, Mongolia, and India. The results are more evident by the day, as the pivot raises the possibility of a major paradigm shift with broad implications for the rest of the world. Among key developments are the agreement on the construction of a natural gas pipeline between Russia and China (which had previously been mired in negotiations for more than a decade), the decision to integrate the Eurasian Economic Union with the OBOR initiative, and China's financing of several major projects in Russia. Russia and China also have increased collaboration in the Shanghai Cooperation Organisation, sided with each other on numerous occasions in the United Nations and other multilateral forums, and increased their military cooperation, including through joint exercises in the South China Sea. Moreover, the two powers support and enable one another on controversial issues such as Russia's interventions in Syria and Ukraine (to which China turned a blind eye) and China's assertive policy in the western Pacific.

Russia's pivot toward Asia coincided with China's own pivot toward Eurasia, first articulated in 2012 by Wang Jisi in his proposal that China rebalance its geopolitical strategy by "marching westward." Beijing accelerated this westward shift in 2013 in the ambitious OBOR initiative that seeks to connect China to Europe and the Middle East through a series of both maritime and land-based infrastructure projects. The AIIB, launched in October 2014, broadened the scope of China's efforts to play a leading role in the economic and political order of Eurasia, this time focusing not just westward but to the east and south as well. In this respect, Russia's pivot to Asia partially aligns, if uncomfortably due to colliding interests, with China's own geo-economic goals.

China's and Russia's national identities, and subsequently strategic cultures, are much closer to one another than is often judged, and they may be growing even closer.[3] There are macrosocietal synergies between the two nations. Geographically, China and Russia share a 4,000-kilometer border that was fully demarcated in 2008. Neither Moscow nor Beijing is interested in territorial gains in Northeast Asia at this time, and both desire bilateral

---

[3] Gilbert Rozman, *The Sino-Russian Challenge to the World Order: National Identities, Bilateral Relations, and East versus West in the 2010s* (Washington, D.C.: Woodrow Wilson Center Press, 2014).

economic cooperation in the development of the decrepit Russian Far East and China's adjacent northeastern provinces. As such, the border area is more a shared interest than an impediment to a productive Sino-Russian relationship. From a historical perspective, the bilateral relationship has experienced both periods of genuine friendship, such as in the 1950s, and periods of deep animosity, such as with the "unequal treaties" of the late nineteenth century and the Sino-Soviet rift of the 1960s. However, the two states share a surprising number of historical similarities. Both Russia and China harken back to periods of great empires when they each exercised hegemony over vast territories in Eurasia. In the twentieth century, both countries were rocked by social revolutions that resulted in the formation of totalitarian states. The two were allies against a common enemy in World War II and competed against the United States in the Cold War. These complementary histories have seeped into the broader cultures of Russia and China. The two societies hold traditional cultural and authoritarian values, are suspicious of a free press, have educational systems based on the same paradigm, and perhaps most importantly, view themselves as distinctly separate from the West's cultural ethos. These similarities are augmented by political characteristics. The authoritarian systems of Russia and China have much in common, especially now that both states are led by a deeply entrenched autocrat whose primary basis of legitimacy is embodying his people's rising national aspirations. These two leaders, Putin and Xi, come from the same postwar generation (being born only six months apart) and seem to have developed a working relationship that is conducive to broader collaboration. Both prize national strength, national feeling, and regime stability ahead of everything else, and utilize paramilitary forces, sophisticated propaganda, and cyberattacks to stifle dissent at home and assert power abroad. They repress once-vibrant civil societies in their countries and target selected expatriates for intimidation or worse. In both states, the decision-making apparatus is controlled by a small coterie of elites who combine business interests with their public duties.

Still, the Sino-Russian partnership is not a full strategic alliance, either formally or in a deeply rooted commitment. Lingering beneath the surface of friendly gestures, speeches, and policies is a general misunderstanding of one another, along with undercurrents of mutual distrust and important conflicting national interests. The two countries clash in some dimensions of their strategic cultures—with different self-images of greatness and humiliation, dissimilar notions of imperial roles, and varying perspectives on the emerging world order. Their political systems do not operate identically, with China's leaders exhibiting more group consultation and decision-making. And no scale of student exchange, language education, and conscientious trust building is likely to overcome the geopolitical competition inherent in sharing the bulk of the Eurasian landmass. Nonetheless, even if long-term alignment is unlikely, cooperation can serve compelling short- and medium-term purposes with crucial strategic implications, such as thwarting U.S. alliances in Europe and Asia and weakening American resolve. It will be important, as we watch the Sino-Russian relationship unfold, to understand how the two countries' strategic cultures—their histories, worldviews, and political circumstances, among other factors—inform their bilateral relations.

The full implications of this emerging Sino-Russian alignment for both U.S. policy and the other countries discussed in this volume are beyond the scope of this preface. Suffice to note, first, that Sino-Russian relations loom large in world affairs. To better understand the potential salience of the bilateral relationship, one only has to ponder the international power shifts and strategic cultural conditions under which a Sino-Russian entente might develop into a vanguard of neo-authoritarianism—a modern-day axis of reactionary states challenging the United States and the liberal order. One has to search hard for more pressing topics in international relations than that of Sino-Russian relations.[4] Second, understanding geopolitical positions, the international distribution of capabilities, and the strategic cultures in China and Russia will provide the United States and its allies with options to temper the threatening aspects of Sino-Russian collaboration, highlight the positive aspects of their collaboration, encourage cooperation with the other countries examined in this volume, and add stability to Eurasia and the Asia-Pacific.

Unlike the games of chess and weiqi, we must assume that history has no actual end. Despite predictions to the contrary, capitalism and democracy did not become ubiquitous in the post–Cold War world. The human condition, historical and cultural legacies, geopolitical considerations, and other factors have allowed some authoritarian systems of government to re-emerge, persevere, or even thrive. And then there are the capitalist democracies, each of which has its own distinctive and changing strategic culture that produces decisions with impacts on international affairs. With these thoughts in mind, *Strategic Asia 2016–17: Understanding Strategic Cultures in the Asia-Pacific* is the second part of a three-volume series exploring the foundations of national power and assessing the future of geopolitical competition in the Asia-Pacific. Last year's edition focused on the material foundations of power, and this year's

---

[4] NBR will address this issue as part of a new multiyear project called "Strategic Implications of Russia-China Relations."

volume explores the ideational dimensions that are so crucial in shaping elite decision-making.

Acknowledgments

This *Strategic Asia* volume on strategic culture was made possible by the work and dedication of the staff and associates that drive all of NBR's projects. This marks the thirteenth year in which Ashley Tellis has provided his extraordinary guidance as the research director of the Strategic Asia Program. The substantive theme, framework, and structure of this year's volume are all a product of his masterful research direction. Alison Szalwinski and Michael Wills likewise played a major role in ensuring the overall success and high caliber of the program as co-editors of the volume. The program has also benefitted from Tiffany Ma's leadership as senior director of NBR's Political and Security Affairs group.

Brian Franchell provided essential research, editorial, and logistical support for the editors and authors. As always, NBR's publications team, led by Joshua Ziemkowski with the assistance of Jessica Keough, Craig Scanlan, Bruno Fiorentini, and Kela Wong, was responsible for formatting, copyediting, and proofreading. Finally, this year's volume also would not have been possible without the contributions of a stellar team of interns and researchers, including Jessica Drun, Mike Dyer, Claire Chaeryung Lee, Xiaodon Liang, Greg Shtraks, and Mengjia Wan. We hope their experience at NBR will serve them well as they embark on their future endeavors as rising leaders in the field of Asian affairs.

The leadership team in NBR's Washington, D.C., office serves as the brain trust of our policy outreach activities. Under the direction of Roy Kamphausen, senior vice president for research, NBR has achieved many impressive accomplishments over the past year and become increasingly effective in integrating policy outreach into projects, including Strategic Asia.

This year's authors have dedicated hours of research and writing to properly explain the nuances of strategic culture in the Asia-Pacific and deserve the highest praise. We appreciate their commitment to adhering to the rigorous schedule that has made it possible to publish their findings in a timely manner. These authors join a community of more than 120 leading specialists who have written for the series. The anonymous peer reviewers, both scholars and government experts, also deserve acknowledgement for offering substantive evaluations of the draft chapters.

Finally, I would like to recognize the Strategic Asia Program's core sponsor, the Lynde and Harry Bradley Foundation. Dating back to the publication of the first volume fifteen years ago, the foundation's support has been absolutely vital to the program's success. It is an honor to have partners at the foundation who share NBR's commitment to strengthening and informing policy. *Strategic Asia 2016–17* will provide scholars and policymakers alike with in-depth, timely analysis of the critical factors that influence strategic choices in the Asia-Pacific. As China's foreign policy becomes increasingly assertive and Russia continues to pivot to Asia, this volume will be a valuable resource for the United States to work with its partners to address these and other challenges.

Richard J. Ellings
President
The National Bureau of Asian Research

STRATEGIC ASIA 2016–17

EXECUTIVE SUMMARY

This chapter explains the theoretical evolution of the concept of strategic culture and how it can be utilized to understand national decision-making in the United States and selected Asian nations.

MAIN ARGUMENT

That cultural attributes shape strategic decisions has been understood for centuries, but modern scientific explanations of international politics have been unable to offer adequate accounts of strategic culture. Although power and the distribution of capabilities offer the best macroscopic insights into competitive international politics, ideational factors are also relevant because even materialist explanations require such overlays at both the epistemological and substantive levels. The door is thus opened for including culture even in realist arguments, an important step in the development of scientific knowledge, because all nations have a strategic culture that manifests itself at the individual, state, and societal levels. By incorporating this ubiquitous factor into analyses of grand strategy, a better understanding of specific state behaviors can be formed, which complements the more generalized understanding typically provided by realism. When done well, studies of strategic culture can help explain how ideational factors shape the acquisition and pursuit of power in international politics.

POLICY IMPLICATIONS

- All states arguably have unique strategic cultures, which invariably shape their political behaviors.

- The accumulation and use of national power, including material military capabilities, are constantly shaped by historical and social context.

- By synthesizing strategic culture with the realist framework, a richer understanding of individual state behavior, which makes for more effective policy responses, is possible.

Overview

Understanding Strategic Cultures in the Asia-Pacific

Ashley J. Tellis

That the security behavior of states is deeply shaped by their culture has been a prominent idea since the very beginning of Western political theory. In his epic history of the Greco-Persian wars, for example, Herodotus sought, among other things, to explain the causes of Greek victory as "the fruit of wisdom and strong law."[1] The Athenians, in Herodotus' reflections, derived their strength from their democracy, which nurtured equality, freedom, and a quest for excellence. The Spartans, in contrast, acquired their power from being enslaved to the law, a bondage that was so indenturing that they trembled before its obligations. As Herodotus had the deposed Spartan king Demaratus tell the Persian emperor Xerxes, the Spartans feared the law "much more than your men fear you. They do whatever it bids; and its bidding is always the same, that they must never flee from the battle before any multitude of men, but must abide at their post and there conquer or die."[2] In Herodotus' judgment, these cultural traits, which were unique to the Greeks, enabled them to muster the courage that made it possible for their smaller armies to defeat the much larger Persian forces marshaled by Xerxes.

Herodotus' *Histories* is much more than a simple narrative that describes the course and outcome of the conflict between the Greek city-states and

Ashley J. Tellis is a Senior Associate at the Carnegie Endowment for International Peace and Research Director of the Strategic Asia Program at the National Bureau of Asian Research. He can be reached at <atellis@carnegieendowment.org>.

[1] Herodotus, *The Histories*, trans. A.D. Godley (Cambridge: Harvard University Press, 1920), 7.102, available at http://www.perseus.tufts.edu/hopper/text?doc=Perseus:text:1999.01.0126.

[2] Ibid., 7.104.

the Persian Empire. Rather, it remains a deeply philosophical reflection that investigates not merely how the greatest powers of his age came into conflict but also how their political regimes were shaped by their worldviews, values, and psychology, all of which affected these states' behavior in the context of their specific political rivalries and material capabilities.[3]

This tradition of explicating the outcomes of security competition through, among other things, cultural attributes was entrenched by Herodotus' immediate successor Thucydides, whose epic analysis of the Peloponnesian War came to constitute, as he had hoped, "a possession for all time."[4] Although Thucydides self-consciously set about distinguishing his own work from that of Herodotus by noting its "absence of romance," he nonetheless extended the tradition established by the latter by also explaining the conflict between Athens and Sparta through more than simply material variables. To be sure, he enshrined one of the foundational insights of political realism for generations to come when he declared that "the real cause [of the Peloponnesian struggle] I consider to be the one which was formally most kept out of sight: The growth of the power of Athens, and the alarm which this inspired in Lacedaemon, made war inevitable."[5] Despite thus signaling the importance of the tangible distribution of power for explaining the conflict, Thucydides proceeded to explore its underlying causes, which he found rooted in the disposition of the two antagonists: the spiritedness of Athens and the passivity of Sparta. The spiritedness of Athens, which Thucydides' Pericles would celebrate in his Funeral Oration, was manifested in the way the polity "present[ed] the singular spectacle of daring and deliberation, each carried to its highest point, and both united in the same persons." The conviction of the Athenians that "vengeance upon their enemies was more to be desired than any personal blessings" is what gave rise to their greatest institutions and achievements, and finally an empire that "forced every sea and land to be the highway of [its] daring, and everywhere, whether for evil or for good, [has] left imperishable monuments behind."[6]

This ethos, in Thucydides' reflection, remained the consequential reason not only for the emergence of Athens as a great power but also for its descent into hubris and the cataclysm it provoked in the form of the Peloponnesian War. Hundreds of years after Thucydides, Machiavelli

---

[3] See Sara Forsdyke, "Herodotus, Political History, and Political Thought," in *The Cambridge Companion to Herodotus*, ed. Carolyn Dewald and John Marincola (New York: Cambridge University Press, 2007), 224–37; and Joel Alden Schlosser, "Herodotean Realism," *Political Theory* 42, no. 3 (2014): 239–61.

[4] Thucydides, *The History of the Peloponnesian War*, trans. Richard Crawley (New York: Random House, 1951), 1.1.

[5] Ibid.

[6] Ibid., 2.6.

similarly explained Roman greatness in terms of strategic culture. Incarnating Petrarch's maxim that "all history is the praise of Rome," Machiavelli's *Discourses on Livy* approvingly concluded that a preoccupation with civic *virtù*—that "competitive pursuit of excellence, expressed in a penchant for turning virtually all social activities into contests with winners, losers, prizes, and trophies"—underwrote Rome's unquenchable thirst for glory and in time created its vast and admirable empire.[7] From Machiavelli onward, a succession of thinkers in the West—including individuals as diverse as Carl von Clausewitz, Max Weber, and Ruth Benedict—explored culture as a key to understanding various social phenomena. Hence, it should not be surprising that armed conflict, perhaps the most troublesome of all human behaviors, has also proved to be appealing territory for cultural exploration in contemporary times.[8]

Strategic Culture and Modern Social Science

Given the distinguished history of analyzing international competition through cultural explanations since antiquity, it may seem surprising that modern studies of strategic culture have not turned out to be entirely persuasive.[9] Strategic culture is understood in this volume as referring to those inherited conceptions and shared beliefs that shape a nation's collective identity, the values that color how a country evaluates its interests, and the norms that influence a state's understanding of the means by which it can best realize its destiny in a competitive international system.[10] Given that these concepts bear on national security managers as they make choices about how to respond internally and externally to their strategic environment, it would be hard to deny that strategic culture matters. How exactly it matters, however, has proved harder to describe.

For the classical theorists from Herodotus to Machiavelli, integrating strategic culture into their larger analyses was not particularly problematic because their philosophical investigations of social behavior naturally

---

[7] Mark Hulliung, *Citizen Machiavelli* (Princeton: Princeton University Press, 1984), 40.

[8] For a useful overview of how culture has been conceived in classical social theory, see Philip Smith and Alexander Riley, *Cultural Theory: An Introduction*, 2nd ed. (Malden: Wiley-Blackwell, 2008), 6–21. The treatment of culture in various contemporary disciplines is surveyed in Lynn Hunt, "Introduction: History, Culture, and Text," in *The New Cultural History*, ed. Lynn Hunt (Berkeley: University of California Press, 1989), 1–22. The role of culture in explaining issues relating to armed conflict in the postwar period is masterfully examined in Michael C. Desch, "Culture Clash: Assessing the Importance of Ideas in Security Studies," *International Security* 23, no. 1 (1998): 141–70.

[9] Desch, "Culture Clash."

[10] Jeannie L. Johnson, "Strategic Culture: Refining the Theoretical Construct," Science Applications International Corporation (SAIC), report prepared for the Defense Threat Reduction Agency, October 31, 2006, 5.

accommodated multiple layers of causation. Thus, for example, their explanations, which incorporated unique cultural variables such as the collective devotion to law or the national restiveness that attains consummation in worldly glory, did not neglect material elements such as the balance of military capabilities or relative national power, nor did they discount individual motivations such as fear, honor, greed, or interest. In other words, the ancients understood that all political phenomena were by their nature complex and, hence, doing analytical justice to them required a layered understanding that subsumed a multiplicity of causes.[11]

The modern descendants of classical theorists, however, have had a harder time in accommodating strategic culture as a worthwhile cause because of their commitment to reductionist explanations. These approaches, which are viewed as the hallmark of "positivist" social science, invariably require culture and its related concepts or hypotheses to be defined precisely, something that has often proved difficult because of the inherent elasticity of these ideas.[12] Furthermore, it is not clear whether the notion of culture, however defined and even if applicable as a good explanation in specific cases, can be universalized sufficiently to produce "covering laws" of the kind required by social scientific approaches that model themselves on the natural sciences.[13] Finally, even if the previous problems can be overcome, a more challenging difficulty facing cultural explanations in contemporary social science is that the outcomes to be explained must be demonstrably attributed solely or primarily to strategic culture over and against any other variables, such as the balance of power or the purposive choices of state leaders in the context of competitive politics. The inability to provide such unique attribution creates problems of "overdetermination"—when two or

---

[11] Ashley J. Tellis, "Reconstructing Political Realism: The Long March to Scientific Theory," *Security Studies* 5, no. 2 (1996): 3–94.

[12] Ronald Rogowski, *Rational Legitimacy: A Theory of Political Support* (Princeton: Princeton University Press, 1974), 13.

[13] The concept of covering law is elaborated systematically in Carl G. Hempel, "Aspects of Scientific Explanation," in *Aspects of Scientific Explanation and Other Essays in the Philosophy of Science* (New York: Free Press, 1965), 331–496. For a good overview of how positivist social science seeks to explain various phenomena through different kinds of covering law explanations, see Arthur L. Stinchcombe, *Constructing Social Theories* (Chicago: University of Chicago Press, 1968). It should be noted, however, that those who reject the possibility of scientific explanation derived from universal laws approach the subject of culture in a different way. For example, Clifford Geertz, one of the most creative and pioneering scholars of culture, argued that "the analysis of [culture is] not an experimental science in search of law but an interpretive one in search of meaning," a judgment that with qualifications fits into the sociological tradition earlier established by Max Weber. See Clifford Geertz, *The Interpretation of Cultures* (New York: Basic Books, 1973), 5; and Thomas Burger, *Max Weber's Theory of Concept Formation: History, Laws, and Ideal Types* (Durham: Duke University Press, 1976).

more sufficient and distinct causes produce the same effect—which, in turn, diminishes the attractiveness of strategic culture as a useful explanation.[14]

The quest for a parsimonious explanation—a distinguishing characteristic of contemporary social science—threatens the viability of strategic culture as a self-sufficient explanation of competitive political behavior because frequently various political outcomes can just as readily be accounted for by other variables. This did not pose any insurmountable difficulty for the ancients because their political investigations were not scientific in the contemporary sense of the term. The emphasis in current social science on establishing hard causality, however, threatens hypotheses based on strategic culture if they cannot provide distinctive explanations that lie beyond the reach of other competing accounts of the evidence.

The Relevance of Strategic Culture in Explaining National Behavior

This volume, *Strategic Asia 2016–17: Understanding Strategic Cultures in the Asia-Pacific*, explores the dominant ideational frames of reference that are prevalent in key Asian states. It thus serves as a companion to *Strategic Asia 2015–16: Foundations of National Power in the Asia-Pacific*, which examined the capacity of various Asian states to produce power through a study of their resource base and their state and societal performance insofar as these bear on the generation of military capabilities.

The studies assembled in this volume are authored on the assumption that strategic culture matters insofar as it constitutes the intangible element of an overarching context that shapes how key national elites, particularly the decision-makers within the countries examined here, understand their strategic environment and the value, purpose, use, and limitations ascribed to their national power—including the application of coercive force—in competitive politics. To modify Ann Swidler's conception of how culture operates in action, strategic culture shapes outcomes both by "providing the ultimate values toward which action is orientated" and by "shaping a repertoire or 'tool kit' of habits, skills, and styles from which people construct 'strategies of action.'"[15] These cognitive frames are transmitted across time merely as a result of a nation's continued persistence, though it is likely that conscious social transference also plays a critical role in many, and certainly

---

[14] For a discussion of overdetermination, see W.C. Wimsatt, "Robustness, Reliability and Overdetermination," in *Scientific Inquiry and the Social Sciences*, ed. M. Brewer and B. Collins (San Francisco: Jossey-Bass, 1981), 124–63.

[15] Ann Swidler, "Culture in Action: Symbols and Strategies," *American Sociological Review* 51, no. 2 (1986): 273.

in all modern, societies. Consequently, all nations, by the very fact of their existence, possess a strategic culture, with the only difference between them being the degree of consciousness about their ideational inheritance, the extent of deliberation characterizing its reproduction, and the sensitivity with which it is applied to policy. Examining a nation's strategic culture, therefore, requires attention to both formal and informal modes of representation that includes a focus on words and actions as well as on all other implied and explicit understandings.

By its very nature, strategic culture manifests itself at diverse levels in a political community: at the level of state, society, and individual. Because of its interest in international politics, this volume will pay special attention to the worldviews of the decision-making segments involved in managing national security, obviously on the assumption that these outlooks are shaped by the ideational inheritance, contestation, and reproduction prevalent in the wider social milieu. The social construction of strategic culture through these processes also highlights the fact that all ideational frames intended to understand the reality of security competition are never static, even when they appear stable. Rather, their incarnation, being owed to the complex interaction between inherited ideas, intra-societal negotiations, state-society bargaining, and the strength of state interests, illuminates the social bases of their generation while highlighting the possibilities of evolution or change.

Despite this expansive view of strategic culture, the ontological assumption underlying this volume remains fundamentally materialist in that it presumes that tangible capabilities are still fundamental to explaining the widest range of outcomes in competitive international politics. Yet the recognition that physical capabilities enduringly matter does not preclude a role for those ideational elements inherent in the concept of strategic culture. This is because the character and the pace of accumulation of material instruments, and the manner of their use—especially when manifested as military capabilities—are shaped by a cognitive inheritance that is possibly unique to every nation.[16]

The rationalist methodology of Popperian social science insists that all observation of the material world is "theory-laden," meaning that it requires some a priori concepts to help the observer make sense

---

[16] How ideas in this sense are linked to material outcomes is explored in Judith Goldstein and Robert O. Keohane, *Ideas and Foreign Policy: Beliefs, Institutions, and Political Change* (Ithaca: Cornell University Press, 1993).

of perceived reality.[17] On this account, treating strategic culture as a methodologically preexistent, but not necessarily unchanging, intellectual frame that helps decision-makers interpret their security environment is essential for the proper understanding of how state managers make decisions about the production and application of national power and the ends to which it may be directed. Explaining even the palpable realities of international politics—the subjects naturally encompassed by any materialist ontology—thus requires an idealist component in its epistemology if it is to satisfactorily account for how states acquire and pursue power in the arena of competitive international politics.[18]

As such, strategic culture serves at the very least as part of the "thick description"[19] of national actions that, when appreciated in their complexity and nuance, contribute toward addressing the question posed by Colin Gray, "What does the observed behavior mean?"[20] At its most ambitious, strategic culture might actually offer possibilities for explaining or even predicting state behavior in the manner intended by covering law models of scientific knowledge. Yet even when successful on this count, its superiority as a social-scientific approach will be determined not only by the verisimilitude of its prognoses in any given case but also by how well it meets the other criteria for good theory, such as comprehensiveness, parsimony, and fecundity.[21]

Incorporating strategic culture in this fashion opens the door to resolving what is often viewed as the antithesis between broadly realist approaches to international politics, which usually employ strict or loose rational choice methods of reasoning, and cultural explanations, which

---

[17] The distinction between Karl Popper's approach and that of positivist social science hinges on this key issue: the positivists believed that scientific laws could be derived solely from experience through induction; Popper not only demonstrated the fallacy of induction as a means of producing scientific knowledge but, following Kant, established that all observation statements (as well as empirical experiments) presuppose prior theory, thus permitting the introduction of deductive logic as a tool of falsification to produce scientific knowledge. See Karl Popper, *The Logic of Scientific Discovery* (New York: Routledge, 1992), 93–111. For a systematic summation of Popper's rationalism as applied to social science, see Ashley J. Tellis, *The Drive to Domination: Towards a Pure Realist Theory of Politics* (PhD diss., University of Chicago, 1994), 18–80.

[18] In a logical sense, then, strategic culture functions as the Kantian "synthetic a priori" in larger social-scientific explanations of state action, even when this activity is concerned entirely with the material realities of power and its application either within or outside the state.

[19] Geertz, *The Interpretation of Cultures*, 6.

[20] Colin S. Gray, "Strategic Culture as Context: The First Generation of Theory Strikes Back," *Review of International Studies* 25, no.1 (1999): 49–69.

[21] See the discussion in Imre Lakatos, "Falsificationism and the Methodology of Scientific Research Programmes," in *Criticism and the Growth of Knowledge*, ed. Imre Lakatos and Alan Musgrave (Cambridge: Cambridge University Press, 1974), 91–196.

often take the form of *sui generis* accounts.[22] If rational state behavior is viewed as culturally conditioned in some way—in that the identity of a nation, the values it prioritizes, and the norms of behavior it judges to be desirable all shape how decision-makers approach the tasks of producing and utilizing power in international politics—then it might be possible to integrate instrumental rationality to explain different kinds of outcomes. These include the lags between structural change and the alterations in state behavior, the failures of states to respond to structural constraints, and the successful pursuit of specific national preferences in the face of weak external hindrances, as Michael Desch has insightfully argued.[23] But it would also explain a much broader range of state behavior, including the differences in styles of statecraft, the choice of particular national strategies, and even the transformation of some configurations of power as a result of determined state action precipitated by unique endogenous ideational factors. If rationalist explanations of political realism can in fact incorporate strategic culture systematically, then the resulting hypotheses would have utility not merely for explaining puzzling outcomes—as is the case now when strategic culture often becomes an "explanation of last resort" that is "turned to when more concrete factors have been eliminated"[24]—but also for explaining the uniqueness of every individual case that is necessarily recessed when the larger regularities of international politics are otherwise satisfactorily explained by the realist research program.

The important point is that such a "thin" rational choice approach, which is willing to admit that strategic culture could shape the expected utility of different choices as a result of some deeply held beliefs, would permit observers to understand the variations in national responses to interstate competition.[25] Consequently, although all nations most susceptible to the rigors of anarchic competition would end up pursuing similar but not necessarily identical strategies of power maximization—an outcome that is best accounted for by the standard covering-law-like explanations of political realism—strategic culture will have made an important contribution to both intellectual comprehension and successful policymaking if it could explicate

---

[22] For an excellent conceptual discussion of this issue, see Sun-Ki Chai, "Rational Choice and Culture: Clashing Perspectives or Complementary Modes of Analysis?" in *Culture Matters: Essays in Honor of Aaron Wildavsky,* ed. Richard J. Ellis and Michael Thompson (Boulder: Westview Press, 1997), 45–58.

[23] For a discussion of some of these outcomes, see Desch, "Culture Clash."

[24] Eric Herring, "Nuclear Totem and Taboo" (paper presented at the BISA annual conference, Leeds, December 15–17, 1997), 8, cited in Theo Farrell, "Culture and Military Power," *Review of International Studies* 24, no. 3 (1998): 409.

[25] The distinction between "thick" and "thin" rational choice theories is well explicated in Michael Hechter and Satoshi Kanazawa, "Sociological Rational Choice Theory," *Annual Review of Sociology* 23, no. 1 (1997): 191–214.

how the preferences and causal beliefs of a state shape the uniqueness of its competitive response.

A good understanding of this kind offers theoretical benefits as well. Beyond providing a textured appreciation of any given state's response to international rivalry—details that are invariably lost in "extensive" explanations that attempt to do justice to numerous cases over space and time—such "intensive" scrutiny of a particular state's behavior could stimulate new hypotheses that explain, among other things, how national institutions mutate as a result of the interaction of external and internal pressures, thus further improving our understanding of international politics. If the focus of strategic culture, therefore, rests in the first instance on providing the best understanding of a specific nation's security behavior, rather than attempting to provide abstract universal generalizations that are trained on "the realist edifice as [a] target,"[26] it could serve as a vital complement to rational choice formulations of political realism, even if it cannot substitute for the latter entirely.

The chapters that follow in this volume are informed by several generations of theorizing on strategic culture, but they do not wade into the academic debates that have surrounded the concept since its inception. These debates continue endlessly, and there is still no consensus on the operational definition of strategic culture, its methods and objects of inquiry, or its scope of explanation. Further complicating matters is the fact that scholars using the notion of strategic culture as an explanation usually seem motivated more by a desire to refute political realism than to demonstrate that cultural explanations can in fact advance our understanding of international politics even if they do not serve as genuine alternatives to realist theories.[27] Attempting to adjudicate these issues lies beyond the province of this volume. Instead, the studies gathered here are aimed primarily at helping policymakers and interested students of Asia understand how ideational factors color the choices of the major Asian states in regard to procuring and using power in international politics. This objective is consistent with Alastair Iain Johnston's judgment that "done well, the careful analysis of strategic culture could help policymakers establish more accurate and empathetic understandings of how different actors perceive the game being played, reducing uncertainty and other information problems in strategic choice. Done badly, the analysis of strategic culture could reinforce stereotypes about strategic dispositions of

---

[26] Alastair Iain Johnston, "Thinking about Strategic Culture," *International Security* 19, no. 4 (1995): 41.

[27] See the discussion in Peter J. Katzenstein, "Introduction: Alternative Perspectives on National Security," in *The Culture of National Security: Norms and Identity in World Politics*, ed. Peter J. Katzenstein (New York: Columbia University Press, 1996), 1–32.

other states and close off policy alternatives deemed inappropriate for dealing with local strategic cultures."[28]

Academic Theorizing on Strategic Culture

The effort to think hard and seriously about strategic culture, as reflected in the individual studies that follow, has benefited greatly from the three generations of scholarship that have marked this paradigm. This section will briefly review these iterations, principally with a view to highlighting the key insights that bear on the chapters that compose this volume.

Although the study of strategic culture received critical impetus during World War II, when the U.S. government employed a large number of leading anthropologists to examine the "national character" of key Axis powers in order to understand their wartime behavior, the importance of culture as an explanatory variable in international security came into its own during the Cold War.[29] The nuclear competition between the United States and the Soviet Union offered fertile ground for the resurgence of interest in strategic culture, in large measure because of what was seen as the confounding Soviet approach to nuclear weaponry and strategic competition.

The devastation caused by nuclear weapons at the end of World War II strengthened the conviction in the United States that the atomic bomb was in fact, in Bernard Brodie's celebrated description, "the absolute weapon."[30] The challenge of managing this new instrument of warfare, whose "capacity…for mass destruction far exceeded any immediately realizable value in enhancing human comfort and welfare,"[31] led U.S. strategists, most notably at the RAND Corporation, to develop thick rational choice theories centered on the presumption that since nuclear war was essentially unwinnable, security competition in the nuclear age would be defined fundamentally by the quest for mutual deterrence rather than asymmetrical advantage. This hope that rivalries even among egoist maximizers would produce conservative strategies in the presence of nuclear weapons was vitiated when the Soviet Union demonstrated a continual willingness to pursue comprehensive nuclear superiority, integrate nuclear warfighting options into its military operations,

---

[28] Johnston, "Thinking about Strategic Culture."

[29] For a succinct summary of the history and logic of "national character" studies, see Federico Neiburg, "National Character," in *International Encyclopedia of the Social & Behavioral Sciences*, ed. Neil J. Smelser and Paul B. Baltes (New York: Elsevier, 2001), 10,296–99.

[30] Bernard Brodie, ed., *The Absolute Weapon: Atomic Power and World Order* (New York: Harcourt, Brace and Company, 1946).

[31] Frederick S. Dunn, "The Common Problem," in Brodie, *The Absolute Weapon*.

and engage in active geopolitical competition that incurred high risks of nuclear conflict.[32]

The failure of American deterrence theorists to anticipate these outcomes opened the door to alternative approaches to explaining Soviet behavior. Before long, Jack Snyder, also then at the RAND Corporation, argued that the traditional Russian obsession with insecurity, when married to Soviet authoritarianism's penchant for absolute control and Marxist-Leninist convictions about the arrow of history, would produce nuclear strategies that emphasized nuclear preemption and the offensive use of force with the intent of procuring victory even in what might be an extensive nuclear war. This difference in attitude explained much about Soviet strategic behavior, which otherwise appeared anomalous to the formal U.S. theories centered on the *ex ante* presumption of a "generic rational man" as an egoist maximizer. By introducing the contrasting notion of "Soviet man"—a calculating creature admittedly, but one influenced by the Soviet Union's unique history, geography, institutions, and meanings—Snyder made a compelling case for the importance of taking strategic culture seriously. He defined strategic culture as "the sum total of ideas, conditioned emotional responses, and patterns of habitual behavior that members of a national strategic community have acquired through instruction or imitation and share with each other."[33]

This notion of understanding strategic culture as instrumental rationality bounded by the ideational constraints emerging from a certain national style was extended by other scholars after Snyder, most notably Colin Gray, David Jones, Carnes Lord, and William Kincade. They located the sources of strategic culture expansively in macro-environmental factors such as geography and factor endowments; in political variables such as history, the character of the state, and state-society relations; in cultural resources such as belief systems, myths, and symbols, as well as textual and nontextual sources of tradition; and in institutional elements, particularly the structure and interests of key military organizations and the character of civil-military relations.[34]

While the sources of strategic culture were admittedly broad in this reading, its logical status as an explanatory device was also

---

[32] The classic examination of such confounding behavior remains Colin S. Gray, *Nuclear Strategy and National Style* (Lanham: Hamilton Press, 1986).

[33] Jack L. Snyder, "The Soviet Strategic Culture: Implications for Limited Nuclear Operations," RAND Corporation, September 1977, http://www.rand.org/pubs/reports/R2154.html.

[34] Colin S. Gray, "National Style in Strategy: The American Example," *International Security* 6, no. 2 (1981): 21–47; Gray, *Nuclear Strategy and National Style*; David R. Jones, "Soviet Strategic Culture," in *Strategic Power USA/USSR*, ed. Carl G. Jacobsen (New York: St. Martin's Press, 1990), 35–49; Carnes Lord, "American Strategic Culture," *Comparative Strategy* 5, no. 3 (1985): 269–93; and William Kincade, "American National Style and Strategic Culture," in Jacobsen, *Strategic Power USA/USSR*, 10–34.

similarly expansive: strategic culture consisted principally of "provid[ing] the *milieu* within which strategy is debated"[35] and as such could not provide unique predictions of state behavior but only "a context for understanding, rather than explanatory causality."[36] Gray insistently held that culture could not be separated from behavior because "all people are 'cultural creatures'. Everything we think and do is performed in the context of culture, perhaps cultures. But culture need not dominate. It is an ever present potential influence, sometimes pressing hard, sometimes not. Its principal function is to make sense of the world for us."[37]

The second wave of strategic culture theorizing, which reached its apotheosis during the 1980s in the work of Reginald Stuart, Robin Luckham, Bradley Klein, and others, was more disparate in its intellectual interests but was unified by a grounding in critical social theory.[38] Stuart's critique of the American national character, Luckham's focus on the militarization of global politics, and Klein's analysis of how strategic cultures come to be manufactured by elites to serve their own particular interests all share the common goal of unmasking the unjust practices prevailing in national and international politics. Klein's work is clearly the most systematic and theoretically self-conscious in this regard, and anchored as it is in post-structuralist and post-Marxist writings, his arguments reveal both an epistemological and a substantive sophistication that greatly enriches the notion of strategic culture.[39]

Unlike the first generation of theorists, who focused on national styles in strategy, presuming that the embedded cultures were unproblematic products of the interaction of various macro-environmental, political, cultural, and institutional variables, Klein's ontology contends that all these elements are socially constituted and at least the human understanding of them requires symbolic communication. Because all sensible communication takes place only through intersubjective exchanges of meaning—which require preexisting social structures to begin with—the power relations embedded in these arrangements shape in accordance with their interests how the diverse

---

[35] Gray, "National Style in Strategy," 35–37. Emphasis added.

[36] Gray, "Strategic Culture as Context," 49.

[37] Colin S. Gray, "Out of the Wilderness: Prime Time for Strategic Culture," in *Strategic Culture and Weapons of Mass Destruction: Culturally Based Insights into Comparative National Security Policymaking*, ed. Jeannie L. Johnson, Kerry M. Kartchner, and Jeffrey A. Larsen (New York: Palgrave Macmillan, 2009), 221–41.

[38] For a useful survey of this work, see Stuart Poore, "Strategic Culture," in *Neorealism Versus Strategic Culture*, ed. John Glenn, Darryl Howlett, and Stuart Poore (Aldershot: Ashgate, 2004), 55–57.

[39] See, for example, Bradley S. Klein, "Hegemony and Strategic Culture: American Power Projection and Alliance Defence Politics," *Review of International Studies* 14, no. 2 (1988): 133–48; and Bradley S. Klein, *Strategic Studies and World Order: The Global Politics of Deterrence* (Cambridge: Cambridge University Press, 1994).

variables that make up any strategic culture are to be understood, internalized, and, by extension, reproduced in the form of political practices. Strategic culture, in this understanding, is accordingly not the natural product of interacting environmental and social causes but rather a socially constituted artifact produced to serve the interests of the powerful in a given society (or the most powerful states in the interstate system).[40]

While this approach to conceptualizing strategic culture has numerous implications at both the epistemological and ontological levels, its practical implications are of immediate relevance here. To begin with, it opens the door to investigating how a strategic culture comes to be created as a social process, requiring the observer to understand which institutions are involved, what societal resources are privileged in this process, and what purposes both outside and inside the state are served by its articulation and promotion. Furthermore, the expectation that a strategic culture is inextricably linked to the structure of power relations in a given society (or in an international system) raises questions about whether a variety of strategic cultures could exist concurrently: a dominant culture complemented by alternatives or a variety of cultures vying for hegemony inside a country (or in international politics). And finally, any reading of strategic culture as socially constituted ushers forward the possibility that strategic cultures could change. This consideration, in turn, challenges scholars to examine the durability of the existing dominant culture, the circumstances that could precipitate change, and the directions in which a culture might evolve and the consequences.

Given the importance of these questions, the second wave of theorizing represented by Klein and others has arguably enriched strategic culture as a research program considerably. Even if its hard ontological claim (that strategic culture is entirely constituted) and its accompanying epistemological assertion (that all understanding is completely intersubjective) are rejected by structuralist-materialist approaches, the core challenges the second wave levies on the latter—namely, the need to explain the genesis of a strategic culture and its robustness insofar as these are linked to existing social formations within a country—cannot but be viewed as productive extensions of the work begun by the first wave of strategic culture theorists.

Whereas the first wave of reflection on strategic culture focused on national styles as the context that shapes strategic action, and the second wave concerned itself with explaining how the perceived context comes to be constituted by elites seeking to preserve and expand their power internally and externally, the third wave of theorizing about strategic culture, which emerged in the 1990s, went in two different directions.

---

[40] For a brilliant summation of Klein's work, see Edward Lock, "Refining Strategic Culture: Return of the Second Generation," *Review of International Studies* 36, no. 3 (2010): 685–708.

Both directions were unified by a commitment to utilizing contemporary social science methodologies to explain certain phenomena. They sought to be rigorous in their explanations and attempted to formulate and test hypotheses in the manner expected by "certain positivist research methods in the social sciences" (and, to that degree, differed from the epistemological assumptions of the second wave).[41] Most interestingly, however, their employment of the scientific approach, with its commitment to providing testable causal explanations, was harnessed in the service of what is ultimately a constructivist ontology.[42]

The first school in the third wave, as represented by the work of Jeffrey Legro, Elizabeth Kier, and Peter Katzenstein, sought to examine strategic culture at the domestic-organizational level.[43] Thus, Legro, for example, explained the restraint exhibited by the British and the Germans toward each other during World War II not as a function of overarching structural constraints but as a product of the organizational cultures—the beliefs and customs—of the military bureaucracies in the two combatants. In a similar vein, Kier focused on how the French military's organizational ethos, interacting with the interests of the political leadership, created the conditions for its defeat in 1940. Beyond seeking to supplant political realism, both approaches in effect argued that strategic cultures formed and nurtured at the domestic organizational level could in fact determine state behavior.

This effort to explain national action as a function of the ideas that dominate key institutions within the state was critiqued by the most articulate representative of the second school in the third wave, Alastair Iain Johnston. He noted that focusing attention on how subordinate institutions affected state policy undermined the objective of demonstrating how "the influences of broader and more deeply historical differences" might shape the formation of strategic culture in and across societies and thus explain the culturally conditioned choices of the core decision-making apparatus of the state itself.[44] By keeping the focus on key elites and security managers who oversee national security policy, Johnston's approach exhibits continuity with the first and second waves insofar as both view the highest

---

[41] Alastair Iain Johnston, *Cultural Realism: Strategic Culture and Grand Strategy in Chinese History* (Princeton: Princeton University Press, 1998), 50.

[42] See the discussion in Emanuel Adler, "Constructivism in International Relations," in *Handbook of International Relations*, ed. Walter Carlsnaes, Thomas Risse, and Beth A. Simmons (London: Sage Publications, 2002), 95–118.

[43] Jeffrey Legro, *Cooperation Under Fire: Anglo-German Restraint during World War II* (Ithaca: Cornell University Press, 1995); Elizabeth Kier, *Imagining War: French and British Military Doctrine between the Wars* (Princeton: Princeton University Press, 1997); and Katzenstein, "Introduction."

[44] Johnston, *Cultural Realism*, 20.

institutions of decision-making within the state as the fundamental locus of the manifestation of a nation's strategic culture.

Consistent with the social-scientific ambitions of the third wave, Johnston produced a body of work that to this day represents the apotheosis of the quest for testable theories of strategic culture. By characterizing strategic culture as the "ideational milieu which limits behavior choices," he not only sought to investigate "the shared assumptions and decision rules that impose a degree of order on individual and group conceptions of their relationship to their social, organizational or political environment."[45] Most ambitiously, he separated culture from behavior to test how the former might causally affect the latter in some falsifiable way. In critiquing the first wave of theorists who failed to force this separation, Johnston held—correctly from the viewpoint of contemporary social science—that any conception of culture as context that included both beliefs and behavior would be unable to demonstrate possible discrepancies between an elite's worldview and actions and, by implication, would be nonfalsifiable. Colin Gray's response to this critique, shorn of its details, essentially boiled down to the contention that the problem of falsifiability represented little more than a theorist's conceit and was of little relevance to policy.[46] Odd as it may seem, both positions are tenable.

If culture could in fact be cleanly prescinded from behavior at a conceptual level, Johnston's position would be persuasive because it would permit a social-scientific examination of the former's impact on the latter either by itself or in comparison with other rival causes. But if such a separation cannot be effected—either because human beings are fundamentally "encultured," meaning that "all strategic behavior is effected by human beings who cannot help but be cultural agents," as Gray contends, or because the distinction between ideational causes and materialist outcomes is both "ontologically and epistemologically problematic," as Johnston admits—then the ambition to create a fully falsifiable theory of strategic culture, however laudable otherwise, necessarily falls short.[47] This challenge is further complicated by the fact that Johnston's own investigations into China's strategic culture—as shaped by its classic texts and consciously socialized by its political institutions—have produced conclusions that are virtually identical to those offered by political realism, except that realism derives China's *parabellum* behavior from various

---

[45] Johnston, "Thinking about Strategic Culture," 45.

[46] Gray, "Out of the Wilderness."

[47] Ibid.; Gray, "Strategic Culture as Context"; and Alastair Iain Johnston, "Strategic Cultures Revisited: Reply to Colin Gray," *Review of International Studies* 25, no. 3 (1999): 520–21.

structural constraints, whereas Johnston concludes that its "realpolitik decisions are cultural."[48]

Given that the realist research program explains much more than just China's strategic behavior, or for that matter vastly more than cultural explanations can account for currently, it must be tentatively judged as superior in terms of its merits as a scientific theory. More pertinently, however, the challenges of hermetically separating material factors from ideational ones in any scientific explanation leave both scholars and policymakers with little more than some version of Gray's approach to understanding strategic culture: a device for "discerning tendencies, not rigid determinants." If used appropriately, this approach could produce as an end result "richer theory and more effective practice."[49]

As Stuart Poore concluded in his masterful examination of the Johnston-Gray debate on strategic culture, the epistemological infirmities of Johnston's positivist methodology imply that any detailed analysis of a country's strategic culture or any cross-national comparisons of strategic culture "can only be elucidated through thick description and insight rather than by searching for and measuring independent cultural variables in the way Johnston suggests."[50] There could be a no more succinct manifesto for this volume. In any event, the third wave of strategic culture theorizing suggests that any examination of this phenomenon would profit greatly from studying whether the key subordinate institutions of a state, such as the military or other important bureaucracies, do in fact have distinctive beliefs and customs that could influence state action in particular ways, and whether and how the highest levels of national decision-making are themselves shaped by the transmitted patterns of meaning found in a country's written texts, oral traditions, or other forms of cultural inheritance.

Shaped by this intellectual heritage spanning many decades, the chapters in this volume examine for each country strategic culture as a product of three broad sets of variables. The first consists of macrosocietal factors, such as geographic location, history, culture (meaning the cumulative deposit of beliefs, values, and symbols of a community that are transmitted across generations), and ethnography. The second encompasses statal characteristics, such as the nature of the domestic political regime, the type and relative capabilities of the economy, the ambitions and worldviews of the elites, and the broad character of state-society relations. And the third includes

---

[48] Johnston, *Cultural Realism*, x. The term *parabellum*, in this context, means violence-prone or warlike.

[49] Gray, *Nuclear Strategy and National Style*, 35.

[50] Stuart Poore, "What Is the Context? A Reply to the Gray-Johnston Debate on Strategic Culture," *Review of International Studies* 29, no. 2 (2003): 283.

intrastatal elements, such as the nature of civil-military relations, the robustness of strategic planning and decision-making institutions, and the effectiveness of the national security bureaucracy.

When examining these sources, insofar as they contribute to the creation, sustenance, and reproduction of strategic culture, the authors of the individual chapters have also paid attention, to the degree possible and relevant, to three specific tasks. One such task is identifying the founding myths, classic texts, and other ideational or social influences (such as religion or caste) that might distinctively shape the cognitive inheritance of a particular nation as expressed in terms of identity, values, and norms. A second is assessing what seems invariant and what might be changing (or seems susceptible to change) because of the transformations in historical, cultural, political, or economic circumstances, as well as what might be the perceived impact of such changes on the evolving strategic culture. Finally, a third task is identifying the elements within a country that run against the grain of the dominant strategic culture, the reasons for their persistence, and the conditions under which they might prevail and with what consequences—in other words, identifying the dissident or subaltern traditions that illustrate the diversity of social elements, even if within an otherwise hegemonic strategic culture. In so doing, these studies do not pretend to be able to uncover specific causal linkages between a country's ideational inheritance and its strategic behaviors—a goal that seems to have eluded even the best theorists of strategic culture thus far. Rather, they offer insights about how the symbolic inheritance and constructs of a nation shape its predispositions and, by extension, color its approach to security competition in international politics.

Surveying Asia's Strategic Cultures

Taken together, the chapters in this volume convey the remarkable diversity of strategic cultures in Asia. They span the range from highly developed and consciously articulated traditions, as in China, to more embryonic efforts at self-reflection, as evidenced in Indonesia, with many variants in between.

Christopher Ford's study of China's strategic culture reinforces the most pointed insights offered by both the first and second waves of academic theorizing on the subject. Ford emphasizes the fact that there is a distinctive Chinese national style "rooted in a uniquely ancient history and political-cultural continuity that legitimates a special and privileged role for Beijing in world affairs as a peace-loving power at the civilizational center of mankind." However, this vision of China, which is viewed as invariant and durable, being built on claims of virtuocratic power, masks the country's strong propensity to use force both domestically and internationally as a way of protecting elite or national interests in any disputes involving power. This ready willingness to use force, which is always visualized reflexively as defensive and justified to the outside as principled, corroborates the most distinctive characteristic of Chinese strategic culture—namely, the reality of "Confucian flesh" covering "realist bones." This "'exacerbated realism' of moralistic coercion" both underlies many of the distinctive traits of Chinese foreign policy behavior and resonates with the insights offered by the second wave of strategic culture theories. As Ford notes, much of this ready willingness to use force in moralistic garb is driven by the interests of the Chinese Communist Party (CCP) in preserving its hegemony over power at home through, among other things, asserting China's claim to primacy abroad. As he argues, a "model of authority" that "is conceptually monist...cannot concede real pluralism and fears alternative loci of virtue." It can be used, however, to "justify CCP autocracy, demonstrate the virtue of the party's leadership, articulate civilizational foundations and precedents for the regime's dreams of status and glory in the international arena, and discredit alien Western values that the regime finds distasteful or threatening" en route to pursuing foreign policies with "power-maximizing geopolitical implications."

Isabelle Facon's discussion of Russia's strategic culture highlights the enduring characteristics of its national style, which she attributes to the complex "geographic, historical, and psychological circumstances" that have shaped the country's dominant leitmotif for several centuries: the quest to become, and to be treated as, a world power that is attracted to, yet often repelled by, the West. This paradoxical attitude, Facon notes, is the result of at least four polarities that have shaped the Russian worldview over time. The first is an assertive religious vision of Russia as a proselytizing Orthodox successor to Rome versus the spatial vision of itself as a vulnerable entity that needs extended territorial buffers for its survival. A second polarity is the tension between offensive and defensive foreign policies for national survival, linked in part to perceptions of domestic weakness and the character of the governing regime at different points in time. Third, Russia exhibits alternating convictions about autarky and integration as desired routes for increasing national power. The fourth polarity is the struggle to balance national focus, interests, and policies between Europe and Asia, given that Russian power has never been potent enough to enable seamless involvement in both regions simultaneously over long periods of time. Navigating these four concurrent polarities has shaped the two characteristics that dominate Russia's strategic style—namely, the enduring emphasis on the primacy of military instruments in its national policy and the perpetual oscillation between spirited activism and torpid retrenchment in its foreign relations. These behaviors lead Facon to conclude that Russia "has always vacillated between a desire for integration with Europe and the West and wariness about the 'importation' of Western political values and socioeconomic ways" and will never become a full part of the West.

Unlike the studies of China and Russia, which both possess a dominant strategic culture that either legitimizes the accumulation and use of coercive power wrapped in moralism or drives the expansion of territory in order to sustain a defensive glacis, Alexis Dudden's chapter on Japan depicts a country that is genuinely struggling with two traditions of understanding security. The currently dominant vision that came to characterize Japan's national style is one that is relatively young and dates back to the end of World War II. It is a strategic culture born of defeat and nurtured by the U.S. occupation that forged, in John Dower's words cited by Dudden, an "alien constitution" that married "monarchism, democratic idealism, and pacifism." Most remarkably, this ethos has been "thoroughly internalized and vigorously defended" by the population as a whole, which appeared content to trade "Japan's right to wage war…for U.S. security guarantees and economic stimulus."

While this cosmopolitanism undoubtedly produced great benefits for Japan, it overlay an older, more traditional understanding that viewed Japan as a maritime state with oceanic borders serving the interests of its island people. This conception, Dudden notes, goes back to the Tokugawa era. Despite the policy failures of that epoch and the periods that followed, it nurtured a specific Japanese self-understanding, namely that the "national space in the seas around Japan is critical" for its identity, interests, and security. The resuscitation of this older idea is led by key elites—a theme that the second wave of strategic culture theorizing would be sensitive to—who seem "committed to again orienting Japan to the sea, as it was positioned during the first half of the twentieth century." This effort underlies the Abe administration's struggles to reform the constitution, increase Japan's contribution to the U.S. alliance system, and more generally push the country toward becoming a more "normal" nation. In short, Dudden notes, despite there being a prior moment in Japanese history when "the idea of the nation as rigidly bordered engendered Japan's collapse," the social consensus that once "held that the country's island nature caused its defeat in 1945" is rapidly eroding. Hence, Japan's strategic trajectory will be determined by the current struggle to define its strategic culture either "as inward-looking and tightly defined or as open-ended and engaged with the world."

David Kang and Jiun Bang's chapter depicts South Korea's strategic culture as characterized by an uncompromising quest for autonomy, which might appear odd given the fact that the country's geography positions it among states that are much richer and more powerful, such as China and Japan. Further complicating the issue is South Korea's relatively greater comfort with China and distrust of Japan—its stronger and weaker neighbors, respectively—an outcome that runs counter to the expectations of balancing postulated by some versions of realism that emphasize the distribution of materialist capabilities as determinative. To explain the distinctiveness of South Korean behavior, Kang and Bang, consistent with the insights of second wave theorists of strategic culture, note that Japan's 35-year colonization of Korea in the modern period, coupled with revulsion about Korea's submissiveness toward China in premodern history, led South Korean elites to construct an early twentieth-century narrative about "how masculine and strong Korea had been in the past." This vision underlies the belief that even contemporary South Korea can pursue strategic independence, while its relative comfort with China over Japan, despite the greater coercive power wielded by the former, is explained by the differences in Korean experience with the two states historically. Even when Korea was a Chinese tributary state, it enjoyed stability and tranquility, whereas the experience of Japanese occupation was cataclysmic.

As a result, Kang and Bang argue that "South Korea's strategic culture has historically viewed China as a major power to be dealt with and Japan as a threat to be defended against" because "if China was the immovable mountain under whose shadow one must live, Japan was the unpredictable and dangerous neighbor that seemed superficially placid but could snap at any time." Further, the need for China's assistance in managing the threat from North Korea today, coupled with the assurance arising from the alliance relationship with the United States, permits South Korea to pursue its policy of preserving independence vis-à-vis larger neighbors while enjoying the benefits of a close relationship with China that often enables Seoul to make common cause with Beijing in opposing the specter of Japanese revanchism.

Ian Hall's discussion of Indian strategic culture captures succinctly the conflicted attitude to power that characterizes New Delhi's conduct in international politics. The chapter views "fatalism, moralism, and activism" as three distinct, but contending, ethical traditions that left their imprint on various political epochs dating back to classical Hinduism through imperial eras (ending in the national struggle against British rule) and culminating in the post-independence era. The behavior that dominated any given period seemed to be shaped greatly by whichever axiological vision was in ascendency at the time. The syncretism that defines Indian civilization, however, ensured that the preeminence enjoyed by any particular worldview at a given moment was insufficient to completely extinguish its competitors. As a result, every hegemony was always transient, and even when it was manifest, the dominant vision was usually tinged with elements drawn from the alternatives.

Hall's analysis elaborates how, in the post-independence period, the three contending strategic cultures in India that remain rivalrous to this day—Nehruvian pragmatism, hard realpolitik, and Hindu nationalism—combine the older ethical traditions in different ways. Yet Hall argues that "strategic restraint," which is a distinctive legacy of Nehruvian practice, is likely to survive even in the face of rising Hindu nationalism. This is not only because it best comports with India's material circumstances presently but because it is also consistent with the Hindu nationalist conviction that without "a unified society that displays the correct degree of manliness and muscularity with regard to both domestic and international politics…a state's military forces will never be able to fulfill their true potential." By thus elaborating both the ideational foundations of India's national style and the purposes that such an operating code is meant to advance, Hall's reading of India's strategic culture comports with the insights offered by both the first and second waves of academic theorizing on the subject.

With perhaps the exception of China, there is no better example in this book of how a strategic culture comes to be deliberately constructed than Yohanes Sulaiman's chapter on Indonesia. Sulaiman emphasizes the fact that Indonesia's archipelagic geography and the hundreds of ethnic groups present on its numerous islands combined to prevent a shared sense of nationality from naturally developing over time. The "latent fear" that "unity could be easily undermined through policies of divide and conquer" amid such diversities led to the construction of a vitalizing founding myth: that modern Indonesia "is the successor state of the two maritime kingdoms of Srivijaya and Majapahit, which are believed to have ruled the entirety of modern Indonesia, as well as the Malay Peninsula, between the seventh and fourteenth centuries." The prestige of the Hindu-Buddhist Majapahit rulers was so great that even the succeeding Islamic kingdoms in the archipelago sought legitimacy by claiming that they were successor states. The political creation of contemporary Indonesia by Dutch colonialism—in the form of the Dutch East Indies—provided fertile ground for the perpetuation of this founding myth as Indonesian nationalists sought to legitimize their anticolonial struggle by claiming that it was aimed at recovering the nation that existed for centuries past in a golden era once enjoyed under Majapahit rule.

While this view was rejected outside Javanese territories, it nonetheless animated the armed resistance to the Dutch colonial forces. Although Indonesian independence was not ultimately secured as a result of any military success, the decentralized guerrilla organization that was entrenched during the anticolonial struggle provided the foundations on which military rule and interests would later come to dominate Indonesia's politics and, by extension, its political culture. The now familiar Indonesian national conviction—nonalignment—is a post-independence artifact that derives from the "free and active" narrative. As Sulaiman points out, this narrative stresses "that in order to be completely free, Indonesia must have an independent foreign policy that is unrestricted by any military pacts or alignments with great powers." This composite edifice, which marries together a historical myth, a particular pattern of political organization, and an ideological principle of foreign policy, remains a remarkable example of how a strategic culture can be consciously constructed to serve the interests of certain elites while advancing the cause of nation-building.

In an assessment that bears some similarities to Hall's analysis of India, Colin Dueck reads U.S. strategic culture as being influenced by two strains. The dominant tradition is classical liberalism, which, anchored in an exceptionalist view of itself, emphasizes that "the United States has a special role to play in promoting a more open, democratic, and interdependent world order." While debates persist about whether this order should be promoted by example or by force, there seems to be no doubt that the U.S. national style is characterized by a liberal worldview and rhetoric that incarnates many of the ideals of the European Enlightenment both in its aims and in the role imagined for reason in political life. Having said this, however, Dueck clarifies that the prevalence of liberal ideals has by no means undermined the ability of the United States to pursue its own interests. Rather, it would be "a mistake to suggest that U.S. strategic culture renders the conduct of effective international strategies impossible. Historically, the United States has often had considerable success in promoting its own position and interests abroad."

If there has been any conspicuous constraint on the pursuit of U.S. interests, it is less the presence of liberal ideals and more the persistence of "a preference for limited liability," which gives rise to a second strain of U.S. strategic culture. When combined with "ambitious classically liberal international goals," the desire to limit liability often creates the "contradictions or gaps between ends and means" that are prominent features of U.S. national security strategy. The common view from abroad of the United States as a country that often seeks grand objectives internationally but remains unwilling to muster either the patience or the resources to realize those aims thus has some foundation in reality because of the tension that Dueck highlights as an enduring characteristic of the United States' national operating style. Furthermore, this stress is likely to survive indefinitely because the realist, progressive, and nationalist subcultures—whatever their other differences—are united in their opposition to expensive overseas crusades designed to promote liberal values internationally. Dueck's analysis, accordingly, adeptly explains both how the dominant liberalism of U.S. strategic culture has been formed, while being continually buffeted by other dissident traditions, and how its transformed iteration shapes the nation's goals, strategies, and patterns of behavior.

Conclusion: Asian Strategic Cultures and U.S. Interests

Although the chapters in this volume cannot provide linear causal connections between strategic culture and specific state behaviors, they do illuminate the key sources that account for the generation of strategic cultures in important Asian states and explain how these ideational frames tend to color various national attitudes toward the accumulation and use of sovereign power, including building partnerships with others and the employment of military force. When these chapters are read synoptically, the challenges posed to U.S. policy in the Asia-Pacific become discernible, even if clear behavioral consequences cannot be derived from strategic culture alone.

If the core task facing the United States in this region consists of coping with the rise of Chinese power and China's accompanying desire to reconstitute its historic continental hegemony—which inevitably entails diminishing the U.S. role as a security guarantor in Asia—this volume's examination of the strategic cultures of key Asian states suggests that the challenges facing Washington will be considerable. The two most important authoritarian powers in Asia, China and Russia, are characterized both by substantial coercive capabilities—in the case of the former, a still steadily expanding economy that supports a dramatic military modernization—and by strategic cultures that emphasize the offensive use of these capabilities, albeit with defensive justifications. Both states also seem inclined to preemptive doctrines, possess relatively brittle governing institutions, are increasingly drawn toward each other because of their grievances with the United States, and are embroiled in several conflicts with their neighbors, many of which are formal U.S. allies. The fact that China and Russia also possess large inventories of nuclear weapons makes the challenges of undertaking successful extended deterrence in Asia all the more burdensome for U.S. defense planners. The strategic cultures of these two countries, therefore, will give both their neighbors and the United States some pause, a disquiet that is only intensified by their burning global ambitions and possession of formidable material capabilities.

The characteristics of the strategic cultures in the democratic states examined in this volume only complicate the picture for U.S. policymakers. Although all these states—Japan, South Korea, India, and Indonesia—are more or less unified by a peaceful strategic culture, which is a great boon from the perspective of regional stability, their more placid attitudes to security competition could make the task of managing China's rise harder than might be expected. Japanese strategic culture is cleaved between traditional realists and postmodern cosmopolitans. While the continued ascendency of the latter might be good for Japan in many ways, it is uncertain whether the country's security and autonomy, as well as its alliance with the United States, will remain robust in the face of burgeoning Chinese power if the reforms desired by the realists cannot be realized. Japan's strategic culture may thus exemplify a cruel conundrum: what is good for its integrity may become subversive of its security, and vice versa. South Korea's greater comfort with China than with Japan further complicates the U.S. task of balancing China.

India's strategic culture, though steadily shifting toward greater nationalism over cosmopolitanism, cannot yet let go of its strong residual commitment to strategic restraint, which produces an ambivalence that makes the task of partnering with the United States quite challenging. As in Japan, a future nationalist hegemony in India may also transform its strategic culture in ways that make more effective strategic balancing possible, but perhaps at the cost of its success as a liberal democracy. Indonesia, by contrast, represents the opposite end of the spectrum: a determined commitment to avoid all semblances of entangling partnerships could threaten its security vis-à-vis a rising China even as Indonesia preserves the purity of its nonalignment.

Finally, there is the issue of U.S. strategic culture itself: the challenges of preserving a global regime that protects the United States' primacy vis-à-vis China or any other state derive from a continued ascendancy of the internationalist constituency within the polity. Yet this very group is under stress in domestic politics today. If its partnership with its nationalist compatriots cannot be repaired—against the opposing views of global order sometimes espoused by progressives and invariably held by isolationists—the larger question of what U.S. strategic goals in Asia ought to be could itself be redefined in ways that would undermine U.S. prosperity, power, and status in the international system. Thankfully, the future of balancing in the region will be determined not solely by strategic culture but equally by material interests. Yet because these latter equities will be discerned greatly through the prisms of the strategic cultures of the nations concerned, a successful geopolitical equilibrium in Asia will arise only to the degree that it is generated through the exercise of U.S. power and statesmanship. To the degree that a better understanding of the strategic cultures of key Asian states makes this task easier, this volume will have served its purpose of both enlarging scholarship and improving policy.

EXECUTIVE SUMMARY

This chapter examines the official narrative and ongoing scholarly debates about Chinese strategic culture and assesses the influence of this strategic culture on China's international behavior.

MAIN ARGUMENT

Though officials in Beijing depict Chinese strategic culture as being shaped by traditional cultural values disinclining it to force and coercion, this culture's key characteristic is actually its realism: calculations of cost and opportunity tied to the balance of power and devoted to the maximization of national power within the international system. Nonrealist factors rooted in Chinese political culture do condition aspects of behavior, such as in creating an obsession with virtue narratives and image as a component of the Chinese Communist Party's political legitimacy. Realpolitik calculation, however—and a notable willingness to use violence when the balance of forces permits—represents the "bones" that underlie the ideational "flesh" of China's strategic culture. This "realpolitik with Chinese characteristics" is more problematic than classical realpolitik because of its soaring ambition for global status, prickly and insecure moralism, inflexible fear of admitting error, and tendency to rationalize and valorize the use of force in self-defense.

POLICY IMPLICATIONS

- A grasp of the idiosyncratic "Chineseness" of China's strategic culture and the party's legitimacy discourse can help foreign leaders pressure the regime more effectively and avoid adopting postures that are inflammatory in unwanted ways.

- Contrary to the official narrative, quasi-Confucian "virtuocratic" traditions may not pull China in the direction of benevolently pacific policy but may instead actually worsen realism's coercive and violence-prone tendencies.

- Some of the worrying effects of this "exacerbated realism" may be attenuated if the parochial interests of the party itself could be played off against the incentives of maximizing realist power in the international arena.

Realpolitik with Chinese Characteristics: Chinese Strategic Culture and the Modern Communist Party-State

Christopher A. Ford

In the official narrative propounded by the Chinese Communist Party (CCP), the People's Republic of China (PRC) has a strategic culture rooted in a uniquely ancient history and political-cultural continuity that legitimates a special and privileged role for Beijing in world affairs as a peace-loving power at the civilizational center of mankind. This role is purportedly sustained by the sophistication of Chinese culture and the benevolence of its rulers. The official narrative continues this "virtuocratic" storyline into the present day, with the CCP as the natural heir to this tradition and China's modern rise as inherently beneficial to all. But this account has problems. The essentialism inherent in its descriptions of Chinese political continuity and its focus on the allegedly unprecedented humiliations of the nineteenth century, for instance, stand up poorly to historical analysis. More importantly, the depiction of Chinese strategic culture as both uniquely Chinese and uniquely focused on harmonious, civilizational "soft power" is also tendentious.

Scholars have debated the role and importance of violence-friendly realpolitik versus pacific- and virtue-focused Confucian elements in Chinese strategic culture. The available evidence indicates that the latter elements

Christopher A. Ford is Chief Legislative Counsel for the U.S. Senate Foreign Relations Committee and is a former U.S. principal deputy assistant secretary of state and intelligence officer in the U.S. Navy Reserve. He can be reached at <fordchristoph@gmail.com>.

The views expressed herein are entirely the author's own and do not necessarily reflect those of anyone else in the U.S. government.

can play an important role in conditioning the views of PRC leaders and their reactions to their environment. Nevertheless, contrary to the official narrative, realist aspects predominate, forming realpolitik "bones" that lie beneath the Confucian-pacifist "flesh" of Chinese strategic culture. On the whole, this culture is notably oriented toward force and coercion, though it accompanies this realism with self-justificatory posturing that stresses the regime's disinterested and violence-averse benevolence.

Despite the predominant role of realpolitik calculation in PRC behavior, distinctively Chinese elements in China's strategic culture do seem to have played some role in making the PRC more sensitive to issues of image, reputation, status-hierarchical national rank, and ideological posturing than one might expect of classic realism. However, most of the PRC's deviations from stereotypical realism do not support the official narrative of "peace-loving" and "harmony-seeking" Chinese strategic culture. Instead, these variations suggest that "realpolitik with Chinese characteristics" can become an "exacerbated realism" of moralistic coercion, more prone to use force and less willing to show flexibility than might otherwise be the case:

- Idiosyncratic elements in Chinese strategic culture have added what are in effect ideological grievances (e.g., Taiwan's mere pronouncement of independence) to the list of more conventionally realpolitik reasons for war.

- Such elements have also encouraged China's fixation on reclaiming its perceived birthright and expunging past humiliation at foreign hands by returning itself to first-rank global status, which may encourage self-assertion driven more by prideful ambition than by careful realist calculation and may make capability-sensitive realpolitik bargaining and compromise more difficult.

- The moralism inherent in the quasi-Confucian virtuocratic conceits that the CCP has inherited from the Chinese imperial tradition may predispose Beijing toward inflammatory positions that highlight China's virtue and its opponents' depravity.

- The Confucian-Mencian tradition has helped nurture a self-justificatory political narrative in which Beijing can rationalize almost any use of force as defensive in nature. This, too, may make conflict easier to contemplate, and compromise harder to justify, than one might expect of a more calmly calculating realist.

Some of the worrying implications of this exacerbated realism might be attenuated if the parochial interests of the CCP itself could be played off against the incentives of maximizing realist power in the international arena.

Sinological awareness may also suggest advantages in soft-power engagement with the PRC. On the whole, however—and very much contrary to the claims of the official narrative—traditionally rooted ideational elements in Chinese strategic culture may make the PRC's international behavior more problematic rather than less.

To explore Chinese strategic culture and its salience in the behavior of the PRC, this chapter begins by examining how the CCP uses narratives about China's strategic culture in a complex process of appropriation, manipulation, and selective remembering. Subsequent sections will assess ongoing scholarly debates between realist and constructivist interpretations of Chinese strategic culture—whether it is principally characterized by power-maximizing calculation and openness to the use of force or governed instead by more culturally idiosyncratic dynamics rooted in China's Confucian and Mencian philosophical and political traditions stereotypically focused on virtue ethics and disinclined toward violent coercion—and explore the influence that strategic culture actually has on the PRC's aims and behavior.

China's Official Narrative

The CCP regime routinely manipulates historical memory for political purposes, devoting considerable time and energy to the systematic reinterpretation, distortion, erasure, or even invention of historical information in order to legitimize and advance regime power. These methods stem from two inherited traditions. First, the Marxist-Leninist tradition has never scrupled to manipulate historical memory to serve present-day ends. Second, the PRC inherited an even older tradition in which each successive Chinese dynasty would write an official history of its predecessor in order to impugn the virtue of that predecessor and justify its own power through the prism of "mandate of heaven" thinking: the ancient notion that authority accrues to those who deserve it and that loss of virtue naturally equates to loss of power.[1]

As indicated backhandedly by Beijing's modern-day fixation on how other countries (e.g., Japan) characterize historical events, and by its prickliness about how others describe Chinese history,[2] the CCP regime devotes considerable effort to trying to control both domestic and

---

[1] Christopher A. Ford, *The Mind of Empire: China's History and Modern Foreign Relations* (Lexington: University Press of Kentucky, 2010), 236.

[2] Christopher A. Ford, "Sinocentrism for the Information Age: Comments on the 4th Xiangshan Forum," New Paradigms Forum, January 13, 2013, http://www.newparadigmsforum.com/NPFtestsite/?p=1498; and Christopher A. Ford, *China Looks at the West: Identity, Global Ambitions, and the Future of Sino-American Relations* (Lexington: University Press of Kentucky, 2015), 455–58.

international interpretations of China's history, culture, and trajectory in the modern world, employing such manipulations to legitimize party power at home and advance PRC interests abroad. An important element of this approach is control over the nature and content of whatever distinctively Chinese strategic culture China is understood to have.

The Narrative of "Chineseness" and Virtue

In recent decades, the PRC leadership has increasingly stressed "Chineseness" as a touchstone of propriety in the sociopolitical arena. This discourse may have begun with circumlocutions designed to obscure early deviations from Marxist orthodoxy—e.g., Deng Xiaoping's description of his market-focused, quasi-capitalist economic program as "socialism with Chinese characteristics"—but what might be described as self-Orientalizing essentialism has now become a crucial component of the CCP's legitimacy narrative. Today, concepts of Chineseness are frequently invoked in contexts ranging from the sublime to the ridiculous. They emerge in such things as the articulation of increasingly Sinocentric political-philosophical themes and the encouragement of Confucian studies beginning in the 1980s,[3] as well as in President Xi Jinping's recent call for the development of a new "system of philosophy and social sciences with Chinese characteristics."[4] Almost nothing, in fact, seems to escape the embrace of virtuous Sinification, with the CCP having recently stepped up efforts to suppress the use of foreign-originating names for property, which are said to damage China's "national sovereignty and dignity."[5]

Such invocations of special Chinese values justify CCP autocracy, demonstrate the virtue of the party's leadership, articulate civilizational foundations and precedents for the regime's dreams of status and glory in the international arena, and discredit alien Western values that the regime finds distasteful or threatening (i.e., civil and political rights, political pluralism, and electorally accountable governance). Depictions of China as having a unique—and uniquely virtuous—strategic culture are part of this campaign, playing a particularly important role in CCP efforts to convince decision-makers in other countries not to worry about, or attempt to impede, China's rise. No less a figure than President Xi has made clear that "several thousand years ago, the Chinese nation trod a path that was different from

---

[3] Valérie Niquet, "'Confu-Talk': The Use of Confucian Concepts in Contemporary Chinese Foreign Policy," in *China's Thought Management*, ed. Anne-Marie Brady (New York: Routledge, 2012), 76.

[4] "Xi Stresses Chinese Characteristics in Philosophy, Social Sciences," Xinhua, May 17, 2016.

[5] "China to Clear Out Foreign, Bizarre Geographical Names," Xinhua, March 22, 2016; and Austin Ramzy, "China Aims to Tighten Borders against Foreign Place Names," *New York Times*, March 23, 2016, http://www.nytimes.com/2016/03/24/world/asia/china-housing-foreign-names.html.

other nations' culture and development," and that this unique path is the basis for the Chinese characteristics that have manifested themselves in modern PRC governance as a result of "our country's historical inheritance and cultural traditions."[6] As Andrew Scobell has summarized, many Chinese today display a "religious-like fervor" about the uniqueness of their own strategic traditions and are "particularly smitten with what they view as China's special gifts to the theory and practice of statecraft and international relations."[7]

So what is the official CCP narrative of China's strategic culture? As it can be discerned not only from official mouthpiece organs but also across a broad range of ostensibly nonofficial media and scholarly sources, this narrative has a number of elements. To begin with, one recurring theme in the PRC's narrative of its own strategic culture is what might be called its essentialist eternalism: the conceit that China, and its strategic culture, has basically always been the same. In conceptual terms, it is assumed not just that there is something special about Chinese thinking but that its distinctiveness has persisted, and in a consistent form, since time immemorial. In geographic terms, territories that are currently part of the PRC—or that the regime declares to be so, even if it does not actually control them (e.g., Taiwan, the Senkaku Islands, and whatever shrinking residua of the South China Sea Beijing has not already seized)—have always been part of China.[8]

This approach implies that a great many things have happened in Chinese history, but in effect remarkably little has actually changed. China is depicted as the embodiment of traditional notions of virtue on the geopolitical stage: a discrete and distinctive civilization that has preserved its brilliant essence and basic geographic contours for "5,000 years of continuous Chinese culture" and that naturally has a unique and privileged role in the world as a result.[9] As if to underline this point, under President Xi's slogan of "revive China," party officials have in recent years even encouraged the revival of the ancient cult of China's mythological "yellow emperor"—the legendary figure said to have begun Chinese civilization 5,000 years ago and who is traditionally thought of as the literal biological forefather of all Chinese people.[10]

---

[6] Didi Kirsten Tatlow, "Xi Jinping on Exceptionalism with Chinese Characteristics," *New York Times*, October 14, 2014.

[7] Andrew Scobell, *China's Use of Military Force: Beyond the Great Wall and the Long March* (Cambridge: Cambridge University Press, 2003), 27.

[8] As State Councilor Yang Jiechi told U.S. secretary of state John Kerry in June 2016, for instance, the islands of the South China Sea "have been Chinese territory since antiquity." Jane Perlez and Chris Buckley, "U.S. and Beijing Offer Competing Views on South China Sea," *New York Times*, June 7, 2016.

[9] Tom Hancock, "From Legend to History: China Turns to a Mythical Emperor," Agence-France Presse, May 19, 2016.

[10] Tatlow, "Xi Jinping on Exceptionalism with Chinese Characteristics."

More importantly, it is axiomatic in the official narrative that there is something not just distinctive and different but actually special about Chinese strategic culture. It is often suggested, for instance, that the country's Confucian past—bound up with a system of sociofamilial virtue ethics that prizes rituals of proper behavior and that historically tended to valorize the gentleman-scholar over the warrior—has given China a generally morality-based and pacifist strategic culture that lacks the "imperialist" or "hegemonic" tendencies found in Western history. (President Xi Jinping himself at one point even suggested that Chinese of ethnic Han origin lack the "invasion gene" that leads to aggression and imperialism in other peoples.)[11]

China's historical predominance in its region, it is thus alleged, was rooted not in intimidation and conquest but rather in civilizational attraction—the gravitational force of a wise and superior civilization that naturally dominated East Asia because it deserved this status. Selective references to the voluminous and sophisticated canon of Chinese strategic writings from the periods that preceded China's first imperial unification reinforce this message and are often used to support the point that traditional Chinese culture disdained the naked use of force and prioritized "winning without fighting" through subtle cleverness.

These notions are consonant with ancient Confucian conceptions in which political authority in effect self-assembles around the virtuous and benevolent leader precisely because of his virtue—rather than as a result of coercion or any actual desire to control—and resonate through modern Chinese tropes about how the country's "peaceful rise" and ambitions for a "harmonious world" offer the planet a "new type of great-power relations" with which to build a strategic environment devoid of hostile competitiveness.[12]

The official narrative gently tiptoes around the idea that these concepts imply a Sinocentric system of global order. Instead, it is emphatic that Chinese strategic culture is qualitatively different from—and notably superior to—the militarized thought that characterizes the strategic culture of the West. It is the very Chineseness of China's strategic culture, in other words, that helps make possible Beijing's selfless leadership in the international community. China's ability to offer the world a locus of "humane authority"

---

[11] Philip Bowring, "A Sense of Destiny Inspires China's Maritime Claims," *Financial Times*, August 20, 2014.

[12] Guo Xinyu and Zhang Lu, "A Nuclear-Free World: An Ideal or a Reality?" *Dangdai shijie*, 2009; and Jane Perlez, "Chinese President to Seek New 'Power Relationship' in Talks with Obama," *New York Times*, May 29, 2013.

inspired by ancient Chinese philosophy will help ensure that the new order makes win-win solutions available for everyone.[13]

A recurring theme is the moralistic nature of the CCP's narratives about itself, China, and the rest of the world. It is not just that China must be depicted in virtuocratic terms, offering the world a qualitatively different and better approach to geopolitics, but also that its leadership—that is, the CCP—needs to be seen as superlatively virtuous at home and abroad. Governments in the West tend to ground their authority in the consent of a sovereign people expressed through periodic elections and protected by the enforcement of political rights against the government. Rejecting this approach, however, but nowadays also unable to take advantage even of the now-obsolete alternative legitimacy discourse of Marxist-Leninism, the CCP has come increasingly to invoke what purports to be an ancient Chinese model of political authority. This model is tied to the benevolence and superlative competence of a self-selected and self-regulating elite, purportedly chosen on the basis of its intellectual and technocratic merits. In effect, the party deserves to rule for the same reason that China deserves to achieve the dream of returning to its ancient position of civilizational and geopolitical centrality: because it is better suited for this role than any other and because its preeminence offers a unique opportunity for all to benefit from a political order of prosperity and harmony.

Moralism and Humiliation

Just as ancient Chinese dynasties once constructed dynastic histories of their predecessors in order to highlight those regimes' moral failures and thereby legitimate their own succession, PRC moralism also involves powerful demonization narratives. Because Chinese status and CCP rule are, in effect, rooted in their virtue, it is imperative that those who disagree with or oppose their dominance be depicted as morally deficient.

This model of authority is conceptually monist, for virtuocratic power cannot concede real pluralism and fears alternative loci of virtue. If their appeal to ordinary Chinese people is to be thwarted, Western conceptions of political rights and democratic process must be decried as decadent, corrupt, intemperate, polarizing, and conducive to either paralysis or instability. Those who resist CCP hegemony within China are tools of "foreign forces" that

---

[13] Samuel S. Kim, "China and the Third World in the Changing World Order," in *China and the World: Chinese Foreign Relations in the Post–Cold War Era*, ed. Samuel S. Kim (Boulder: Westview Press, 1994), 128, 142, 161; Michael B. Yahuda, *China's Role in World Affairs* (London: Croom Helm, 1978), 281; Yan Xuetong, *Ancient Chinese Thought, Modern Chinese Power*, trans. Sun Zhe (Princeton: Princeton University Press, 2011); and Cai Tuo, "China Should Have a Part in the International Order's Transition," *Xiandai guoji guanxi*, 2009.

wish China ill and threaten chaos.[14] Those who oppose Chinese designs in East Asia are acting out of hegemonic intentions, militarizing the region, and setting the stage for an unnecessary and catastrophic confrontation. (Japan, for example, does not merely control islands that China wishes to control but denies the evil demons of its own history and flirts with a revived militaristic revanchism that threatens the stability of Asia.) The demonization of foreign and nonconformist domestic others is an essential part of the narrative.

In the Chinese context, the storylines of indigenous virtue and foreign malevolence are tied together in the idea that China suffered a "century of humiliation" at foreign hands from the period of the First Opium War (1839–42) at least until the CCP's triumphant arrival in power in 1949—a discourse encouraged by successive Chinese governments from 1915 to the present day. (There was, for instance, National Humiliation Day in Republican China from 1927 to 1940, and the PRC's National People's Congress readopted the idea in 2001.)[15] This persistent narrative of humiliation, which received renewed emphasis in official propaganda as part of the patriotic education campaign organized by party officials in the wake of the Tiananmen Square massacre of 1989, ties together a number of key elements. It invokes and validates the idea of virtuous China's natural and destined position as the "middle kingdom" at the center of global affairs, while at the same time excusing the country's lack of such status at present as the result of unfair and undeserved foreign depredations. Carefully nursed memories of humiliation also provide the regime with a claim to political legitimacy rooted in the stewardship of China's return to glory, as well as a locus of nationalistic grievance with which to fuel political mobilization against whatever the government declares to stand in the way of such progress, either at home or abroad.

The century of humiliation narrative invokes, perpetuates, and takes advantage of the psychic shock created in the nineteenth century when China encountered a more vibrant and powerful foreign "other"—in the form of European power, then in the full flower of its Industrial Revolution exuberance—that had conceptions of political authority and global order very different from Chinese imperial thinking and that seemed, as a sociopolitical system, to have physical, economic, intellectual, and spiritual resources superior to those China could then claim for itself.[16]

---

[14] Cary Huang, "Chill Wind Blows through Chinese Academy of Social Sciences," *South China Morning Post*, August 2, 2014; and "Conscientiously Preserving Social Harmony and Stability," *Beijing Daily*, March 5, 2011.

[15] William A. Callahan, "National Insecurities: Humiliation, Salvation, and Chinese Nationalism," *Alternatives* 29, no. 2 (2004): 199, 202–3, 201–11.

[16] Christopher A. Ford, "The Past as Prism: China and the Shock of Plural Sovereignty," *Joint Force Quarterly* 47 (2007): 14.

This encounter was a tremendously debilitating politico-moral blow for an ancient, proud, and vain empire with virtuocratic pretensions within a Confucian political culture. China has yet to entirely recover from this blow.[17] The official narrative of past national humiliation—with its corollary of a self-assertive collective destiny in "rejuvenating the Chinese nation and Chinese civilization"—remains an important part of modern China's self-perception.[18]

Chinese Strategic Culture beneath the Cloak

Puncturing Conceits

Before getting to the more strategically central and policy-relevant parts of the official Chinese narrative, it is worth examining some of its lesser manifestations. What should one make, for instance, of the official PRC narrative of Chinese eternalism? In reality, of course, the Chinese state has not always existed for five thousand years. There has certainly been civilization in China for a very long time, and in many eras it was one of considerable complexity and sophistication. Similar things, however, could be said of other areas of the world. It is not immediately obvious why China's claims of historical continuity and distinctiveness are inherently more compelling than those of other states and regions—including Europeans who invoke the intellectual and spiritual legacy of Greece, Rome, and Jerusalem; Indians who look back to Harappan culture and the Mauryan Dynasty; and Middle Easterners whose first empires and great monuments predate anything of significance anywhere else. China's historical cultural core also constitutes only a small portion of modern-day China. The first real imperial unification of a feuding patchwork of rivalrous smaller states did not occur until 221 BCE under the first emperor of the Qin Dynasty (221–207 BCE), and China has oscillated between unification and a sometimes notably chaotic disunity ever since, with two significant periods of unification being the result of foreign conquest. Modern Chinese essentialism may make for fine rhetoric, but it is poor history.

Though a fixation on claims to possession rooted in the distant fog of history is perhaps unsurprising for a regime that can claim no foundation

---

[17] As Charles Horner has observed, a key objective for every Chinese regime since the fall of the Qing Dynasty has been to escape this "Chinese predicament." See Charles Horner, "Historical Perspectives upon Chinese Perceptions of the United States" (remarks at a Hudson Institute workshop, Washington, D.C., December 14, 2011).

[18] Fei-Ling Wang, "Beijing's Incentive Structure: The Pursuit of Preservation, Prosperity, and Power," in *China Rising: Power and Motivation in Chinese Foreign Policy*, ed. Yong Deng and Fei-Ling Wang (Lanham: Rowman and Littlefield Publishers, 2005), 19, 32.

in democratic consent by a sovereign population, there is also some irony in the importance that the modern CCP narrative attaches to the idea of an indissoluble Chinese nation-state that occupies the frontiers that modern China inherited from the Qing Dynasty (1644–1912) and that has ancient historical claims to all of this territory. The two dynasties that give rise to the most sweeping of the PRC's modern territorial claims, the Yuan Dynasty (1271–1368) and the Qing Dynasty, were actually non-Chinese conquest dynasties, created when outside "barbarian" peoples—Mongols and Manchus, respectively—invaded and defeated China, thereafter ruling it as merely one component (albeit a very large and important one) of their sprawling empires. It is Yuan and Qing precedents, however, that are most often invoked to ground the claims to sovereignty over areas such as Tibet, Taiwan, and Manchuria. To many observers, this logic seems somewhat problematic—as if France were to claim Belgium because at some point they had both been conquered and ruled by Germany.

The eternalist and essentialist narrative of the modern-day PRC has, in other words, fixated on territorial frontiers associated with the military hegemony of China's past conquerors and has entangled this border with a reification of the nation-state that seems to have been imported from nineteenth-century Europe but that would scarcely be recognizable to the ancient peoples about whom it is today asserted. Some modern scholarship based on Manchu archives from the Qing period, for example, has indicated that China's Manchu rulers did not view themselves as Chinese, administered China as only one part of a multinational empire, and did not Sinicize their other territorial possessions.[19] Such historical accounts are starkly inconsistent with the official narrative of Chinese political-cultural eternalism keyed to Qing-era boundaries. The modern PRC has tried to deal with such inconsistencies through vituperative denial or by depicting the Mongol and Manchu invaders as "Chinese peoples,"[20] but even this official narrative is—ironically—inconsistent with China's own ancient Confucian tradition. This tradition tended to view Chineseness not in stark territorial-nationalist terms but instead along a graduated civilizational continuum according to each people's degree of Sinicization, proceeding outward from populations

---

[19] Pamela Kyle Crossley, *A Translucent Mirror: History and Identity in Qing Imperial Ideology* (Berkeley: University of California Press, 1999); and Beatrice S. Bartlett, *Monarchs and Ministers: The Grand Council in Mid-Ch'ing China, 1723–1820* (Berkeley: University of California Press, 1991).

[20] "A Righteous View of History," China Media Project, http://cmp.hku.hk/2015/04/22/38664; Frank Langfitt, "Why a Chinese Government Think Tank Attacked American Scholars," National Public Radio, May 21, 2015, http://www.npr.org/2015/05/21/408291285/why-a-chinese-government-think-tank-attacked-american-scholars; Ben Dooley, "U.S. Scholars in Crosshairs over Interpretation of China's History," Kyodo News, May 13, 2015; and Tang Zongli and Zuo Bing, *Maoism and Chinese Culture* (New York: Nova Science Publishers, 1996), 38–39.

at the cultural core through concentric circles of ever-increasing barbarity.[21] To point out these facts, of course, is not to gainsay the subjective experience of historical distinctiveness and ancient continuity as perceived by modern Chinese. But it does appear that the PRC's eternalist narrative has only an ambiguous relationship with historical reality.

The official Chinese narrative of national humiliation also does not stand up to scrutiny as well as its proponents might expect. China did, of course, suffer at foreign hands in its encounters first with European and then with Japanese imperial power in the nineteenth and twentieth centuries. Much pain and indignity was unquestionably inflicted, and modern Chinese understandably remember the period with bitterness. Nevertheless, the centrality of humiliation narratives in modern Chinese political life seems extraordinary and stands out in disproportion to how such tropes have featured in the political culture of a number of other peoples who also suffered tremendously when they crossed swords with imperial states empowered by the Industrial Revolution.

Indeed, with the exception of the grim brutalities inflicted on China by Japan in the 1930s, China does not seem to have fared extraordinarily badly at imperial hands compared with other areas of the world that fell at various points under the imperialist yoke. Sub-Saharan Africa suffered slavery and all but complete colonization; the peoples of the Americas faced displacement, conquest, and depopulation; and most of the Middle East and South Asia endured conquest and foreign rule. By contrast, China retained political independence, albeit constrained within a framework of unequal treaties and foreign economic concessions. China even retained its traditional governance structures for decades after European imperial contact, shedding them only when internal Chinese revolution replaced these structures with more modern forms in the republican period after 1911.

In reality, the power of the narrative of China's national humiliation owes as much to the soaring nature of the old empire's self-regard—and to the peculiar sociocultural dynamics of interactions with European culture, which seem to have produced a much more acute psychological predicament for China than did the country's actual conquest on two occasions by more localized barbarians—as it does to the horrors inflicted on China during most of the period commencing when the First Opium War began in 1839. Successive Chinese regimes' emphasis on the concept of humiliation is itself telling, for the term suggests not so much concrete injury inflicted at someone else's hands as it does an abasement of pride: being forced from a state of grandeur into a position of being humbled and

---

[21] Ford, *The Mind of Empire*, 33–38.

reduced to lowliness. The humiliation narrative long nourished by Chinese political leaders, therefore, is as much a construction of modern Chinese politics—an effort to structure and ascribe meaning to the past in light of perceived failures in the present day to live up to what China was meant to be, and a shifting of blame to others for this painful gap—as it is a historical account of actual events.

Debating the Nature and Extent of Chinese Realpolitik

In scholarly circles outside China, experts have debated the degree to which the country can indeed be said to have a distinctive strategic culture and what its contours might be. Some scholars have argued that far from China having traditionally taken only a pacifist, selfless, and civilizational approach to its neighbors, the record of its many imperial dynasties and thousands of wars is replete with self-aggrandizing conflict.[22] Alastair Iain Johnston, Michael Swaine, and Ashley Tellis have contended, for instance, that much of Chinese history demonstrates not so much a Confucian approach to issues of war and peace but in fact a realism that actually preferred military force as a means of resolving disputes when that option was available, and that pursued what today might be known as soft-power competition only when the balance of forces left the empire no other choice.[23]

Peter Perdue, for one, has pointed out that "Chinese dynasties never shrank from the use of force."[24] He argues that the "civilizing force" model of ancient Chinese imperium—in which China acquired expansive dominions as the result of benign "cultural influence" rather than force—is not in fact an ancient verity. Instead, this concept originated among nationalist Chinese thinkers in the 1920s and 1930s as anti-Japanese propaganda discourse designed to whip up patriotic feelings of support for reclaiming an imagined ancient unity of harmonious Chinese peoples. According to Perdue, the "ideological view of Chinese history" created by such apologetics was transmitted to early Western scholars trained in nationalist China, among them John King Fairbank, and hence moved into the Western mainstream.[25] According to Scobell, it was only in the 1990s that historians began to peer

---

[22] There are claims that China has been involved in 6,539 conflicts over the course of its long history. For more on this, see Wang Zhenmin, "Different U.S.-China Conceptions of the Role of Law: Chinese Views," in *The United States and China: Mutual Public Perceptions*, ed. Douglas G. Spelman (Washington, D.C.: Woodrow Wilson International Center for Scholars, 2011).

[23] Alastair Iain Johnston, *Cultural Realism: Strategic Culture and Grand Strategy in Chinese History* (Princeton: Princeton University Press, 1995); and Michael D. Swaine and Ashley J. Tellis, *Interpreting China's Grand Strategy: Past, Present, and Future* (Washington, D.C.: RAND Corporation, 2000).

[24] Peter C. Perdue, "The Tenacious Tributary System," *Journal of Contemporary China* 24, no. 96 (2015): 1,002–14.

[25] Ibid., 1,002, 1,011–14.

behind such assumptions and recognize that a more "assertive, aggressive China" may in fact have existed.[26]

Taking an approach that might seem to split the difference between the archetypes of "parabellum realism" and Confucian-pacifist, "civilizational force" models,[27] Huiyun Feng has argued that structural realism provides only a "partial explanation" for Chinese behavior. According to Feng, Chinese strategic culture is influenced by both the realpolitik statecraft literature of China's pre-unification Warring States period (475–221 BCE) and Confucian ethical-moral traditions. Accordingly, she argues for a "realism-plus-beliefs framework" of analysis in which such Confucian traditions qualify what realism exists in China's strategic culture. In this analysis, Chinese behavior shows a "balance between Parabellum and Confucian propensities," with individual leaders each exhibiting different admixtures of realist and Confucian inclinations. (Feng argues that Mao Zedong exemplified realism, for example, while Deng Xiaoping tended more toward Confucianism.)[28]

In Feng's view, the net result of this balance is to make China not an "offensive" realist but instead a "defensive" one. Yet beyond simply her use of the term realist, Feng's account differs little from the PRC's own self-justificatory and ostensibly Confucian-pacifist interpretation. According to Feng, for instance, although it is realist, China does not orient its foreign policy behavior around power or against threat but instead focuses on building constructive partnerships with other major powers. "Peace-loving" and "nonviolence," she contends, are also "key characteristics of China's strategic culture."[29]

A third approach might be found in the work of Scobell. He agrees with Feng that Chinese strategic culture is dualistic, in that both conflict-averse and defensively minded Confucian elements and more military-focused and offensively oriented realpolitik elements coexist, ensuring that China is neither inherently pacifist nor inherently warlike. For Scobell, however, the realist elements seem more important, for these layers of strategic culture result in a Chinese "cult of defense" in which "realist behavior dominates but is justified as defensive on the basis of a pacifist self-perception." In practice,

---

[26] Scobell, *China's Use of Military Force*, 16–17.

[27] Johnston explains the term "parabellum realism" as deriving from "the realpolitician's axom 'si pacem, parabellum' (if you want peace, then prepare for war). This parallels a Chinese idiom, 'ju an si wei, wu bei you huan' (while residing in peace, think about dangers; without military preparations there will be calamity)." Alastair Iain Johnston, "Cultural Realism and Strategy in Maoist China," in *The Culture of National Security: Norms and Identity in World Politics*, ed. Peter J. Katzenstein (New York: Columbia University Press, 1996), 217, note 2.

[28] Huiyun Feng, *Chinese Strategic Culture and Foreign Policy Decision-Making* (London: Routledge, 2007), 4–6, 15, 17, 25, 67, 78.

[29] Ibid., 4, 26.

he notes, while Chinese elites view China as being a defensive power and "deliberate in calculating" the use of force, it is nonetheless "prone to resort to force in a crisis." For Scobell, the "shared myth" of China's fundamentally defensive orientation allows leaders "to rationalize virtually any military operation as a defensive action."[30]

Just as Feng's account ends up being more or less congruent with constructivist Confucian-pacifism, so also does Scobell's analysis thus end up being fairly congruent with Johnston's account of Chinese strategic culture. According to Johnston, for instance, while China has exhibited fairly consistent "hard realpolitik or *parabellum* strategic culture," even into the Maoist period—including "a preference for offensive uses of force, mediated by a keen sensitivity to relative capabilities"—this is not an abstract, structural realism but rather an "ideationally based hard realpolitik" in which a Confucian-Mencian strand and a zero-sum, coercion-oriented parabellum strand coexist. Yet for Johnston, the Confucian-Mencian element is simply an "idealized discourse" important in Chinese rhetoric and self-image, whereas the hard realpolitik elements persist in actual Chinese practices.[31] Scobell, one suspects, would broadly agree, as would Perdue, who observes that Chinese imperial rulers "waged war constantly against rival powers, although they often masked their campaigns as defensive actions against 'pirates' or 'rebels.'"[32]

Confucian Flesh, Realist Bones

How, then, should one assess the relationship between realpolitik and more culturally idiosyncratic Sinic elements in Chinese strategic culture? To begin with, it is hard to deny that there is a powerful realism even in some of the most self-consciously Chinese elements of China's strategic culture. As Michael Pillsbury and others have noted—and as we have seen even Huiyun Feng freely concede—metaphors and statecraft concepts from China's Warring States period have recurred frequently in the writings of Chinese scholars attempting to understand the modern international arena.[33] Extensive references to classics from that period are embedded throughout modern Chinese strategic writing and are used to provide lessons or metaphors with

---

[30] Scobell, *China's Use of Military Force*, 15, 38, 192–93, 197–98.

[31] Johnston, "Cultural Realism and Strategy in Maoist China," 216, 217, 219–20. Emphasis is in the original.

[32] Perdue, "The Tenacious Tributary System," 1,008.

[33] Michael Pillsbury, *China Debates the Future Security Environment* (Washington, D.C.: National Defense University Press, 2000), 4–5, 315.

which to assess the future, making Warring States–era concepts "the prism through which Chinese thinkers have viewed the post-Westphalia world."[34]

While this connection to and continuing invocation of ancient canonical sources may seem to add weight to the notion that Chinese strategic culture is indeed, in some sense, deeply and historically Chinese, it is important to remember just what a stereotypically realist strategic discourse much of this literature provides. It seems to have been all but unquestioned in Warring States–era texts, for example, that any system of plural state sovereignties is naturally a zero-sum, Hobbesian rivalry for position and status in which the goal of statecraft is to achieve not just hegemony but in fact political unification.[35]

To be sure, China's venerable canon of Warring States–era texts also contains ethical-moral works, including works in the Confucian tradition. The PRC's modern narrative of itself often draws on them, such as by using Warring States–era concepts and language in suggesting that China's "humane authority" can lead and bring to fruition a new era of "harmonious" international relationships. Indeed, some of the PRC's modern cheerleaders expressly invoke ancient authors as sources of inspiration, purporting to ground their views in inspiration drawn from pre-Qin thinkers such as Confucius, Mencius, Guanzi, and Xunzi.[36] Nevertheless, the moral ambitiousness of the Confucian-Mencian tradition was itself heavily laden with power-maximizing geopolitical implications, insofar as even this strand of Chinese thinking took it as a given that possessing virtue equated to acquiring political power, that supreme virtue would lead inexorably to the unification of "all under heaven," and that the state rivalries of the Warring States era were thus fundamentally about the question of which ruler would come to dominate the Sinic world system.[37]

These ethical traditions also did not shy away from using force against those who resisted the all-unifying prerogatives of virtue. No less a figure than Confucius himself, in fact, advocated the use of punitive military expeditions against barbarians who refused to accept guidance from their Chinese geopolitical betters.[38] China's ancient ethical-moral discourses may not have

---

[34] Ford, *The Mind of Empire*, 245–47.

[35] Ibid., 53–57.

[36] Yan, *Ancient Chinese Thought*, 35, 41, 45, 48, 92, 84.

[37] Confucius himself, in fact, made his livelihood as a purveyor of statecraft advice to the princes of China's rival states, on the grounds that if only a properly wise (or wisely counseled) ruler were to arise, the entire system would orient itself around him. "He who exercises government by means of his virtue may be compared to the north polar star, which keeps its place and all the stars turn toward it." Confucius, *Confucius: Confucian Analects, The Great Learning and The Doctrine of the Mean*, trans. James Legge (Oxford: Clarendon, 1893), 145.

[38] Ibid., 310.

used the language of cynical realpolitik, therefore, but as Scobell has suggested in discussing the "cult of defense" he sees in Chinese strategic culture, they offer intellectual resources that appear quite capable of rationalizing almost any sort of power-maximizing conduct. Indeed, in Beijing's modern penchant for demonizing foreign powers such as the Soviet Union and the United States for seeking self-serving hegemony of a sort China itself naturally eschews, one can discern a self-reinforcing fusion of realist power-balancing and quasi-Confucian moralism.

A clearer window into the importance of the realist strain within Chinese strategic culture, however, can be found in actual Chinese practice, and here some historical perspective is in order. One of the key examples cited by PRC officials in explaining how their country would never threaten another state, even if it were to possess military power with global reach, is the remarkable oceanic voyages of the Muslim eunuch Admiral Zheng He at the beginning of the Ming Dynasty in the early fifteenth century. Yet these officials disingenuously rely on foreign audiences' unfamiliarity with the historical record. Far from being a romantic model of peaceably awe-inspiring engagement, Zheng's voyages included notable episodes of gunboat diplomacy, such as sending marines to intervene in favor of the pro-Chinese faction in a Sumatran civil war and taking a local Sri Lankan ruler back to China in chains.[39] On the whole, Chinese imperial history provides remarkably little support for the notion that there is anything particularly unique or pacifist about China's interactions with the rest of the world.

Nor does China's modern history easily support the narrative of harmonious Confucian pacifism. Where opportunities presented themselves to use force, it would appear, the PRC has not hesitated to do so. This was the case against India, which China invaded in 1962 in connection with a territorial dispute. It was the case against Vietnam as well, which China invaded in 1979. Beijing also used attacks with tactical aviation and amphibious units to compel the surrender of a Vietnamese garrison in the Paracel Islands in 1974, thereby seizing control of that island chain, and captured a reef in the Spratly Islands from Vietnam by force in 1988, taking a handful of prisoners and killing several dozen Vietnamese soldiers. The official narrative is also not particularly consistent with the PRC's present-day behavior in the South China Sea, where in order to justify its tendentious claims to enormous expanses of ocean—claims that have now been authoritatively rejected by an arbitral tribunal of the Permanent Court of Arbitration convened under the UN Convention on the Law of

---

[39] Geoffrey Wade, "The Zheng He Voyages: A Reassessment," Asia Research Institute, Working Paper, no. 31, October 2004, 11, 16, 18.

the Sea—Beijing has been constructing new islands out of almost nothing in areas claimed by other countries, and then garrisoning these new bastions.[40] Even if one were to quibble with the exact calculations of scholars such as Jonathan Brecher, Michael Wilkenfeld, and Sheila Rosen—who found the PRC to have used force more frequently in foreign policy crises during 1949–85 than did the United States, the Soviet Union, or the United Kingdom between 1927 and 1985—it is hard not to agree with Johnston that the PRC has, in practice, been "quite prone to use force."[41]

The PRC's relative weakness during most of the CCP's tenure may often have encouraged leaders in Beijing to take strategically nonconfrontational positions for fear of provoking reactions for which China was unprepared—as indeed Deng Xiaoping himself urged in his famous exhortation to his countrymen to "bide our time and build up our capabilities."[42] This hardly implies, however, that one should expect any such allegedly Confucian pacifism to continue as Beijing's power grows. Given the "tradition of exceptional tactical flexibility" that Mao Zedong is said to have bequeathed to his successors,[43] early nonprovocation under Deng is not surprising, but one might also expect the PRC's growing power to result in more aggressive behavior. Deng's aphorism about biding time clearly implies that China was merely awaiting a point when it would be able to assert itself. Far from being an enduring element of Chinese strategic culture, therefore, nonconfrontational postures appear through this prism to be simply a tactical expedient: a prudential choice to be abandoned when favorable changes in the balance of power make confrontation feasible and success likely, and thus a fundamentally realist approach.

Additional evidence for this tactical expediency can be found in the CCP's turn from congenial relations with Japan in the 1970s and 1980s to shrill Japanophobic demonization in the 1990s as Chinese perceptions of that country's relative position and trajectory on the geopolitical stage shifted. At a time when Japan was regarded by Chinese (and Americans) as a rising superpower that would lead the economic future of Asia—and when Beijing clearly had much to learn from Japan as the PRC began to open its economy to the outside world—the Chinese party-state engaged in friendly and cooperative relations. In the 1990s, however, as Japan slipped into a long

---

[40] Derek Watkins, "What China Has Been Building in the South China Sea," *New York Times*, October 27, 2016, http://www.nytimes.com/interactive/2015/07/30/world/asia/what-china-has-been-building-in-the-south-china-sea.html. The arbitral tribunal's ruling is available at https://pca-cpa.org/wp-content/uploads/sites/175/2016/07/PH-CN-20160712-Award.pdf.

[41] Johnston, "Cultural Realism and Strategy," 252.

[42] Susan L. Shirk, *China: Fragile Superpower* (Oxford: Oxford University Press, 2008), 105.

[43] Orville Schell and John Delury, *Wealth and Power: China's Long March into the Twenty-First Century* (New York: Random House, 2013), 255.

period of debt-ridden stagnation and political dysfunction, the PRC felt free to mobilize a harshly anti-Japanese "patriotic education campaign" and today continues to indulge in all manner of condemnatory rhetoric.[44]

China's current spasm of territorial seizure in the South China Sea, moreover, has only been mounted at a point when no other player appears able or willing to challenge China's growing military strength. It is no coincidence that this upsurge coincided with the U.S. financial crisis of 2008—and the period of U.S. indebtedness, budgetary impasse, paralyzing political polarization, and geopolitical retrenchment that the crisis helped engender—and with China's acquisition of increasingly robust naval power-projection capabilities. In short, little in the PRC's behavior suggests that there is anything distinctively or inherently peaceable about China's strategic culture, at least beyond tactical prudence.

Deng Xiaoping's exhortation for China to "bide our time and build up our capabilities" may sound distinctive when expressed in a tersely portentous form reminiscent of ancient strategists such as Sun Zi. It is less clear, however, that there is anything distinctively Chinese in the concept apart from this phrasing. Much of Deng's meaning, for instance, might alternatively be conveyed as either the recommendation of a technocratic modern think tank ("engage in strategic misdirection") or a pithy homily worthy of an American cowboy ("don't kick 'em 'til you can lick 'em"). The tactics and strategy of Chinese statecraft may be developed, expressed, and implemented in idiosyncratically Sinified ways, in other words, but one should not mistake them for something more unique than they are.[45] Beneath its self-consciously Orientalized flesh, a skeleton of classically realist calculation runs through Chinese strategic culture.

The Weight of Culture

However, one should not simply dismiss the PRC's historically tenuous official narrative—or the less propagandized idea that Chinese strategic culture is shaped in important ways by distinctively Chinese elements—as irrelevant, for it is not. If there is a story to be told about strategic culture in China today, it is more complicated than simply a tale in which a classically cynical realism disguises itself in the garments of virtue. For one thing, even

---

[44] Ford, *China Looks at the West*, 227–33.

[45] Huiyun Feng, one fears, committed the methodological error of judging modern Chinese leaders entirely based on their utterances, mistaking PRC officials for "Confucian leaders with very cooperative orientations" simply because they expressed themselves and defended their actions in such terms. Compare Feng, *Chinese Strategic Culture*, 87, 98, 106, 121, 124, with Ford, *China Looks at the West*, 124. Feng judges only Mao himself as a truly realist leader, a specific conclusion with which Johnston would agree, for Mao's writings are suffused with the language of violence and struggle. For more on this, see Johnston, "Cultural Realism and Strategy," 229, 234–48.

if it is factually problematic and in large part politically engineered, the self-Orientalizing official narrative may help shape and constrain otherwise realist PRC behavior by making some policy conclusions or courses of action more difficult to explain or justify than others.[46] Countries dealing with modern China should pay more attention to how CCP narratives constrain Beijing's behavior, and might even constitute exploitable vulnerabilities. Even within the realm of essentially realpolitik interactions, moreover, Sinic idiosyncrasies in strategic culture might also affect the dynamics of crisis stability—e.g., influencing what sorts of posture or rhetorical positions are particularly likely either to provoke or to mollify Chinese elites (or the public) in a tense situation—and help condition how Beijing views or prioritizes its objectives. It might also be that culturally idiosyncratic elements in Chinese thinking accentuate certain behaviors to which more conventional realpolitik power maximization may already predispose the PRC.

There do seem to be some elements of long-term continuity in Chinese strategic culture that are rooted in distinctively Chinese traditions and are analytically separable from the more abstract impulses of structural realism. Though it is in key ways historically problematic, the PRC's official narrative overlies a set of old cultural norms and assumptions that establish aspirational values that each Chinese regime—including the modern party-state—tends to accept as the necessary foundations for legitimate authority, and to which, whatever its actual practice, each regime needs to make its approaches appear to conform. The Confucian assumption that political authority grows out of virtue, for instance, has already been noted, but it is worth emphasizing the degree to which the actual realism of Chinese behavior has for a long time been compelled to exist within a justificatory framework of moralistic virtuocracy, helping create some of the more distinctive aspects of Chinese international behavior.

Because in this context any lack of virtue on the part of China's ruling elite would tend to undermine its claims on power, the CCP has continued an ancient Chinese dynastic tradition of needing its actions to be portrayed—and, at least rhetorically, accepted and validated (or at a minimum not challenged)

---

[46] At least at the margins, it may be that the PRC's behavior can sometimes be constrained by the contours of what its propaganda narrative has decreed must be the case about China. Some have suggested, for instance, that the PRC felt it necessary to pull out of its invasion of Vietnam as rapidly as possible in order to prevent the appearance that China was engaging in imperialism or hegemonism of the sort that it decried in other states but to which party officials made clear that their country was entirely immune. Compare, for example, the accounts given of the Vietnam invasion in Chün-tu Hsüeh, ed., *China's Foreign Relations: New Perspectives* (New York: Praeger, 1982), 7; Shee Poon Kim, "China and the ASEAN States: From Hostility to Rapprochement," in Hsüeh, *China's Foreign Relations*, 72, 80; John W. Garver, *Foreign Relations of the People's Republic of China* (Englewood Cliffs: Prentice Hall, 1993), 314; and "Full Text of Hu Jintao's Report to the Seventeenth Party Congress," Xinhua, October 24, 2007, http://news.xinhuanet.com/english/2007-10/24/content_6938749.htm.

by others—as benevolent and virtuous.[47] These imperatives have helped accentuate the ideological totalitarian state's natural instinct for propaganda message control and the manipulation of historical memory, adding to them a remarkable obsession with controlling narratives about China and the CCP not just domestically but overseas as well.

Virtuocracy is also not a concept of political authority that tends naturally to accept territorial frontiers, and it has proved difficult for Chinese leaders to defend their rule at home without asserting some special claim to status and prominence on the world stage—first as the ancient civilizational monopole of humanity (under multiple dynasties) and later as the revolutionary standard bearer for the dawning of a brilliant new age (under Mao). Today, the CCP regime projects itself as the translator of traditional Chinese virtues into the global arena, in leading the construction of a new system of interstate relations characterized by harmony and prosperity for all (under Hu Jintao and Xi Jinping). Gripped by this political imperative of defending its rule by advancing such a discourse of special destiny, the CCP appears to feel that other countries' narratives of China are very much China's business, making it common for PRC leaders to demand that other states refrain from "hurting the feelings of the Chinese people" by expressing thoughts about China that are not congruent with the PRC's virtuocratic narrative of itself. These virtue themes, connecting the regime's domestic insecurities to how the CCP and China are perceived and described even in the outside world, also help explain apparent quirks of PRC behavior, such as Beijing's fixation on securing "apologies" from any who are deemed to have wronged China.[48]

Alloyed with traditional Confucianism's emphasis on the "rectification of names"—the assumption that societal order can be understood, and is in a sense actually constituted, by the articulated ascription of social identities into which particular roles are encoded—these themes also help explain the modern party-state's fascination with calculations and rankings of comprehensive national power (CNP). To be sure, part of CNP theory derives from notions inherited from the Soviet Union about the "correlation of forces"—concepts with which Marxist dialecticians, understanding historical events as the epiphenomenal manifestation of changes at the level of substructures in political economy, sought to assess what the gradual unfolding of socialism in world history meant for the global balance of power at any given moment. This Communist heritage was powerfully reinforced,

---

[47] For an example, see *The First Chinese Embassy to the West: The Journals of Kuo Song-t'ao, Liu His-Hung, and Chang Te-yi*, trans. J.D. Frodsham (Oxford: Clarendon Press, 1974), 24.

[48] For examples, see "China Court Tells Writer to Apologise for Challenging Propaganda," *Hong Kong Free Press*, June 28, 2016, https://www.hongkongfp.com/2016/06/28/china-court-tells-writer-apologise-challenging-propaganda; and Ford, *China Looks at the West*, 456.

however, by the ancient Confucian emphasis on the rectification of names, which held it to be critical that participants in the social order be properly described and that all concur with these labels and the roles they signified. Just as Confucius believed that simply describing a son as a son and a father as a father ensured proper governance by establishing respective duties and responsibilities in the family and the Confucian social system, so also could one understand the operation of the international system by correctly describing the hierarchy of its participants.[49] Since around 1984, theorists of CNP have tracked the shifting rank ordering of states in the international system as if calculating league standings in professional sports.[50] Encouraged by such tabulations, Chinese thinkers have looked forward to the day when their country will reach the rank they feel it deserves—and from which China will be able to play the principal guiding and norm-shaping role in the geopolitical arena.[51]

In this regard, it is also worth emphasizing how important to modern Chinese strategic culture—and how closely linked to the country's ancient conceits of self-image and civilizational primacy—is the idea of China being restored to the position of global status the country feels it deserves, and of which it assumes it was robbed by European and Japanese imperial power. This leitmotif of returning to preeminent global status—what I have elsewhere called the "great telos of return"[52]—is a powerful locus of continuity in long-term attitudes and policy agendas, serving both as a strategic objective and as a justification for all manner of choices in domestic and international policymaking since the late nineteenth century.

The first generation of such thinking can be found in the work of the late nineteenth-century political thinker Kang Youwei, who at a time of obvious Qing Dynasty weakness vis-à-vis foreign barbarians wrote about the importance of "increasing the country's power" and advocated a "self-strengthening program" that would help China regain its lost power and prestige.[53] It also forms the basis for the suggestion by early twentieth-century political theorist Liang Qichao, for example, that, notwithstanding China's debilitating international weakness of that era, the United States and China would ultimately have to confront each other

---

[49] Confucius, *Confucian Analects*, 256.

[50] Pillsbury, *China Debates the Future Security Environment*, 9–11, 256.

[51] Tuo, "China Should Have a Part in the International Order's Transition."

[52] Christopher A. Ford, "China Views America: Aspiration, Opposition, and the Telos of China's Return," Hudson Institute, Security and Foreign Affairs Briefing Paper, August 2012, 2, http://www.hudson.org/content/researchattachments/attachment/1062/chinaviewsamerica--ford0812.pdf.

[53] Jonathan D. Spence, *The Gate of Heavenly Peace: The Chinese and Their Revolution, 1895–1980* (New York: Viking Press, 1981), 8–9, 13, 67.

for mastery of the Pacific.[54] Similarly, the writer Lin Yutang projected that China would in time be so strong that "nothing the western nations can do can stop her or keep her down."[55]

The founder of the Republic of China, Sun Yat-sen, similarly lamented in 1924 that whereas once China had "called herself 'the majestic nation,' [and] thought that she was situated at the center of the world," she had now become weak, with her "old national spirit…asleep." Sun's aim, he proclaimed, was to awaken that spirit and "restore our national standing." This was an objective echoed by nationalist president Chiang Kai-shek, who announced in his 1943 manifesto *China's Destiny* that it was "the unanimous demand of the people…to avenge the national humiliation and make the country strong."[56]

Concepts of the great telos of return also formed the conceptual predicate for Mao's triumphant proclamation in 1949 that China had once again "stood up" and would no longer be a nation subject to insult and humiliation.[57] Achieving China's "return" was likewise an unspoken objective animating Deng's exhortation for China to "bide its time" until some future turning point, and even underlay the agenda of some of Deng's critics during the Democracy Wall movement of the early 1980s. Some of these critics, for example, saw autocracy as a limiting factor on China's progression of national ascendancy and assumed that China could only achieve its longed-for return through democratization.[58]

More recently, such thinking seemed to underlie Hu Jintao's imaginings of a "harmonious world" modeled on the CCP's own domestic politics.[59] According to Hu, because "history and reality tell us that 'backwardness incurs beatings by others,'" it was "the unswerving goal that each Chinese generation has striven to realize" to bring about "the great rejuvenation of the Chinese nation."[60] Today, the quest for *fuqiang* (wealth and power)—a term that is a modern shorthand for the Warring States–era phrase *fuguo qiangbing* (to enrich the state and strengthen its military power)—lies at the conceptual and emotional core of President Xi Jinping's "Chinese dream" of a "strong nation,"[61] his use of modern endeavors such as the One Belt, One Road initiative to invoke and recreate

[54] R. David Arkush and Leo O. Lee, eds., *Land without Ghosts: Chinese Impressions of America from the Mid-Nineteenth Century to the Present* (Berkeley: University of California Press, 1989), 89.

[55] Schell and Delury, *Wealth and Power*, 4.

[56] Ibid., 131, 189.

[57] Yongjin Zhang, *China in International Society since 1949* (New York: St. Martin's Press, 1998), 18.

[58] Andrew J. Nathan, *Chinese Democracy* (New York: Knopf, 1985), 4–6, 10, 37, 94.

[59] Yu Keping, *Democracy Is a Good Thing: Essays on Politics, Society, and Culture in Contemporary China* (Washington, D.C.: Brookings Institution Press, 2009), 169, 171.

[60] Schell and Delury, *Wealth and Power*, 386.

[61] Ibid., 5–6; and "Reaching for the Moon," *Economist*, December 21, 2013, 68.

the glory days of Chinese political-economic centrality in Eurasia, and the modern CCP's self-justificatory contention that only under its rule can "the great rejuvenation of the Chinese nation" be achieved.[62]

Policy Implications

So what is the net impact of all of this? To the extent that Chinese strategic culture can be understood as having realist bones, one should expect that PRC decision-making will continue to be fundamentally focused on classically realpolitik concerns of relative power, and that its leaders will generally shape their choices according to the ever-evolving calculus of risk and opportunity that such power balances imply. The Confucian-moralist flesh of Chinese strategic culture, however, still exerts influence on Beijing's behavior, causing it to differ in some regards from what one might expect from classical realism. These deviations need to be understood, particularly to the degree that Confucian moralism may in reality tend to push behavior in directions different from the peace-loving benevolence predicted by the CCP's official narrative.

Ideological Sensitivity

Traditional cultural elements help make the PRC more sensitive to matters of image, reputation, and ideological justification than one would presumably expect of a purely realist power. This is the result of a confluence of elements within Chinese strategic culture. It is an important idiosyncrasy of that culture, for instance, that foreign and domestic matters are entangled in significant ways. The Chinese cultural heritage of virtuocratic political pretension blurs the distinction between these realms—both because the authority-organizing power of virtue in political affairs is not envisioned as stopping at state frontiers and because any defects in the order created by one's virtue carry implications for the legitimacy of one's authority—while making it difficult for China's rulers to admit anything but omnicompetent benevolence in either sphere.

Particularly since the CCP lacks any other foundation on which to legitimize its rule, the regime must maintain the quasi-Confucian legitimacy narrative of virtuocratic merit at all costs, and this has implications across the breadth of Chinese public policy. Among them, it has a significant impact on censorship and propaganda, both at home and, increasingly, abroad. The international aspects of what officials call "grasp[ing] the discourse power...to capture position" are particularly interesting, for they are closely

---

[62] "Our Bulldozers, Our Rules," *Economist*, July 2, 2016, 37–38; and Wang Faan et al., *Zhongguo heping fazhan zhong de qiangjun zhanlue* [China's Strategy for Invigorating the Armed Forces amid Peaceful Development] (Beijing: Military Science Press, 2011), chap. 1.

bound to imperatives of the great telos of return.[63] For a successful return, China apparently needs not only to depict itself as a virtuous paragon state on the international stage but also, in a postmodern wrinkle on ancient tribute state psychodynamics, to have others acknowledge it as such (or at least acquiesce by not challenging China's assertions).

Even domestically, within the virtuocratic framework, to concede the existence of major problems is to raise questions about the CCP's claimed right to rule, which grounds itself in economic development, political harmony, and China's growing status. Such legitimacy-imperiling political dynamics are less acute when the CCP can describe difficulties as not being the party's fault—e.g., when they are cast as ills inflicted by malevolent "foreign forces" with "ulterior motives."[64] Even where notional blame can be shifted, however, this can still create challenges, inasmuch as problems that the regime cannot simply deny by hiding them behind veils of censorship can produce increasingly repressive party postures against real or imagined domestic opponents, not to mention a grievance-mongering xenophobia against foreign adversaries that inflames Chinese nationalist sentiment and may encourage international belligerence.

For a regime that professes such certitude about its own merits and course, the CCP seems deeply insecure not only about things directly bearing on its own monopolization of power in China (e.g., the "spiritual pollution" of Western political values) but also even about seemingly minor aspects of image maintenance and perceived status.[65] For example, despite emphasizing the distinctive merit of China's ancient culture and invoking the importance of Chinese values, the regime seems to delight in validation by eminent (or purportedly eminent) Westerners, with "international observers" credited wherever possible with "marveling at the sustained vigor and vitality of the Communist Party of China…and the glorious achievements it has made."[66]

---

[63] David Bandurski, "Listen to the Citizens, and Control them," China Media Project, June 22, 2010.

[64] Wang Jisi, "From Paper Tiger to Real Leviathan: China's Images of the United States since 1949," in Chinese Images of the United States, ed. Carola McGiffert (Washington, D.C.: CSIS Press, 2005), 9, 13, 18; "Conscientiously Preserving Social Harmony and Stability," Beijing Daily, March 5, 2011; and David Bandurski, "Beijing Daily: The Masses Support Stability," China Media Project, March 6, 2011, http://cmp.hku.hk/2011/03/06/10679.

[65] See Nathan, Chinese Democracy, 123.

[66] Yao Jianing, "Senior PLA Official Meets with Former U.S. Secretary of State," China Military Online, March 21, 2016, http://english.chinamil.com.cn/news-channels/2016-03/21/content_6970195.htm; and "Chinese Communist Party Lauded for Strength, Achievements on 95th Birthday," Xinhua, July 1, 2016. The PRC eagerly latches on to "foreign expert" opinions congruent with its message, even when the experts are obscure and the position tendentious. See "UK Law Expert: South China Sea Arbitration Lacks Legal Basis," People's Daily, June 22, 2016; and Fu Jing, "South China Sea Tribunal Has No Validity," China Daily, June 27, 2016. Chinese press accounts also delight in depicting elements of traditional Chinese culture, such as Spring Festival (New Year) celebrations, as being "no longer celebrated only by Chinese people" but as having "an ever larger effect internationally." Gao Yinan, "Chinese New Year Carries Weight Worldwide," People's Daily, February 15, 2016.

Understanding the virtuocratic pretension and politico-moral insecurity of the modern Chinese regime gives insight into why Beijing considers it so important to try to control such things as descriptions of World War II in Japanese textbooks, a mural painted on a private building in a small Oregon town that highlights Chinese brutality in Tibet and advocates Taiwanese independence, or website data from the U.S. embassy in Beijing that contradicts official Chinese air pollution figures, among other examples.[67] Modern Chinese leaders are extraordinarily interested in what they call "grabbing the megaphone" of public discourse even overseas, reportedly spending $10 billion a year trying to place propaganda messages in foreign media and reacting with notable bitterness and anger to perceived slights.[68]

Almost all governments care about their international image, of course, and make its promotion part of their public diplomacy. Few, however, seem to care about it as much as the CCP regime or turn with such vicious intensity against those who "hurt the feelings of the Chinese people" by disrespecting China's virtue and status.[69] There seems to be no *de minimis* threshold for what can count as a grievance against the PRC's dignity.

I would suggest, however, that this characteristic behavior is not the result of any actual immaturity. Rather, it is the natural and foreseeable result of the CCP's lack of any democratic legitimacy capable of providing a foundation for state authority independent of the monist and virtuocratic conceits of a Confucian political tradition that tends to prize virtue-based claims to political power, to stress role-ascriptive articulations of social hierarchy and see agreement on such positional status as essential to social order, and to fear disorder and pluralism as indicators of the leadership's moral failure and hence lack of a right to rule. In this fashion, some of the distinctively Chinese elements within Chinese strategic culture have made the PRC more sensitive to matters of image, reputation, and ideological justification than one would expect of a classically realist power.

---

[67] See the foreword by Quansheng Zhao in Xuanli Liao, *Chinese Foreign Policy Think Tanks and China's Policy towards Japan* (Hong Kong: Chinese University Press, 2006), ix; Bennett Hall, "Mural Draws Fire from China," *Corvallis Gazette-Times*, September 8, 2012, http://www.gazettetimes.com/news/local/mural-draws-fire-from- china/article_22529ace-f94a-11e1-bf2a-0019bb2963f4.html; and Tanya Branigan, "APEC: China Blocks Access to U.S. Air Pollution Data for Beijing," *Guardian*, November 10, 2014, http://www.theguardian.com/world/2014/nov/10/apec-china-blocks-access-us-air-pollution-data-beijing. Nor do Chinese authorities shrink from such things as demanding rosier assessments from economists and other analysts "whose public remarks on the economy are out of step with the government's upbeat statements." Lingling Wei, "China Presses Economists to Brighten Their Outlooks," *Wall Street Journal*, May 3, 2016.

[68] "Grabbing the Megaphone," China Media Project, http://cmp.hku.hk/2010/04/20/5436; and "Who Draws the Party Line?" *Economist*, June 25, 2016, 36.

[69] Biwu Zhang, *Chinese Perceptions of the U.S.: An Exploration of China's Foreign Policy Motivations* (Lanham: Lexington Books, 2012), 56.

The Exacerbated Realism of Moralistic Coercion

In contradistinction to the official narrative of a Confucian moral tradition that pulls China away from a classically violence-focused realpolitik, the PRC's cultural inheritance could exacerbate the problems of potential belligerence already implicit within the realist paradigm for any increasingly muscular rising power. Here, I see four principal reasons for concern.

Ideological incentives to violence. On top of the ideological sensitivity discussed in the preceding section, elements of Sinic idiosyncrasy may make China more prone to violence over particular issues than a more conventional realism would suggest is warranted. The case of Taiwan is illustrative. A traditional realist would presumably not be averse to territorial self-aggrandizement if the associated costs and risks did not make attack prohibitively dangerous. Yet that same traditional realist would surely also not seek out confrontation with powerful opponents in order to seize territory that presents no threat and the forcible possession of which is unlikely to bring significant concrete benefit.

Nevertheless, Beijing is almost fanatically committed to the principle that Taiwan—an island that has enjoyed de facto independence for generations and presents almost no military threat to the PRC—must be prevented from declaring *de jure* independence at virtually any cost, and that Taiwan's eventual joinder with the mainland must be ensured by force if necessary. Nor is this just a rhetorical posture. Ensuring the capability to defeat Taiwanese "splittism" has been an organizing principle of the PRC's military posture for decades and has long been a driver for its anticipation of a possible conflict with U.S. naval forces if they are sent to save Taiwan from invasion. Indeed, PRC officials have repeatedly signaled that they would attack Taiwan even if it did nothing more than officially declare itself independent. Unless this is all entirely a calculating realist's bluff—which seems unlikely, since a predictable result of this posture is to make both Taipei and Washington more concerned about and prepared for war with Beijing than would otherwise have been the case—the PRC's bellicose approach to Taiwan is hard to understand as fundamentally realpolitik behavior. To make sense of it, one must turn to more ideational factors.

Here we circle back to the essentialist eternalism so prominent in the PRC's official narrative of China. The legitimacy discourse of the contemporary CCP cannot permit any admission that what has been declared to be "China" has any destiny other than unification under party control. In the Chinese tradition, as we have seen, political authority is both virtuocratic and inherently monist. Accordingly, if China has always been by its nature one and indissoluble and if Taiwan has been part of China in the past, then the CCP cannot concede that the island's destiny today is anything other than reunification, because to do this would impugn its legitimacy to rule at all. Taiwan's development from a one-party Kuomintang dictatorship to a vibrant democracy over the last quarter-century has only made this problem worse. For the CCP to accept the legitimacy of a Taiwan that is both independent and democratic would be to admit that electorally accountable governance is an option available and appropriate for Chinese people—a position that is obviously anathema to CCP authorities.

Thus, ideological imperatives linked to Chinese political culture and party legitimacy narratives have helped push the regime's calculation of its interests in directions different from what one might expect of a more thoroughgoing realism. Significantly, this "realism with Chinese characteristics" seems more aggressive and conflict-prone as a result of the admixture of these ideational elements.

Unrealistic global ambition. Second, virtuocratic pretensions and an obsession with positional hierarchy—coupled with and fed by officially promoted narratives of past national humiliation that it is China's destiny to rectify and overcome—seem to have encouraged the CCP not just to build up China to the point where it can resist international "bullying" and protect its sovereign rights, but in fact also to go much further: to seek an ambitious revision of the structure and norms of the international system so as to privilege China and achieve its long-awaited return to geopolitical primacy. This line of thought has been encouraged by modern Chinese thinkers' frequent recourse to models of statecraft with roots in canonical works from the Warring States period, which in their own time spoke insistently to the imperative of systemic primacy. Moreover, it gains momentum from Confucian-Mencian traditions of monist, virtuocratic political authority and has been nourished by generations of regime propaganda focused on the great telos of return.

The impact of the CCP regime's fetishization of humiliation-redressing return and rejuvenation—coupled with longings for the status and civilizational supremacy that imperial China is imagined to have enjoyed in the ancient world—may push the PRC toward prideful assertion and unreasonable ambition, making it less conflict-averse and less likely to settle for sub-maximalist positions and outcomes than would a state with a more conventionally realist approach. Where one might expect the behavior of a pure realist to be modulated depending on the circumstances, sensitive to both positive and negative shifts in relative power, the modern PRC's realpolitik with Chinese characteristics may find self-restraint more challenging and the prospect of reverses more difficult to accept because of its emotional investment in a romanticized concept of national destiny and the great telos of return. In this way, ideological imperatives may push

Chinese strategic culture in a direction very different from what the official PRC narrative would lead one to expect.

Inflammatory moralism. The third type of potential problem lies in the link between virtuocracy and two related forms of moralistic oppositionalism: the demonization of opponents (to forestall the emergence of competitors in virtue) and the depiction of all significant problems as being someone else's fault (to forestall suspicions that one does not deserve to rule after all). To the degree that virtuocratic pretension, and its associated modern performance metrics of ever-advancing Chinese power, prosperity, and international status, form critical components of the CCP regime's legitimacy narrative, one should expect any unfavorable perturbations in China's trajectory to give rise to more vituperative and heavy-handed treatment of dissenters at home and to more shrill opposition to and blame-shifting demonization of real or imagined adversaries abroad.[70]

Moreover, because virtuocratic politics do not permit leaders to concede error or incompetence, and because the CCP's hostility to democratic values denies the party a claim to legitimacy grounded in anything more than the Confucian conceit that unaccountable power is the natural result of omnicompetent benevolence, the regime may be tempted to take unusually risky courses of action for fear of otherwise having to admit that some major plank of its policy agenda had been wrongheaded. As Scobell has suggested, despite its self-image as being conflict-averse, traditional Chinese society nonetheless approved of the use of force and coercion by state and authority figures against those that threatened "the correct order of things"—a position that seems reinforced by China's adherence for many decades to Marxist-derived conceptions of class struggle, which tend to valorize violence against "enemies of the people."[71] Such vituperative moralism is seldom conducive to moderation.[72]

The virtuocratic pretensions of Chinese strategic culture, therefore, may be less conducive to the peaceful pursuit of harmonious coexistence than to a moralistic irascibility likely to inflame tensions more than soothe them. This is thus another way in which realism with Chinese characteristics might derogate from what one might expect from the realism of traditional imagining, but this departure is not in the direction of peace-loving harmoniousness. Instead, emphasis on the axiomatic righteousness of

---

[70] As China's debt burden mounts and the economy slows under President Xi Jinping, for instance, there seems to be not just an ever-harsher crackdown upon dissent but also an increasing emphasis on the CCP's role in providing "ideological guidance" across the breadth of Chinese politics. See, "The Return of Correct Thinking," *Economist*, April 23, 2016, 35–36.

[71] Scobell, *China's Use of Military Force*, 22–24.

[72] Perdue, "The Tenacious Tributary System," 1008.

China's cause and the depravity of any who stand in its way may serve to reinforce, rather than counteract, the sort of violence-friendly parabellum instincts identified by Johnston and others.

The "cult of defense." The Chineseness of China's strategic culture might also exacerbate parabellum tendencies in a fourth way: by providing a discourse in which the PRC can essentially rationalize any use of force as necessary for self-defense, that most upright of moral principles justifying violence. As discussed above, Huiyun Feng sees Chinese strategic culture as fundamentally "defensive in nature."[73] While this view correctly identifies a defensive focus as being an important part of how PRC leaders articulate and defend their policies, Scobell's account is more consistent with what we have seen both in actual Chinese practice and in the ideological imperatives of virtuocratic legitimation—what he terms a cult of defense, through the prism of which whatever China does is defensive and fundamentally benevolent in nature.

Such a mindset, however, does not merely make it easier to rationalize or publicly defend violence one might wish to undertake for other reasons. As Scobell suggests, the cult of defense may impede China's ability to manage crises and conduct foreign and national security policy in ways that are in fact realistic, for it threatens to leave Beijing intellectually "incapable of recognizing that actions it views as purely defensive may be construed as offensive and threatening in other capitals."[74] But the problem might actually be worse than Scobell suggests. Framing the use of force as a matter of self-defense also undermines arguments against using violence, making such force seem non-optional and making moderation in its employment sound like a kind of self-betrayal.

Just as the moralism of Chinese virtuocracy can impede compromise or bargaining with opponents that it obliges the regime to portray as depraved threats to the natural order of things, China's discourse of infinitely malleable "defensive" self-justification could make violence seem more attractive or necessary in the first place. These ideological factors may thus reinforce each other, potentially creating a strategic culture that is both intemperate and immoderate, perhaps eventually even to the point of pathology—a parabellum paradigm both comfortable with the use of force and predisposed against the traditional realist's willingness to be flexible, or even to retreat, when circumstances require.

---

[73] Feng, *Chinese Strategic Culture*, 2, 74, 80.

[74] Scobell, *China's Use of Military Force*, 198.

The Realism of Party Self-Interest

In at least one way, however, China's legacy of quasi-Confucian virtuocratic political culture could help moderate the moralistic bellicosity of such a system of exacerbated realism. In certain circumstances, it might be possible to elicit restraint where the interests of the CCP itself can be pitted against the broader interests of the country as a power maximizer in the international arena. This possibility derives from seeing in the PRC's decision-making process a very specific sort of realism: a party-focused realism rather than one that necessarily revolves around the interests of the Chinese state or the Chinese people. The CCP, in other words, prizes its own continued survival and monopoly of power irrespective of whether this is good for China as a whole.

Understanding this partial relocation of the locus of realist calculation opens up new avenues for analysis and may also offer opportunities to influence Chinese behavior by playing on this distinction. To the degree, for example, that foreign bellicosity seems incompatible with the party's own domestic self-interest—such as if the CCP were to perceive that in the event of conflict it would be faced with conditions inside China in which party officials would no longer be able to guarantee their own continued control[75]—it might be possible to elicit moderation from party-centric realists in Beijing even when a more state-centric realism might still counsel war.

Indeed, in the right circumstances, it might be possible to leverage the fragility of quasi-Confucian political authority against the party, inasmuch as the CCP's performance-based legitimacy narrative is a brittle one likely to have trouble handling undeniable setbacks or failures. If a situation were to confront the party, in other words, with a sufficiently high likelihood of failure in a major international undertaking—or even a sufficiently high likelihood that aggressive action would result in a diminishment of China's international status and thus a reversal on the road to real civilizational return and global respect—this might suffice to deter that undertaking. This, after all, seems to have been part of the thinking behind Deng Xiaoping's warning about biding time, which was all the more essential for fear that the CCP's authority could not survive leading China unprepared into another Qing-style humiliation in a confrontation with barbarian outsiders. Looking forward, it might be possible to induce a return to Dengist strategic caution by confronting the CCP itself with the risk of regime calamity triggered by international failure.

---

[75] One example of such a scenario is if a foreign adversary seemed likely in wartime not just to target traditional military assets and facilities but also to disrupt the regime's instruments of coercive political control, such as its Internet monitoring, censorship, and message control system, or the command-and-control network of its domestic security police.

Conclusion

Chinese strategic culture is an amalgam: a fundamentally realist system, but one nonetheless shaped by ideational elements with roots in China's ancient history and the assumptions its people have traditionally made about the nature of power, authority, and China's role in the world. It is important to understand this realpolitik with Chinese characteristics, both because its contours help explain actual PRC behavior and because such an understanding may help foreign leaders in dealing with a rising China.

It follows from the foregoing analysis that just as the core of Chinese strategic culture is a realist one, so presumably should responses to China follow a basically realist logic—one alive to the impact of shifting power balances, including the role of hard power and deterrence-based strategic signaling as key components of competitive behavior, and dedicated to adjusting the ingredients and manifestations of countervailing national power for best advantage. This is a discourse that Chinese leaders understand, one that shapes their own behavior, and one to which they are likely, on the whole, to respond. At the same time, however, a sophisticated understanding of the Chineseness that is nonetheless present in Chinese strategic culture can point us to the ways in which Chinese realism is likely to differ from realist expectations, for good or for ill.

Understanding these wrinkles can help improve policies for dealing with a rising China. As we have seen, one important way in which this may occur is through efforts to deter aggression through an awareness of—and a systematic effort to target—the insecurities inherent in the party-centric realism of the CCP's calculations and the ways in which these weaknesses might perhaps be manipulated to elicit a return to less provocative and more Dengist forms of strategic caution. In the realm of soft power and diplomatic engagement, moreover, Sinologically informed policies might also affect the PRC beyond what traditional realism would suggest is possible.

As one example, precisely because discourse control is so important to PRC leaders—and because their strategic culture seems to drive them in somewhat idiosyncratic directions in diplomacy and propaganda—one might expect that other powers' public diplomatic engagement with China could play with some effectiveness, in both positive (affirming) and negative (oppositional) ways, on the peculiar predilections and sensitivities of the modern CCP's quasi-Confucianized virtuocratic narrative. Although it is common for Western leaders to criticize the PRC for censorship and human rights abuses, the CCP might find it more painful to be accused of failings that more directly challenge the party's legitimacy. Exposing the endemic corruption of China's party-state system and the personal venality and moral turpitude of CCP leaders, for instance, might do more to rattle party grandees and undercut their legitimacy within China than simply decrying their use of heavy-handed tactics against dissidents. After all, ruthless coercion against those who threaten social "harmony" has always been practiced in China and has traditionally been considered acceptable and appropriate even within the system of Confucian ethics. By contrast, being exposed as corrupt, selfish, and immoral—and as being incompetent or incapable enough so as to allow disorder and injustice to flourish in society—would drive directly at the core of the virtuocratic legitimacy narrative of every Chinese regime, including the contemporary CCP. Such criticism strikes, in effect, at its "mandate of heaven."[76] The ability to play on such narratives could be a useful tool.

That said, while there is a great deal to admire in China's venerable civilization, this chapter's exploration of Chinese strategic culture suggests that troubling pathologies can arise from this ancient culture's interaction with the modern circumstances of CCP rule. Of particular concern is the emergence of a dogmatic moralism and virtuocratically insecure irascibility that may tend to create an exacerbated realism that is potentially more prone to violence even than classic realpolitik would suggest. This chapter has examined some of these dynamics in the hope of prompting deeper engagement by policymakers and scholars with these important issues.

---

[76] Christopher Ford, "Puncturing Beijing's Propaganda Bubble: Seven Themes," New Paradigms Forum, November 20, 2015, http://www.newparadigmsforum.com/NPFtestsite/?p=1993.

EXECUTIVE SUMMARY

This chapter examines the influence of key features of Russia's strategic culture on its international behavior and discusses the potential for Russia to focus more attention on Asia.

MAIN ARGUMENT

Russia's strategic culture is deeply rooted in the geographic and spiritual parameters of its history. An important element of this culture has been a search for security through territorial expansion due to an absence of natural physical buffers. This expansionist tendency has been reinforced by a messianic mission tied to Russia's Orthodox path. These elements have combined to solidify the exceptionalist vision underlying Russia's claim to be recognized as a great power. Russia's vast territory, perceived security vulnerabilities, and heterogeneous population have helped entrench a centralized autocratic type of governance aiming to keep internal tensions in check while resisting external pressure through the alternation of defensive and offensive behaviors. These enduring elements of Russia's strategic culture have resulted in a wavering between feelings of superiority and inferiority toward the West, with this Western-centrism producing relative neglect of the Asian vector of foreign policy; a strong reliance on military tools in national policy; and a continuous balancing between retrenchment and engagement in international affairs.

POLICY IMPLICATIONS

- Prolonged periods of antagonism between Moscow and Washington risk intensifying the pace at which Russia seeks partners outside the West, and especially in Asia.

- Given the central place that the United States occupies in Russian strategic preoccupations, Washington must strike the right balance between asserting principles, defending interests, and protecting allies while continuing to engage Russia on a vast array of topics.

- Dialogue and engagement by the United States may ease tension and help the Kremlin take a more relaxed approach on the international stage.

Russian Strategic Culture in the 21st Century: Redefining the West-East Balance

Isabelle Facon

In 2016, Russia's attitude on the world stage is characterized by a number of features that disconcert many of its partners, if only because their consequences appear rather counterproductive from the point of view of Moscow's interests. Russia's diplomacy appears excessively focused on relations with the West, which Moscow has approached confrontationally. Russia's discontent with Western policies in the post–Cold War era seems to know no bounds, while Western countries assert that they have done their best to accommodate Moscow's frustration with the heavy degradation of its status in world affairs and its concern with a number of shifts in the Euro-Atlantic and Eurasian spaces, sometimes risking Western consensus.[1] Moscow has put increasing pressure on the former Soviet republics and seems unable to assert its influence through noncoercive means, leading even its most reliable partners (Belarus and Kazakhstan) to try to lessen this influence. Russia's annexation of Crimea and crucial role behind the development and entrenchment of separatism in Donbass create additional doubts about the rationality of its regional strategy.[2] By reneging blatantly on commitments to

Isabelle Facon is a Senior Research Fellow at the Paris-based think tank Fondation pour la recherche stratégique. She can be reached at <i.facon@frstrategie.org>.

[1] Among other examples, see the NATO-Russia Founding Act in 1997 that allowed for restrictions on military deployments in the territory of the new member states, Russia's admission to the group of eight (G-8) in 1998, the downplaying of Western capitals' criticism of Russia's military operations in Chechnya in 2001, and the reset of U.S.-Russia relations in 2009.

[2] Alexander J. Motyl, "How Far Will Putin Go?" *Foreign Policy*, March 1, 2014; and Julia Ioffe, "Putin's Press Conference Proved Merkel Right: He's Lost His Mind," *New Republic*, March 4, 2014.

the UN Charter and Helsinki principles, Moscow has taken the risk of not only losing Ukraine but also isolating itself politically and economically and complicating the achievement of its foreign policy goals. Russia's positioning in Asia raises further questions. As seen from the outside, its proclaimed turn to the region looks overwhelmingly China-centered, and it is not clear whether Russian institutions are really willing to devote the necessary political energy to this endeavor or whether the turn is primarily a reaction to the current stalemate in relations with the West. Finally, Russia's growing inclination to resort to military intimidation and the use of force does not seem conducive to better international integration of the country at a time when its successive governments have not managed to seriously modernize the domestic economy.

Various categories of explanation are plausible. As a former KGB colonel, President Vladimir Putin has gradually increased the weight of representatives of the various force structures, the *siloviki*, in his decision-making. This has certainly contributed to heightening Moscow's defiance toward the West's actions in its neighborhood and presumed willingness to destabilize the current regime. Putin and his political allies are certainly not averse to using coercive means (such as manipulation, pressure, and, if need be, military force) to achieve national interests. Another explanation lies in Russia's deep frustration with its loss of influence all over the world after 1991. This explains Moscow's aggressive promotion of the idea of "Russia's comeback" once oil-related revenues replenished the state's coffers, enabling, among other things, significant investment in the modernization of the military.

At the same time, without opting for a determinist vision of Russia's foreign policy, one has to recognize the enduring influence of ideas and concepts framed by specific historical, cultural, and geopolitical experiences on many aspects of Moscow's international vision and behavior and the definition of its national interests. They shape in large part the hierarchy of the sources of national power that Russia considers it should pursue in order to assert its interests and standing on the world stage. This historical and intellectual legacy, the traces of which could be felt in the Soviet era and during the Yeltsin epoch (although this latter period has often been presented as quite atypical by traditional Russian strategic standards), has oriented the way that Russia has adjusted its role in the new world order that has taken shape after the end of the Cold War.

This chapter first provides an overview of the way Russia currently positions itself on the world stage, of the major strategic goals of its foreign policy, and of the main themes, visions, and perceptions that shape these goals. The chapter then presents the basic elements of Russia's strategic culture to better understand its behavior and aspirations on the international stage in the early 21st century. The following section focuses on a key aspect of Russian strategic culture—the strong reliance on military instruments to assert the country's international interests. Finally, the conclusion assesses the domestic and foreign policy trends in Russia that should be followed closely because they may gradually open the way to serious breakthroughs in its international behavior. The implications for U.S. interests of both continuity and potential change in this behavior are also explored.

Russia's Vision of Major International Challenges and Interests in the 21st Century

If one looks at the history of Russia's foreign and security policy since the end of the Cold War and reads through the major strategic documents that present the underlying motives and goals of this policy (for example, its national security strategy, foreign policy concept, and military doctrine) or major speeches by top Russian officials, several important dimensions appear quite stable: Russia's claim to be recognized as a great power with global responsibility; its tendency to position itself primarily in relation to the West; its desire to remain the leading power in the post-Soviet space, which partially overlaps the borders of the former Russian and Soviet empires; and its growing interest in closer interactions with Asian powers. These policies have been accompanied by an acute threat perception: all strategic documents describe Russia's strategic landscape as highly volatile and competitive, with challenges coming from many directions, including from the interplay between domestic problems and the international situation.

The idea that Russia should be recognized as a great power is a key parameter that has driven Moscow's posture on the world stage for several centuries—a posture that nowadays many officials and scholars abroad do not see as justified given Russia's serious structural weaknesses.[3] President Barack Obama's declaration that Russia is merely a regional power constitutes

---

[3] This status has been pursued since at least Peter the Great, who developed relations with European powers while strengthening Russia's economic and military potential. It was after the Congress of Vienna in 1815 that Russia was considered "a power with system-wide interests as well as a say in matters pertaining to the management of the system" of leading powers. Later on, the Soviet Union obtained the status of being the second world superpower. See Iver B. Neumann, "When Did Russia Become a Great Power? Realist, Constructivist and Post-Structuralist Answers" (paper presented at the International Studies Association 48th Annual Convention, Chicago, February 28, 2007), quoted in Norbert Eitelhuber, "The Russian Bear: Russian Strategic Culture and What It Implies for the West," *Connections* 9, no. 1 (2009): 6. For an analysis of Russia's structural weaknesses, see Andrew C. Kuchins, "Russian Power Rising and Falling Simultaneously," in *Strategic Asia 2015–16: Foundations of National Power in the Asia-Pacific*, ed. Ashley J. Tellis with Alison Szalwinski and Michael Wills (Seattle: National Bureau of Asian Research, 2015), 125–58.

an indirect and negative (but conscious) "tribute" to this aspiration.[4] Even the supposedly pro-Western foreign minister during the early Yeltsin era, Andrei Kozyrev, shared this belief, declaring that Russia had to become "a normal great power."[5] To justify such a claim, Russian leaders (and many political scientists) constantly underscore the prestige and leverage that nuclear weapons and a seat as a permanent member of the UN Security Council provide the country. Russia has consistently worked to sustain the strength of these assets by promoting a nonproliferation agenda, together with the other members of the Security Council, and by displaying no real interest in reforming the Security Council's membership. The possession of huge reserves of hydrocarbons and other raw materials is often mentioned as another pillar of Russian power, albeit in an increasingly ambivalent manner, as will be discussed later. Russia also tends to suggest that its geography, which spans several key strategic regions—Europe, Asia, Eurasia, and the High North—de facto contributes to its international clout.[6]

With the same perspective in mind, Russia has highlighted its ability to develop strong relations with all leading powers of the emerging "polycentric system of international relations."[7] In the 1990s, its stated project of integration with the West was underpinned by many factors, one of which was the fact that by then the West was indisputably the club of leading powers. Therefore, being admitted into this club was, from the Russian perspective, one of the best arguments to support the country's great-power claim. In recent years, seeking a strategic partnership with the European Union has become less prominent in Russia's general strategy, not only because of conflicting views about the future of the shared neighborhood but also because the EU is now seen as increasingly weak economically and strategically.[8] Therefore, partnership with this entity, although still relevant geopolitically and economically, has become

---

[4] President Obama stated that "Russia is a regional power that is threatening some of its immediate neighbors, not out of strength but out of weakness." Julian Borger, "Barack Obama: Russia Is a Regional Power Showing Weakness over Ukraine," *Guardian*, March 25, 2014.

[5] "Andrei Kozyrev: Rossiya dolzhna stat' normal'noy velikoy derzhavoy" [Andrei Kozyrev: Russia Must Become a Normal Power], *Kommersant*, November 28, 1992.

[6] The length of Russia's total land boundaries is 22,408 kilometers and its coastline is 37,653 kilometers. *The World Factbook 2016* (Washington, D.C.: Central Intelligence Agency, 2015), https://www.cia.gov/library/publications/the-world-factbook/geos/rs.html.

[7] Ministry of Foreign Affairs (Russia), "Concept of the Foreign Policy of the Russian Federation," February 12, 2013, http://archive.mid.ru//brp_4.nsf/0/76389fec168189ed44257B2E0039B16D.

[8] Russia long hoped for the EU to take on a more serious security identity and to develop defense and security cooperation with Russia, which over the longer term the Kremlin thought might undermine NATO's relevance in Europe. Moscow no longer counts on such a turn of events, which has probably contributed to the hardening of its negative interpretation of the EU's policy of partnership with former Soviet republics. See Karin Anderman, Eva Hagström Frisell, and Carolina Vendil Pallin, "Russia-EU External Security Relations: Russian Policy and Perceptions," Swedish Defence Research Agency, February 2007.

less beneficial for Russia's international standing than strategic convergence with China and other major rising powers.[9]

Given this background, it is hardly surprising that in the post–Cold War context Moscow has never ceased to try to demonstrate that it has an impact on U.S. foreign policy despite the immense power gap between the two countries. Russia has become highly frustrated every time it has appeared clearly that this is not the case (for example, with the wars in Kosovo and Iraq or on the issue of antimissile defense), while being galvanized when it could demonstrate an ability to weigh in U.S. decisions (as has been the case with the war in Syria).

Since the end of the Cold War, Russia seems to have worked on its new international identity and built its positions on global issues primarily with respect to Western powers. On this, its agenda has taken different forms, however. Initially, Moscow's aspiration to be integrated into the club of Western powers was partially satisfied when it was added as a member to the group of seven (G-7) in 1998, which was renamed the G-8. However, membership in this forum was not enough to compensate, from a Russian perspective, for the gradual restructuring of the European political, economic, and security space around two organizations—NATO and the EU—that Russia could not credibly join. This translated into resentment as Moscow believed that the situation was potentially creating security problems on its Western border and represented a conscious effort to isolate it on the European stage. Yevgeny Primakov, Russia's foreign minister from January 1996 to September 1998, orchestrated a diplomatic approach that, focusing on the slogan of the need to establish a "multipolar world order," expressed Russian discontent through seeking "comrades" in soft opposition to Western policies. Russian foreign policy remained very much motivated by goals to be attained in relations with the West but from a more antagonistic standpoint. This became more explicit after Russian leaders decided once and for all that the West would never take Russia's interests into consideration. In their view, the rejoinder to Moscow's cooperation with Washington after September 11 was the United States' unilateral rejection of the Anti-Ballistic Missile Treaty in 2002, the war in Iraq in 2003, the Baltic states' membership in NATO in 2004, and the color revolutions in Georgia and Ukraine in 2003 and 2004, among other developments. The most emblematic rhetorical benchmark signaling this change in vision was Vladimir Putin's speech at the 2007 Security Conference in Munich. The Russian president accused the United States and the West in general of undermining the international rules established after World War II,

---

[9] Bobo Lo rightly points out that for Russia "membership—or co-leadership with China—of the BRICS [Brazil, Russia, India, China, and South Africa] confers a success by association." See Bobo Lo, "The Illusion of Convergence—Russia, China, and the BRICS," Institut français de relations internationales, Russie.Nei.Visions, no. 92, March 2016, 8.

ensuring their own security in a way detrimental to the security of others, and displaying a propensity to use disproportionate force.[10]

A key element behind Russia's rather hostile attitude toward the West resides in its perception that Western powers and organizations have been trying to actively weaken its influence and interests in the post-Soviet space. With the exception of a very brief period in the first years of the 1990s, during which most of the former Soviet Union was considered as a burden that Russia should not take on given its own huge reform agenda, Moscow under Presidents Boris Yeltsin, Vladimir Putin, and Dmitri Medvedev has worked to keep all the levers it can to prevent the loss of the Newly Independent States to other powers. These levers include multilateral institutions that tend to limit or constrain the interaction of these countries with other players—for example, the Eurasian Economic Union (EEU) for trade and political issues and the Collective Security Treaty Organization for security and military issues. When Moscow has considered the prospect of such a loss particularly tangible—for example, after NATO's declaration in 2008 that Georgia and Ukraine would become members of the alliance, the EU's development of specific partnerships with countries of the shared neighborhood, and the United States' and the EU's official support for the leaders of the Revolution of Dignity in Ukraine against President Viktor Yanukovych—the set of levers and tools has expanded to include the use of military force. Russia sees this geopolitical space as strategically important—as a platform to project its influence beyond the borders of the former Soviet Union and as a key to its ability to remain a center of power in the future polycentric world order. Indeed, Russia seems to consider that it can be one of the poles only in association with EEU partners.[11]

In the aftermath of the global financial crisis, and in a context where Western military operations in Iraq and Afghanistan faced growing criticism, the Russian international discourse started to refer more systematically to the idea that the West's leadership is doomed to decline. At the same time, Russian leaders seem to think that this could make the United States and Europe more aggressive toward "challengers" such as Russia. Russian diplomats

---

[10] Vladimir Putin (speech at the Munich Conference on Security Policy, Munich, February 10, 2007), http://en.kremlin.ru/events/president/transcripts/24034.

[11] For the NATO declaration, see "Bucharest Summit Declaration," NATO, Press Release, April 3, 2008, http://www.nato.int/cps/en/natolive/official_texts_8443.htm. As correctly stressed by Samuel Greene, Russia sees the EU's association agreements with the Eastern partnership countries (Ukraine, Moldova, Armenia, Georgia, Azerbaijan, and Belarus) as geopolitically threatening in the sense that their "successful implementation…would…[transform] these countries from a zone where Russia's elite can do business into one where they cannot" because of the democratic and good governance practices that these states would absorb gradually. For more on this issue, see Samuel A. Greene, "Future Approaches to the U.S.," in *Russian Futures: Horizons 2025*, ed. Hiski Haukkala and Nicu Popescu (Paris: EU Institute for Security Studies, 2016), 43.

convey this idea to their counterparts at BRICS meetings and summits with Chinese leaders.[12] According to Sergey Karaganov, a leading Russian foreign policy scholar whose statements are generally considered as representing the mainstream line in the Kremlin, "the 'old' West, which dramatically lost ground in the 2000s after a seemingly spectacular victory in the 1990s, is now trying to reconsolidate its position" by recreating confrontation in Europe and through negotiating trade agreements such as the Trans-Pacific Partnership and the Transatlantic Trade and Investment Partnership.[13] Western sanctions have also been presented in this light. In other words, Russia expects (and welcomes) weaker Western leadership but also assesses that this is associated with risks for competitors, including Russia.

These persistent misunderstandings and tensions with the West are among the factors that have encouraged Russia to turn to Asia in a much more resolute way while making this turn more complex. This process actually started in the 1990s with the development of a strategic partnership with former foe China. Driven by the two countries' desire to concentrate on domestic and international consolidation rather than on geopolitical competition, this partnership gradually became a platform for Russia to promote its ambitions to contribute to the establishment of a multipolar world order, the essence of which was solidarity vis-à-vis perceived Western hegemony. In 1999, Prime Minister Primakov initiated the Russia-China-India strategic triangle, which, gathering once a year at the foreign minister level, was supposed to be another incarnation of the multipolar order. In the early 2000s, however, Putin pushed for a more active Asia policy with other, less Western-oriented factors in mind. In 2003, a strategic energy study concluded that future demand for Russia's oil and gas exports would be far higher in Asia than anywhere else. At the same time, the Kremlin grew increasingly concerned about the situation in its far eastern territories. The global recession of 2008–9 reinforced this "Asian vector," and significant shifts in trade and investment followed its promotion, taking into account shifting economic and strategic international balances, Russia's effort to increase its participation in the globalized economy, and the development needs of the eastern part of its territory.

Many of Russia's international behaviors and priorities reflect the prevailing influence of realism among the conceptual drivers of Russian foreign and security policies and in Moscow's constant search for a balance of power among the states it considers to be major international players. This is

---

[12] The BRICS grouping comprises Brazil, Russia, India, China, and South Africa.

[13] Sergey Karaganov, "How the World Looks from the Russian Perspective," Huffington Post, February 15, 2016. "Confrontation in Europe" is a reference to the adjustments that NATO has made in its defense posture in the aftermath of the conflict in Ukraine.

probably attributable to the strong geopolitical outlook that has historically characterized Russia's world vision, and is unsurprising given the central importance of the territorial dimension in Russian state-building. Combined with other influential factors such as the country's Orthodox Christian identity, this focus has given Russia a specific geopolitical personality and strategic culture. In many ways, Russia's conditions in the immediate post–Cold War period (i.e., declining diplomatic influence on the European and international stages, poor integration into the globalized economy, and the collapse of its military) jostled strategic reflexes that traditionally drove Russian behavior on the world stage. Judging by the apparent resurgence of some of these reflexes in recent years, what Western scholars saw as a rapid (though painful) adaptation of Russia to the new world order in the 1990s was likely perceived by Russians as a loss of identity and sovereignty—a feeling that was probably fueled by the poor economic, social, and international outcome of such "normalization."

Russian Strategic Culture: Alive and Well

Some of the features of Russia's international behavior described above reflect the country's discontent with its degraded international status after the fall of the Soviet Union and a willingness to restore at least part of its lost position in regions deemed strategic. It is also indisputable that Russia's foreign policy under Putin has been influenced by KGB culture, characterized by a more distinct defiance toward the outside world. The interplay and competition between economic lobbies and oligarchs have left an imprint on how Russia attempted to insert itself into the global economy. However, certain elements of continuity tend to indicate the impact of other, deeper-rooted structural factors. Russian leaders who were considered more liberally minded by the West have not differed much on some key issues from Putin, to whom the current toughness of Russian diplomacy is often attributed. Yeltsin, for example, who was viewed as Western-oriented, condemned NATO's enlargement and deployed troops to solve the separatist problem in Chechnya. He also claimed a special role for Russia in the post-Soviet space. Medvedev proved to be tough on Ukraine while pursuing closer ties with the West; he worked to get Europe's cooperation to promote Russia's economic modernization but accepted this only on Russia's terms. And it is indeed striking to see in the post–Cold War era the continuation of a number of patterns of the Russian state's international conduct that are typical of a certain tradition of Moscow's approaches to the international stage, to the role it deserves on it, and to how to uphold this role, including through military means. This derives from key pillars of Russia's strategic culture and reflects the nature of the power system that it has produced throughout the centuries. While exaggerating the importance of this strategic culture would overlook the diverse personal backgrounds of Russia's successive leaders and understate their efforts to adapt to the post–Cold War order, not taking this culture into account would mean a flawed understanding of Russia's international postures.

One scholar gives the following account of Russian strategic culture since the beginning of the sixteenth century:

> Russia's strategic thinking has been articulated around two dimensions, religious and spatial, which are intrinsically linked to the dialectics of kinship and alterity of Russia in relations to Europe, on the one hand, and Asia, on the other hand. The Orthodox legacy of the Byzantine Empire and the geographic position between Europe and Asia determined the idea of Russia having a specific geopolitical mission and provided for the conceptual framework of [Russia's] strategy throughout the Tsarist epoch.[14]

Although it would take more than a few lines to sum up the strategic thinking and self-perception of Russia, this quote identifies the fundamental elements of Russian strategic culture that still leave a strong mark on Moscow's international ambitions and behavior. This culture is deeply rooted in the geographic and spiritual parameters of Russia's historical path. These parameters explain, among other things, why Russia has built itself over the past centuries on a complex combination of defensive and offensive outlooks, the traces of which can be observed up to the present day in Russian diplomacy and military policy.

Russian Exceptionalism: Sources and Impact

One of the generally accepted characteristics of Russia's strategic culture is that the state has consistently searched for security through territorial expansion, be it through colonization or military campaigns, due to the absence of natural physical barriers strong enough to protect Russia from invasions and attacks. Over time, the persistence of the perception that Russia is exposed to multiple external threats and challenges has led Moscow to view neighboring spaces and countries as buffer zones that it must control either militarily or politically. This strategy is also underpinned by the fact that such control ensures fuller access to and greater influence in a number of strategic regions. Control of these buffer countries by other players would undermine or even suppress Russia's indirect access to the "bigger world," a

---

[14] Elena Morenkova Perrier, *Les principes fondamentaux de la pensée stratégique russe* [The Fundamental Principles of Russian Strategic Thinking] (Paris: Institut de recherche stratégique de l'Ecole militaire, 2014), 8.

key condition of its great-power claim. This background is one of the invisible forces that drive Moscow's readiness to resort to coercion (political, economic, or military) to defend what President Yeltsin called the "near abroad" and President Medvedev termed Russia's "sphere of privileged interests" in countries and regions that constitute both a security buffer and a platform for projecting Russia's influence all over the world. Here, the defensive/offensive dialectic that is historically so characteristic of Russia's international conduct is at play. It indeed seems clear that "from Moscow's perspective, its actions in Ukraine represented quintessentially a series of necessary defensive, rather than offensive and expansionist, measures that were intended to prevent an even more severe geopolitical imbalance on the continent resulting from NATO and EU expansion into Central and Eastern Europe."[15]

In order to explain Russia's clear-cut expansionist tendency, some scholars focus on the deep-rooted approaches originating from the adoption of Orthodox Christianity in 988. Russia's aspiration to present itself as the "third Rome" when it became the heir of the Byzantine Empire and the last bastion of Orthodox Christianity after the fall of Constantinople to the Turks in 1453 supposedly motivated Russia's feeling of spiritual superiority vis-à-vis others. According to some explanations and interpretations, the messianic impulses that Russia drew from this fueled its expansionism.

What is certain is that over the centuries these two dimensions—the accumulation of territory and messianic conviction—have combined to solidify the country's exceptionalist vision of itself underlying its claim to be recognized as one of the greatest world powers. When Russian experts accuse the West of undermining the "rules of the second half of the 20th century...absolute respect for sovereignty and territorial integrity, non-interference, at least openly, in the internal affairs of other states," they do not see this position as contradicting Russian's own interventionist behavior toward its neighbors, since for them what is crucially important is "respect for the interests and security of *at least* big powers."[16]

The construction of the Russian state through territorial expansion has also nurtured the conviction that Russia's identity must be distinct from anything that exists elsewhere, including in Europe and Asia, at the crossroads of which its territory stands. Some recent currents of Russian strategic thinking even consider that Russia is not situated between two

---

[15] Eugene Rumer, "Russia and the Security of Europe," Carnegie Endowment for International Peace, June 2016, 4.

[16] Karaganov, "How the World Looks from the Russian Perspective." Emphasis added. Examples of Russia's interventionist behavior include the recognition of separatist entities on Georgia's territory as independent states, the provision of economic aid and the distribution of passports to these same entities, and support to the separatists in Donbass.

continents but is itself a continent.[17] This attitude, combined with the need to protect the "purity" of Orthodox Christianity, has fueled the distinct autarkic tendencies that have appeared from time to time throughout Russian history. This attitude is all the more persistent because Russia's immense territory almost allows the country to live only on its own resources. The discourse about self-sufficiency as an attainable goal (at least in such sectors as agriculture) and about Russia's ability to quickly produce substitutes to imported products has rapidly spread in the context of Western sanctions and Russian counter-sanctions and may be considered as an avatar of this attitude. Sanctions will probably stimulate resentment from segments of society toward the supposed dangers of tying Russia too closely to the globalized economy. In general, the persistence of this mindset explains the salience of such concepts as independence, sovereignty, and national interest in Russian foreign policy discourse.[18]

The West as the Primary Challenge to Russian Integrity and Power

All these parameters combined are important factors in the strong ambivalence that Russian leaders have always maintained toward Europe and the West—an ambivalence that has historically been manifest in the recurrence of the "question of Russia being in Europe or outside."[19] This issue has historically been strongly associated with a constant wavering between a feeling of superiority and a sentiment of inferiority and with the perception that major security challenges are to be expected in the western strategic direction. Europe is the universe that Russia has persistently tried to catch up with, including, since the time of Peter the Great, through welcoming European specialists and technicians and importing European technologies and expertise. This historical phenomenon was echoed by, among other things, the "modernization partnerships" that Russia under Medvedev proposed to the EU and its member states in the late 2000s.

When imperial Russia started developing its ambition to be recognized as a power with global reach, it naturally focused on how relations with

---

[17] Andrei Kolesnikov deplores this view as an "archaization of conscience" that has gained strength in the context of the West-Russia crisis triggered by the conflict in Ukraine. He explains that once again the Russian man, after being "a typical European man," is now being "persuaded that he is not European, that he is unique and exceptional." For more on this issue, see Andrei Kolesnikov, "Why the Kremlin Neglects Strategic Thinking," interview by Pavel Koshin, *Russia Direct*, September 14, 2015. This is an ongoing cycle that Russia's foreign policy has experienced since the end of the Cold War. After maintaining for years that Russia is part of Europe, Russian discourse is now focusing on the idea that the country should develop its Eurasian identity and become a bridge between a more dynamic Asia and a rather apathetic Europe.

[18] One should remember here the eagerness with which Putin worked to reimburse Russia's sovereign debt after he became president.

[19] Morenkova Perrier, *Les principes fondamentaux de la pensée stratégique russe*, 13.

the major European powers of that time could influence the realization of this ambition. At the same time, it viewed materialist and liberal Europe as a major force from which Orthodox Russia had to be protected. Thus, when in 2016 the Kremlin asserts that Russia is the defender of real European values, while deploring the "decadence" observable in European countries, this position is the product not only of Russian propaganda explicitly aimed at dividing European societies but also of Russia's historical self-perception of its relation with Europe.

The country's deep-seated sense of vulnerability vis-à-vis the West is due to the fact that, from Moscow's perspective, European powers have represented the most persistent threat to Russian integrity and been the most frequent invaders. Historically, Russia was invaded by Poland, Sweden, France, and, in less than a quarter of a century, twice by Germany. The threat of a direct military confrontation in Europe between NATO and the Warsaw Pact anchored the perspective that the western part of the territory is the most vulnerable. Russia's fierce reactions to the post–Cold War evolution of NATO—both the alliance's geographic enlargement and its move to take on more expeditionary missions, which Russia sees as making NATO an offensive organization—are certainly a product of this view.

In the contemporary world, this historically embedded approach to Europe has also included the United States, the Soviet Union's main competitor during the Cold War and, from Russia's perspective, an unwelcome player in Europe since the founding of the Atlantic alliance. The fact that the Soviet Union could be considered as the equal of the United States fueled Russians' traditional feeling of superiority, while the ideological competition stimulated messianic impulses. Conversely, the large power gap between Russia and the United States after the fall of the Soviet Union and the fact that China rapidly took on the role of the main challenger to the United States came as shocks to Russian elites desperately trying to recreate some form of a duopoly with Washington on at least some key international issues. The failure of Moscow's attempts at achieving strategic equivalence with Washington fueled its determination to exploit any sign of U.S. strategic weakness and to impose on Washington at least some form of coordination, as has been the case in Syria.

All these factors combined to form a very ambiguous posture of attraction and distrust vis-à-vis the Western world, as well as to create tension between sentiments of inferiority and superiority in relation with it. This is reminiscent of the well-known discussion between Westernizers and Slavophiles in the nineteenth century—the latter arguing, among other things, that Russia should not try to imitate the "decaying" West but should make an original contribution to human civilization and world affairs. Some of their ideas clearly inspire today's "neo-Eurasianists," who believe that while the West is doomed to decline, Russia as a unique civilization will create a new political and cultural pole that will enlighten humanity.[20] One illustration of this posture is Moscow's lack of interest in seeing its integration with Europe be driven by norms decided elsewhere.[21] Another "symptom" is its strong reluctance to accept any kind of interference from Western institutions and states in domestic affairs, including criticism of its record on human rights and political freedom. The divergence between Russia and the EU on the nature of the partnership for modernization has expressed this quite clearly—with the former hoping for technological transfers and industrial partnerships, and the latter being more concerned with democratization, economic liberalization, rule of law, and governance issues.[22]

Russia's posture has taken highly antagonistic forms in recent years. After the color revolutions that took place in Georgia and Ukraine in the first half of the 2000s, Russia, exaggerating the role of U.S. NGOs in these popular revolts, started to consider that the West's inclination to interfere in other states' internal affairs constitutes a real security challenge. This view persists in the latest editions of Russia's security strategy and military doctrine and is reflected in some Russian analysis of current global problems.[23] Typically, the events in Ukraine in 2014 were presented by officials in Moscow as an armed anti-constitutional coup supported by the West.[24]

---

[20] See Alexander Dugin, "L'idéologue de Poutine" [Putin's Ideologist], interview by Galia Ackerman, *Politique Internationale*, Summer 2014.

[21] As a Russian political scientist observes about discussions on a new EU-Russia partnership and cooperation agreement, "Brussels must realize that over the years of Putin's presidency Russia has given up the unsavory role of a beggar at the doors of the EU and the West in general, as it used to be in the past decade, and has ceased to be a secondary co-participant in relations, when it was addressed as 'partner' only out of kindness. In this new situation, Russia does not and will not recognize the validity of the EU's claims to the role of senior partner, the more so mentor." Vladimir Pankov, "Options for the EU-Russia Strategic Partnership Agreement," *Russia in Global Affairs* 6, no. 2 (2008): 172–84, http://eng.globalaffairs.ru/number/n_10933.

[22] See Laure Delcour, "The EU and Russia's Modernisation: One Partnership, Two Views," LSE Ideas, April 5, 2011, http://blogs.lse.ac.uk/ideas/2011/04/the-eu-and-russia%E2%80%99s-modernisation-one-partnership-two-views.

[23] Russian Federation, "Military Doctrine of the Russian Federation," December 2014; and President of Russia, "National Security Strategy of the Russian Federation," December 2015. In the Kremlin's view, competition among powers now has ramifications in the field of political values. Moscow has used such discourse to condemn Western military interventions in Iraq and Libya, which Putin mentioned at the UN General Assembly in September 2015. Vladimir Putin (speech at the 70th session of the UN General Assembly, New York, September 28, 2015), http://en.kremlin.ru/events/president/news/50385.

[24] "West's Support for State Coup in Ukraine Prime Cause of Crisis in Ukraine—Putin," TASS, June 19, 2015.

What Is Asia's Place in Russia's Eurasia Policy?

The traces of this debate can also be found in the stance of Russian representatives in frameworks such as the BRICS or the Shanghai Cooperation Organisation (SCO). Russia maintains that these organizations guarantee their members free choice of political and economic development while the European and Euro-Atlantic institutions do not. The "Shanghai spirit," the informal doctrine of the SCO, suggests that by promoting "mutual trust, mutual benefit, equality, consultation, respect for diverse civilizations and pursuit of shared development," members are committed to rejecting any interference in each other's internal affairs. This is another element that suggests that Asia is important to Moscow primarily as a function of what the region can help Russia achieve in relations with the West. The secondary nature of Russia's interest in Asia has always been striking, given the importance that Russian leaders give to the status of their country as a bridge between Europe and Asia. Russians, including Putin, have always defined their country's identity as European, which has probably determined the clear historical prioritization in Russian diplomacy of relations with Europe and the West.

In the early 21st century, such a legacy makes it difficult for Russia to improve its position in Asia, where it is now increasingly acting on the basis of interests that are not only connected to the Western vector of its foreign policy. Russians themselves seem to be skeptical about this new goal. Putin apparently had to push hard for the Russian bureaucracy to implement seriously the agenda of rebalancing diplomacy and international economic relations toward Asia.[25] Russia faces specific difficulties in adjusting its Asian agenda. Its foreign policy toward the region is heavily determined by the partnership with China, where Russia now occupies the junior seat, and hampered by the close connections of many Asian states with the West, which constrain their cooperation with Russia. In a quite competitive strategic environment, Russia will have to leverage its increasingly closer ties with China through a diversification of partners in the region (for example, India, Japan, and Vietnam). The Association of Southeast Asian Nations' rejection in spring 2016 of Russia's request to become a strategic partner says much about how long the road might be before Russia's regional commitment is deemed predictable and constructive by Asian states. Even the Chinese leadership, at least until the recent events in Ukraine, remained wary that Russia might betray China for the sake of consolidating ties with the West.

---

[25] Dmitri Trenin, "Bureaucracy and Corruption Stand in Way of Russia's Shift to Asia," *Global Times*, March 29, 2015.

In the future, an important point to follow will be the internal discussion in Russia about the contribution of Asia not only to the country's economy or security but also to its identity. Here, one may wonder whether the words of Alexander Dugin, who recently said that "Eurasianism consists in valorizing the contribution of Asia to [Russia's] culture and mentality," should be considered as an important political signal.[26] Dugin, whose influence on Russian decision-making is certainly overrated, may have in mind a philosophy close to that of the Slavophiles in which the term Eurasia is defined in connection with and opposition to Europe rather than Asia. When Russian officials speak of the Eurasian focus of Russia's diplomacy, strategy, or even identity, they are not in fact stressing the dual identity of their country. What they generally are referring to is "a geopolitical principle—that is Russia's claim to be the 'pivotal' state and 'engine' of the post-Soviet world."[27]

However, it is important to pay attention to the increasingly widespread idea in Russia that the example of China—and other countries in Asia—shows that economic growth can be achieved under nondemocratic systems. Such an approach fits well with the authoritarian nature of the regime in Russia. In any case, the current situation that sees China increasingly turning toward the West, through the "new Silk Road" projects, and Russia more systematically looking east will probably enhance Moscow's interest in promoting its central role in the looming reconfigurations in the Eurasian space.

The Besieged Vulnerable Fortress: The Authoritarian Solution

To explain the disconcerting coexistence of defensive and offensive accents in Russia's international discourse and actions on the world stage, one should keep in mind the fact that Russia's gradual expansion of its territory has paradoxically aggravated its feeling of vulnerability vis-à-vis the outside world. Indeed, the more the Russian empire enlarged its space—again, in part as a reflex to build buffer zones, and in part out of messianic impulses—the more it had to manage the social, ethnic, and religious heterogeneity of its population, as well as engage in a constant struggle to control an elastic space, much of which is remote from the major political and economic centers. This is still true today: for example, Russia's turn to Asia is hampered by the lack of infrastructure tying the Russian Far East to the rest of the country. Likewise, Russia's demographic decline triggers serious discussions about how the country will preserve its territorial integrity when it is not capable of inhabiting its territory fully. This latter argument is often used concerning

---

[26] Dugin, "L'idéologue de Poutine."

[27] Marlène Laruelle, "Eurasia, Eurasianism, Eurasian Union: Terminological Gaps and Overlaps," PONARS Eurasia, Policy Memo, no. 366, July 2015, 3.

Russia's border with China. The Russian side is increasingly subject to deindustrialization and depopulation trends that are in striking contrast with the demographic dynamism on the Chinese side of the border.

Domestic weaknesses are considered factors that external powers can exploit to try to take control of Russia's resources or to break its international clout. Such anxiety about the possible risks that can stem from these internal and external dynamics was evident in Putin's statement in the aftermath of the Beslan tragedy in September 2004 when he accused external enemies of "trying to seize a juicy morsel from Russia."[28] The same mindset was also at work when, in reaction to the unprecedented demonstrations that took place in 2011–12 in Moscow and other Russian cities, Kremlin officials accused the West of trying to meddle in Russian politics, including through U.S.-funded NGOs. The unrest sparked the adoption of a new law in November 2012 compelling organizations that receive foreign funding and are deemed to engage in "political activity" to register as "foreign agents." In September of that same year, the government had expelled USAID from Russia.

While this policy may look like a product of Putin's KGB background, it also reflects another classical trait in Russian strategic culture. Russian leaders have long conceived of an authoritarian organization of power as the only way to keep internal tensions and fractures in check while resisting external pressure. The size of Russia's territory, the perception that the country is surrounded by security challenges in all directions, and the multiethnic nature of the population due to the progressive addition of non-Slavic populations have all helped entrench a highly centralized autocratic type of governance. Such a system was supposed to allow for optimal control over the heterogeneous and dispersed populations of the empire (now the federation) to ensure their assimilation, as well as for the concentration of the resources of the country, state, and society with a view to efficiently addressing external challenges while also promoting Russia's great-power ambitions.[29]

Military Instruments as the Mainstay of Russia's Power Strategy: Past and Present

The set of geographic, historical, and psychological circumstances described in the preceding section contributed to shaping the nature of the

---

[28] Quoted in Richard Sakwa, *Putin: Russia's Choice*, 2nd ed. (New York: Routledge, 2008), 142.

[29] The perception of the need to ensure the state's strength to manage its large territory and diverse population was fed by history. In Russian understanding, "internal conflicts among the principalities that constituted Russia and between different groups in Russian society" facilitated outside military incursions. See Eitelhuber, "The Russian Bear," 5. This also explains, without justifying it, the forceful policy that Russia pursued to answer Chechnya's separatist aspirations.

political system in Russia. As one scholar has observed, "from Imperial times to the Soviet era, the notion that its territory and resources were the object of neighboring and enemy states' expansionist and bellicose ambitions not only shaped Russian threat perceptions, but also contributed to forge a strong nationalism, which is part and parcel of the Russian national identity."[30] This factor explains why Western sanctions, for example, have not undermined the population's support of Putin: in fact, sanctions "helped to mobilize people around the governor of the besieged fortress."[31] This is typical of the relationship between power and society in Russia, one that has allowed Russian leaders to make the population accept the limitations imposed on its political and social rights and the prioritization of foreign policy and military power over social and economic needs. In this second decade of the 21st century, the Russian population seems content to accept a heavy economic burden to pay for national defense. The military operations in Ukraine and Syria have not harmed Putin's popularity. This is strongly connected to the fact that military tools have been prioritized over social objectives for centuries, which is a key factor in accounting for why Russian society has remained less free than other European societies. As one scholar explains, "since the end of the fifteenth century until the formation of the Soviet Union, all major reforms in Russia were spurred by the question of how to obtain money and increase the strength of the armed forces. In the final analysis, all reforms were dictated by foreign and military policy needs."[32]

Some schools of thought define strategic culture "in terms of military strategy and the use of force in International Relations" and as "a deeply held cultural predisposition for a particular military behavior or thinking, derived from a country's history, geography, national myths and symbols, political traditions and institutions, among other sources."[33] Russia constitutes an interesting case study in this specific frame of analysis given its strong militaristic tradition.[34] This probably has much to do with the fact that "the Russian state and empire emerged and expanded in conditions of almost constant warfare, initially defensive, then increasingly offensive as the empire expanded."[35] The gradual accumulation of territories has nurtured

---

[30] Marcos Degaut, "The Russian Strategic Culture and the Annexation of Crimea: The Empire Strikes Back?" Mundorama, May 10, 2014.

[31] See Kolesnikov, "Why the Kremlin Neglects Strategic Thinking."

[32] Eitelhuber, "The Russian Bear," 6.

[33] Degaut, "The Russian Strategic Culture."

[34] See Alexander M. Goltz and Tonya L. Putnam, "State Militarism and Its Legacies—Why Military Reform Has Failed in Russia," *International Security* 29, no. 2 (2004): 121–58.

[35] Fritz W. Ermarth, "Russia's Strategic Culture: Past, Present, and in Transition?" Science Applications International Corporation (SAIC) report, prepared for Defense Threat Reduction Agency, October 31, 2006, 3–4.

the centrality of military power in Russia's general strategy. From the Russian perspective, controlling the huge territory that Russia has built up over the centuries requires a big army and a profusion of military equipment. The Soviet experiment, in which the buildup of military power became the driving force of political and economic development, can be understood as an extreme continuation of this mindset.

Military tools have also played a key role in securing the periphery, with a number of interventions abroad to keep control of territories sending signs that they could quit Moscow's embrace—for example, Hungary in 1956, Czechoslovakia in 1968, Georgia in 2008, and Ukraine in 2014. A Russian defense specialist has suggested that the decision in 2015 to beef up Russia's military presence along the border with Ukraine means that the Russian government, aware that it has durably lost "all substantial levers of influence over Ukraine," believes that it can only "bet on military levers" in the new post-Euromaidan circumstances.[36]

Phases where Russia deprioritized military instruments have been very rare, with the most recent one being the Yeltsin era. Although the leaders of the "new Russia" consciously tried to normalize the place of the military and the military-industrial complex in the country's distribution of resources, the cause was ambiguous. First, a key reason for drastically reducing the armed forces and state defense orders was the economic crunch after the collapse of the Soviet Union. Second, the various attempts at military reform undertaken in that period did not lead to a profound restructuring of the armed forces, which overall kept their Soviet outlook, albeit in a much degraded form. This lack of real reorganization was of course due to the lack of financial resources available to modernize and professionalize the military forces. But there was also palpable passive resistance (and not only in the military) to any radical change, including slashing military personnel and abandoning conscription.[37] It was also not too long before government officials formulated a discourse presenting the military-industrial complex as a locomotive of Russia's industrial and technological future that should be preserved and supported in the global arms market.[38]

Thus, the demilitarization of foreign policy and the economy that occurred in the 1990s was at least partially imposed on Russian leaders, and

---

[36] Ruslan Pukhov, "Rossiya-NATO: Nasha karta Afriki" [Russia-NATO: Our Map of Africa], *Vedomosti*, July 15, 2016.

[37] On what this period meant for the Russian armed forces and civil-military relations, see Dale R. Herspring, *The Kremlin and the High Command: Presidential Impact on the Russian Military from Gorbachev to Putin* (Lawrence: University Press of Kansas, 2006).

[38] Many key firms of the Russian military-industrial complex were salvaged in the 1990s by the Asian market as Indian and Chinese orders substituted for domestic contracts. This contributed to the deepening of Moscow's relations with these countries.

there was no consensus that de-emphasizing military instruments was the right path to follow. Russian officials started suggesting that the West would have been more respectful of Russia's interests had the country been able to maintain a credible armed force; as a result of its feeling that it was more exposed to external pressure due to the weakness of its conventional forces, Russia relied increasingly on nuclear weapons in its defense policy.[39] Since 2000, Putin has repeatedly stressed that in the complex security environment in which Russia is evolving, it must possess credible military instruments to resist pressure (primarily from the militarily more advanced West) and to defend its legitimate strategic and security interests abroad.[40] Since Russia has been able to invest again in its armed forces and defense industrial complex as a result of high international prices for its key export item, hydrocarbons, it has done so in a way that puts a heavy burden on the national economy.[41] Defense expenditure accounted for 19.7% of the total budget in 2015 and 4.0% of GDP in 2014.[42] In the context of military operations in Crimea and later Syria, Russian officials started again focusing in their speeches on their country's international greatness based on its military power and achievements. Russian military aircraft now test NATO air defenses at a pace that is unprecedented since the end of the Cold War, and at times in a very provocative way (including by violating the airspace of NATO members). Russia also devotes huge financial and material resources to organizing military exercises, including snap inspections, at all levels and in all military districts; some of these exercises involve tens of thousands of troops and masses of military equipment.[43]

In the post-Soviet period, the deep-seated habit of prioritizing military instruments of power has been entrenched by the fact that Russia has not recorded very tangible achievements in its effort to diversify the sources of its

[39] Stephen J. Blank, *Russian Nuclear Weapons: Past, Present, and Future* (Carlisle: Strategic Studies Institute, 2011).

[40] "The world is changing. The processes of global transformation currently underway may carry all sorts of risks with them, many of them unpredictable. In a situation of global economic and other kinds of hardships, it may be very tempting for some to resolve their problems at others' expense, through pressure and coercion. It is no wonder that we already hear some voices saying that it is 'only natural' that resources of global significance should soon be declared as being above national sovereignty…[W]e should not tempt anybody with our weakness." Vladimir Putin, "Byt' sil'nymi: Garantii natsional'noy bezopasnosti dlya Rossii" [Being Strong: The Guarantees of National Security for Russia], *Rossiyskaya Gazeta*, February 17, 2012.

[41] For an overview of the transformation of the Russian armed forces under Putin, see Roger N. McDermott, Bertil Nygren, and Carolina Vendil Pallin, eds., *The Russian Armed Forces in Transition: Economic, Geopolitical and Institutional Uncertainties* (New York: Routledge, 2012); and "Voennaya reforma: Na puti k novomu obliku Rossiyskoy armii" [Military Reform: Towards a New Look for the Russian Army], Valdai Discussion Club, July 2012.

[42] Ruslan Pukhov, "Is Russia Punching Above Its Weight?" (unpublished slide presentation, January 2016).

[43] Johan Norberg, "Training to Fight—Russia's Major Military Exercises 2011–2014," Swedish Defence Research Agency, December 2015.

national power strategy—although it has definitely tried to. In the late 1980s and early 1990s, Soviet and later Russian leaders grasped that a rebalance was occurring among the main criteria for power and international authority at a time when the international community was hoping to reap the dividends of peace—with a clear valorization of economic power. Putin initially "was explicit and consistent in his view that a strong Russia had to be prosperous, and that prosperity could not be achieved without deeper international economic integration."[44]

In the early 21st century, however, Russia's share in global trade has remained rather marginal for reasons that likely include the tensions between its national strategic culture and contemporary realities.[45] In 2014 the country accounted for only 2.6% of total world exports, and its share of total world imports was only 1.6%.[46] Russia does not export a lot of high-value-added and high-tech products.[47] The energy levers that dominated Russia's international power posture in the 2000s are quite ambivalent resources in terms of its great-power claim. First, Russian leaders consider that a great power should not become a reserve of raw materials that supports the growth of others. This constitutes a powerful driver behind the Russian government's promotion of arms exports. As a result of the historical prioritization of defense needs, some of the major items other than raw materials that Russia can sell on world markets are weapons and military equipment.[48] The same reasons have pushed Russian leaders to identify the defense sector as one of the major sources moving the Russian economy toward a high-tech, innovative, and knowledge-based structure. Thus, the Russian government will continue to encourage arms exports that it perceives as a source of economic prestige and strategic influence over its clients. In recent years, moreover, the *force de frappe* of Russia's "energy weapon" has lost some of its leverage due to important shifts in international energy markets (such as the U.S. shale oil revolution and the EU's effort to lessen its dependence on Russian gas). In addition,

---

[44] Gould-Davies, "Russia's 'Sovereign Globalization,'" 1.

[45] For example, Russian elites and society have not been unanimous in accepting the implications of increased integration with the globalized economy. In their view, this "meant easing control of commercial and financial flows across borders, increasing dependence on external actors, and binding Russian entities to contracts and jurisdictions beyond Russia's control," all things not squaring very much with the country's classical defiance of, or at best cautiousness toward, the outside world. See ibid.

[46] World Trade Organization, "Russian Federation," Statistics Database, September 2015, http://stat.wto.org/CountryProfile/WSDBCountryPFView.aspx?Language=S&Country=RU.

[47] The latter accounted for only 1.5% of Russia's net exports in 2012. Kuchins, "Russian Power Rising," 137.

[48] According to data from the Stockholm International Peace Research Institute (SIPRI), Russia's share of international arms exports in 2011–15 was 25%, ranking second behind the United States (33%). Aude Fleurant, Sam Perlo-Freeman, Pieter D. Wezeman, and Siemon T. Wezeman, "Trends in International Arms Transfers, 2015," SIPRI, Fact Sheet, February 2016.

the windfall of oil revenues in the 2000s and 2010s has significantly reduced incentives for the Russian government to invest in diversification across the economy and reduce its dependence on hydrocarbons. The consequences become obvious when oil prices stay durably at relatively low levels. (Russia faced a 3.7 % decline in GDP in 2015 as a result of reduced oil prices since fall 2014.) In other words, Russia has not come to terms with its "enduring weakness," which has "always been its relative economic backwardness."[49] In addition, Russia's nascent—and sometimes clumsy—attempts at establishing a soft-power strategy have not made the country sufficiently attractive, even in the near abroad, where it could have relied much more smartly on the influence of Russian language and culture.

The way Russia assesses the relative role of military power has nonetheless recently shown signs of adaptation. The military reforms that the government has pursued since 2008 have produced smaller and more professional forces, and this transformation has focused on developing the ability to move forces swiftly to any exposed spot. Russia still sees itself as threatened from many directions by challenges covering the spectrum of military action—from high-tech combat operations to the fight against jihadists or even the handling of social upheavals and color revolutions in the near abroad. To address such a complex situation, Russia has shifted its focus from accumulating military power to devising new concepts to integrate conventional, nuclear, and unconventional elements of military power in order to build a complex toolkit for facing various contingencies.[50] In a way, Russia is not an exception on this front. The integration of nuclear, conventional, and unconventional tools of military power as part of a unified strategic vision is a notion that has also percolated in the United States and France. There are differences, however. The first one is the amount of resources, particularly financial, that the Kremlin will be able to invest in these three interrelated capacities. It will never manage to match Western capabilities, notably U.S. ones. The other key difference lies in the political-military structures of the Russian state. Its authoritarian tendencies give Putin greater margins of action, given that no official mechanism requires him to justify his use of military or unconventional means, as was shown by the Crimean takeover in March 2014. However, despite this advantage at the outset of a crisis, should the crisis last, Russia would have the greatest difficulties in sustaining its efforts due to a rapid shortage of means, including financial industrial constraints.

---

[49] Gould-Davies, "Russia's 'Sovereign Globalization,'" 3–4.

[50] Diego A. Ruiz Palmer, "Back to the Future? Russia's Hybrid Warfare, Revolutions in Military Affairs, and Cold War Comparisons," NATO Defense College, Research Paper, no. 120, October 2015; and András Rácz, *Russia's Hybrid War in Ukraine: Breaking the Enemy's Ability to Resist*, FIIA Report, no. 43 (Helsinki: Finnish Institute of International Affairs, 2015).

Analysis of the debate about the Russian military also shows that the leadership now seems to be looking for concepts that allow for only limited use of force against adversaries, even those who are stronger militarily, in combination with (and often as the last resort) other means such as information campaigns, cyber operations, economic measures, and political interference. Another important shift concerns Russia's status as a nuclear superpower, which has to some extent offered the country greater strategic comfort in the face of a multifaceted external threat. However, from a longer-term perspective, recent advances in U.S. military technology (especially in antimissile defense and strategic conventional weapons) have the potential to undermine Russia's confidence in its nuclear deterrent. As suggested by its tough diplomatic posture on these issues and the active countermeasure programs that Russia has pursued in recent years, these new challenges probably reinforce the country's historical feeling of vulnerability to external, and especially Western, pressure.

Conclusions

The Path Forward for Russia

Russian strategic culture is rooted in several centuries of history that have been characterized by political, technological, and ideological ruptures, as well as fluctuations in Russia's alliances with foreign powers and numerous conflicts and wars. The process of circumscribing this strategic culture is all the more complex an undertaking because there exists an abundant and contradictory, if not controversial, literature about Russian strategic culture and thinking, with many different interpretations. And yet some fundamental elements have proved very resilient and still exert a strong influence on the way Russia assesses the world situation and its place in it, defines its national interests, and perceives the intentions of other players. This strategic culture is significantly determined by the territorial dimension of Russia's evolution. Territorial expansion was intended to meet both defensive and offensive objectives dictated by a complex mix of attitudes: a sentiment of vulnerability connected to the absence of strong natural borders and validated by a history of invasions; a feeling of superiority and messianic impulses linked to Russia's vision of itself as the moral guarantor, defender, and promoter of Orthodox Christianity; and a combination of exceptionalism and isolationism.

Schematically, this legacy has produced at least two major effects that still permeate Russia's behavior on the world stage. One is the massive reliance on military tools for both the protection of the national territory and the advancement of Russian interests in the near and, at times, far abroad. The other result of this ambivalent set of motivations is that Russia has always balanced—usually not in alternating phases but simultaneously—retrenchment, and at times even isolationism, with a desire to have input on all major international issues. Yet although it has always wanted to influence the course of world affairs and has encroached on the sovereignty of a number of states, Russia is viscerally hostile to interference (whether real or imagined) with its own internal affairs and international interests. It has always vacillated between a desire for integration with Europe and the West and wariness about the "importation" of Western political values and socioeconomic ways.

Russia has also fluctuated between an inferiority complex—partly tied to its traditional relative technical, social, and economic backwardness in relation to Europe—and a feeling of superiority both toward Europe (based in a sense of moral superiority) and toward Asia (based in its European identity). The latter has endured, although it may have been shaken or modulated by China's rise and Russia's being compelled to seek international clout through association with Asian powers. The diagnosis of Russian strategic culture proposed by a U.S. expert is instructive in this context: "defensiveness bordering on paranoia, on one hand, combined with assertiveness bordering on pugnacity, on the other."[51] In particular, the Russian habit of resorting to offensive policies and means (e.g., through tough diplomacy, economic coercion, and the use of force) to respond to a very defensive perspective vis-à-vis the international stage makes negotiating with Russia very difficult for its partners.

Russia's perception of itself as a great power, which was solidified during the Cold War by the Soviet Union's status as the second superpower, was brutally shaken by the multiform crisis the country endured in the 1990s. Russia had become a secondary diplomatic power and proved unable to shape the evolution of strategic areas where it at one time had strong positions. Even on the European stage, Russia felt that its voice was not heard, which reactivated one of the classical themes of Russian strategic thinking—the idea that Western powers are not prepared to welcome Russia as a legitimate part of Europe.[52] The traditional sentiment of vulnerability toward the outside world, in particular the West, was intensified by Russia's harsh military crisis. It was also substantiated by the fact that the buffer had become not only unstable and

---

[51] Ermarth, "Russia's Strategic Culture," 7.

[52] This argument is present in Alexander Dugin's rhetoric. He has stated that "Atlanticists and Eurocentrists will always see Russia as a barbarian country and as an enemy," adding that "we are 'the other Europe'" and that should an alliance occur between the two Europes, "it should be an alliance of equals." See Dugin, "L'idéologue de Poutine." By saying so, he does not seem to see a contradiction with Russia's constant assertion that given its millennial history and specific identity, it should not have values and rules of the game imposed on it by Western powers.

rife with potential risks but also, in the perception of Russian leaders, a place for geopolitical rivalry with outside powers, the most proactive of which were the United States and the EU. Russia's partial failure to integrate itself into the globalized economy, or, from Russia's perspective, to receive a dignified place in it, has sparked a deep-seated frustration with the international order.

In recent years, Russia's behavior on the world stage has again taken on traits that give the impression that it is reverting rapidly to its traditional geopolitical postures, which are marked by a strong reliance on hard power. This makes strategists wonder whether Russia might start using force more frequently to expand its territory and impose a new, less Western-centric world order. Strategists wonder whether Russia might increasingly consider resorting to military tools as an extension of diplomacy to force adversaries and partners to heed its interests and to preemptively protect itself from perceived threats.

While in many ways the broad outlines of Russia's international strategy reflect the endurance of elements of its strategic culture, its environment has evolved and continues to evolve. This may over the longer term rebalance the weight of traditional parameters. In the context of the Ukrainian conflict, Russian officials have used rhetoric about, in substance, the "sovereignization" of the economy and took additional measures aimed at reducing the social and political presence of foreign (primarily Western) actors on its soil, which is reminiscent of Russia's quasi-autarkic instincts. Yet it is striking to see that at the same time Moscow has attempted to show that it is not acting in isolation, working to diversify its economic foreign relations and trying to use its involvement in the Syrian conflict to establish the conditions for mending the broken ties with the West. Russia's efforts to promote multilateral platforms such as the BRICS grouping and the SCO to enhance its own international authority are another new development. Russia has historically preferred to rely solely on its own forces and is probably not fully comfortable with this new role, as evidenced by its desire to present itself as the "guide" in these forums.

One important condition for Russia seriously departing from its strategic culture could be the country's success, or failure, in rebalancing its foreign policy through the strengthening of its Asian vector. Russia's historical concentration on European partners and adversaries is one of the main arguments used by those who express strong skepticism about the possibility for Russia to achieve its proclaimed "turn to Asia." One of the consequences of Russia's focus on its strategic relations and problems with the West is its traditional neglect of foreign policy in Asia. As a result, Moscow has earned a reputation in Asia and the Middle East for being an unreliable partner because of its clear-cut tendency to use the non-Western vectors of its diplomacy primarily for the sake of achieving goals in relations with the West. Putin now seems to be determined to enforce the shift to Asia, which has been accelerated by the profound crisis in relations with the West caused by the Ukrainian conflict. One may speculate that over the longer term, a less unbalanced (i.e., less Western-centric) foreign policy could make Russia feel more comfortable in its international shoes and less frustrated by misunderstandings and differences in ties with Western countries. After speaking first of integration with the West and Europe, then of itself (plus the former Soviet states regrouped in the EEU) as the second pole of greater Europe (the first pole being the enlarged EU), Russia is now reviving a discourse about its role as a bridge between Asia and Europe. It has explicitly, albeit reluctantly, accepted that in this strategic scheme China will play an important role, including through the development of its presence in Eurasia (through the new Silk Road project).[53] Russia is also trying to develop positive relations with other Asian powers such as Vietnam, India, and Japan. Should this picture be realized, Europe will not be excluded, but the region may over the long term be increasingly deprioritized by Moscow, which will be freer than today to propose cooperation with Europe on its own terms.

Key parameters of Russian strategic culture have survived because Russia's adjustment to the post–Cold War international setting has been painful as a result of the country's economic weaknesses and the nature of its political system. The ability, or inability, of Russia to break the dependence of its economy on hydrocarbon exports will also be a determinant of possible redefinitions of Moscow's national power policy. As discussed above, Russian officials have often declared that the country's over-reliance on exports of raw materials was not compatible with its claim to great-power status, which has led them to aggressively promote military and nuclear technologies abroad as a symbol of industrial and technological strength. Overall, a more diversified economy could help Russia feel more confident and lessen its reliance on military power. On this latter front, Russian leaders have recently pursued options that depart quite dramatically from traditional practices such as relying on abundant manpower and redundant military equipment. In other words, they have accepted that some dimensions of the country's traditional military practices have been challenged by technological change, demographic hurdles, and economic constraints. The result is, as was underscored previously, a restructuring of the toolbox of coercive means, in

---

[53] Timofey Bordachev, "Rossiya i Kitay v Tsentralnoy Azii: Bolshaya igra s pozitivnoy summoy" [Russia and China in Central Asia: The Great Win-Win Game], Valdai Club, Valdayskiye Zapiski, no. 50, June 2016.

which military options are no longer the only, or even primary, instruments in a number of contingencies.

Finally, Russia's traditional messianic impulses have recently subsided. Moscow has no ideology to export; in fact, the general principles it tries to promote on the world stage—basically centered on the necessity for all states (at least big ones) to choose their own path of political and economic development—are more defensive than proactive. Above all, Russia is trying to build an informal alliance with other states on various continents that share these principles in the hope that unity is strength. However, the tough line, up to the use of military force, that Moscow has been pursuing in recent years to promote a world order that it perceives as more protective of its interests has made Western observers conclude that Russia is aggressive (to some, more aggressive than the Soviet Union) and should be resolutely countered. For its part, Russia is firmly convinced of the specificity of its identity and strategic role and rejects any outside attempts at restricting it to the status of a regional power. The country will probably not be westernized in the way that had been expected in the 1990s.

Implications for the United States

Given the central place that the United States occupies in Russian strategic calculations, Washington has a special responsibility in trying to make Russia an easier player and partner. Any prolonged period of serious antagonism between Moscow and Washington risks intensifying the pace at which Russia will look for additional partners outside the West, which will see its leverage over Russia erode further. This will not make the strategic landscape any more stable, be it in Europe or in Asia. In the Asia-Pacific, Russia could become a more active participant in great-power strategic competition. Despite all the objective difficulties and ambiguities, efforts to integrate the Chinese Silk Road projects and the EEU should be followed closely. The lack of a bilateral strategic dialogue based on a sound and realistic approach to what Russia is and wants is fraught with security risks, especially given that Russia's nuclear arsenal continues to pose an existential threat to the United States.

Hence, it seems that Washington has to navigate between asserting its principles, defending its interests, and firmly protecting its allies, while at the same time continuing to engage Moscow on a vast array of topics. This probably means adjusting the U.S. posture in such a dialogue to acknowledge Russia's specific world outlook, where it is feasible and has little political cost. For example, signaling that Moscow matters on a number of specific dossiers, which it does, is a cheap way to help push ahead discussions by satisfying Russia's great-power aspirations without betraying any ideals and principles. This may also help attenuate the strong negative interaction between the constant tension with "the only superpower" and Russia's historical encirclement and feeling of insecurity.[54] Thus, the U.S. response to a defiant Russia will probably not only comprise better weapons, better intelligence, and better technology. Dialogue and appeasement, which are not equivalent to compromise of principles, may help the Kremlin envision a more relaxed approach on the international scene and defuse tension that is rooted in obsolete visions. However, this approach can work only if Russia manages to overcome or circumvent the internal economic and political hurdles to its full participation on the world stage. On both fronts, Moscow currently believes that options and solutions can come from closer interaction with Asia. Depending on the circumstances, the impact of this approach on relations with the West could vary considerably and deserves close attention.

---

[54] "Putin Admits U.S. Is the Only Superpower Today," TASS, June 17, 2016.

EXECUTIVE SUMMARY

This chapter examines the divisions in Japan's strategic culture and assesses the implications for U.S. security interests.

MAIN ARGUMENT

Japan is deeply divided over the issue of how best to use its first-rate military. Article 9 of the constitution forfeits the right to wage war, yet recently enacted security legislation circumvents this proscription by upholding the constitutionality of collective self-defense. Nonetheless, a majority of Japanese continue to oppose the deployment of troops overseas for combat missions. At the same time, a broader historical shift is taking place that defines Japan again as a maritime state. A strategic division manifests in this context between two views of Japan's strategic culture. The first is espoused by those who would dispatch the Self-Defense Forces abroad for combat missions. The second sees a more cosmopolitan role for Japan in Asia and the world. In the latter view, Article 9 of the constitution serves as the cornerstone of a deeply realized social contract eschewing war for dependence on the U.S. protective shield.

POLICY IMPLICATIONS

- The outcome of the debate over the constitution will define Japan's place in both the region and the world for the foreseeable future.

- Policymakers should understand the contours of the opposing positions within Japan's policy community and society at large and take seriously the depth of commitment that Japanese citizens have to the constitutional proscription against waging war beyond Japan's borders.

- Policymakers need to recognize that the so-called history issues—the living legacies of Japan's empire and war in the Asia-Pacific—are entwined with security interests and specifically Japan's debate over the use of its armed forces.

Two Strategic Cultures, Two Japans

Alexis Dudden

During much of the past 70 years, Japan's understanding of its strategic culture coalesced under the protective umbrella of U.S. military might. Most people both within and outside Japan held that such a demilitarized strategic culture facilitated a stable, peaceful period of economic and societal recovery from the devastation of World War II. Many have come to understand this condition, moreover, in relation to the devastation that Japanese troops visited throughout the Asia-Pacific more than 70 years ago—less as punishment or atonement than as a way of redirecting Japanese society forward. Today, however, those seeking to shape the nation's strategic culture are deeply split. Japan has a world-class military, and amid a shifting balance of power and possibility in Asia, the nation's leaders are profoundly at odds over a core issue: when, where, why, and how the Japanese military should be deployed. A nation's strategic culture can be a primary unifying feature, or it can divide a troubled populace. The outcome of this debate will define Japan's place in the region and world for the foreseeable future.

At the forefront of any discussion of Japan's strategic concerns is the awareness that although the United States' occupation authorized Japan's famous war-renouncing constitution in 1947, U.S. patronage nonetheless has encouraged Tokyo to develop the Japan Self-Defense Forces into a first-rate military.[1] Additionally, the constitution has always provided for the right to self-defense. Yet there has been no amendment to the constitution, making some view it as an ossified stumbling block that does not reflect the reality

Alexis Dudden is a Professor of History at the University of Connecticut. She can be reached at <alexis.dudden@uconn.edu>.

---

[1] For more on this issue, see Kenneth B. Pyle, *The Japanese Question: Power and Purpose in a New Era*, 2nd ed. (Washington, D.C.: AEI Press, 1996).

of Japanese troop capabilities.[2] At the same time, for many Japanese people, Article 9 defines their national identity and is the cornerstone of Japan's strategic culture.

Even with the parliamentary victory in July 2016 bolstering the ruling Liberal Democratic Party (LDP) that supports changing the nation's military posture to allow the deployment of troops overseas, public opinion polls continue to show that an overwhelming majority of the population nonetheless favors preserving the law that prevents such action.[3] Despite this gap, the current administration of Prime Minister Shinzo Abe appears determined to overturn Article 9 and other key provisions of the constitution.[4] During a speech on May 3, 2016—when Japanese commemorate the promulgation of the constitution in 1947—Abe declared, "Let's work together to revise our Constitution."[5]

At first glance, the divergence in approaches to Japan's future strategic outlook seems straightforward: one camp would send Japanese troops abroad for the first time since World War II to engage openly in wars alongside allies, while the other—the majority of people, albeit not the party in power—would uphold Article 9 of the constitution, which limits Japanese troops to defending the homeland. (A majority of the latter camp sees merit, however, in permitting Japanese forces to aid in overseas humanitarian relief operations under the United Nations' command, which has happened in places such as Cambodia and Haiti.)[6]

At the same time, a profound historical shift is at stake. Japan's recent security debates reveal competing visions for the nation's place in the world. In essence, the divide pits those who would define the state of Japan rigidly against those who understand its role in more cosmopolitan terms. Regarding this issue, Sheila Smith has observed that "within Japan the debate is less about strategy and more about the efficacy of broader

---

[2] Kenneth Mori McElwain and Christian G. Winkler, "What's Unique about the Japanese Constitution? A Comparative and Historical Analysis," *Journal of Japanese Studies* 41, no. 2 (2015): 249–80.

[3] Gavin Blair, "What Abe's Stunning Win Means for Japan's Pacifist Constitution," *Christian Science Monitor,* July 11, 2016.

[4] While Article 9 garners most attention in discussions of strategic culture, the proposed constitution favored by the current prime minister would also fundamentally redefine the emperor, returning the throne to a position of political power not seen since the wartime era.

[5] Tomohiro Osaki and Ayako Mie, "Abe's Revisionist Agenda Subject of Opposing Rallies on Constitution Day," *Japan Times,* May 3, 2016.

[6] A series of special measures further augmented the Japanese military's overseas capabilities in the immediate wake of September 11 without changing the constitutional prohibition against war. As will be explained in this chapter, measures such as refueling U.S. ships built on prior shifts in Japanese strategic culture, which political scientist Richard J. Samuels labels the "salami slicing" method of snipping away at Article 9. See Richard J. Samuels, *Securing Japan: Tokyo's Grand Strategy and the Future of East Asia* (Ithaca: Cornell University Press, 2007), 82–104.

civil-military relations instituted in the wake of Japan's devastating defeat in World War II."[7] Japanese planners who most fervently support a hard-edged approach for Japan's place in the world favor scrapping Article 9 to return Japan to so-called normal nation status. At the same time, those with more fluidly defined understandings of their country—in terms of immigration and Japanese citizenship, among other things—would uphold the constitutional refusal of war, while at the same time developing differently conceived humanitarian purposes for the Japan Self-Defense Forces at home, within the region, and around the world.

This chapter will tease out salient features of these two views against the arc of modern Japanese history. The first section will offer a brief discussion of the historical backdrop against which Japanese are debating the future of their country, while the next section will examine the broader features of Japanese planners' collective shift toward defining Japan anew as a maritime state. Finally, the last section will summarize current debates, emphasizing the importance to U.S. policymakers of taking seriously the depth and contentious nature of the discussion of these issues within Japanese planning circles and society at large. Key to the success of U.S.-Japan policy is understanding the reasons for and the tenacity of division within Japan over defining Japanese strategic culture.

The Evolution of Japanese Strategic Culture

Recognizing Strategic Possibilities and Limitations

The ocean surrounding Japan brought the country into being. It is the water that connects the thousands of islands that make up Japan, and over time, travel and trade brought about the richly complex society that is Japan today. In this vein, its rulers have long understood that their country's island nature affords security, but strategists have regularly disagreed about what this entails or how to exploit this advantage.[8] At certain junctures in Japanese history—particularly during eras of decentralized rule—Japanese officials, adventurers, scholars, and entrepreneurs traveled relatively freely throughout regional coastline areas and beyond to India and Europe, even crossing the Pacific Ocean in the sixteenth century to learn about the world and their country's place in it. When rulers have decided to curtail the island

---

[7] Sheila A. Smith, "Reinterpreting Japan's Constitution," Council on Foreign Relations, Asia Unbound, July 2, 2014, http://blogs.cfr.org/asia/2014/07/02/reinterpreting-japans-constitution.

[8] The long-standing analysis of Japan's maritime nature by political scientist Masataka Kosaka is paramount. In Japanese, see Masataka Kosaka, "Kaiyo kokka Nihon no koso" [The Concept of Japan as a Maritime State], *Chuo Koron* (1964): 48–80. In English, see Masataka Kosaka, "Japan as a Maritime Nation," *Journal of Social and Political Ideas in Japan* 3, no. 2 (1965): 49–56.

nature of Japan—in essence to circumscribe what we know today as Japan and its people within a tightly drawn perimeter—history shows that social forces eventually push back. Put simply, the Japanese people have repeatedly demonstrated that the reality of living on an island necessitates staying in motion and engaging openly with the world beyond the surrounding seas. When borders and definitions of who belongs as a member of Japanese society have become too tight, the system has collapsed under its own demands.[9]

Similar to contemporary conversations about safeguarding Japan, nearly two hundred years ago the country's planners wrestled with redefining Japan as a maritime state in response to encroaching powers, which was as salient then as it is now.[10] Throughout much of the Tokugawa era (1603–1868), official policy mandated that foreign visitors to Japan be limited to Chinese, Korean, Ryukyuan, and Dutch envoys and traders, all of whom could come ashore only at fixed entry ports, mainly in the south, far from the capital (then called Edo and now Tokyo). Russian incursions caused the greatest stress to this policy, yet well into the early 1800s Japan's rulers were able to keep even Russia at bay through a strategy that boiled down to what one historian described as, "It would be better to have no relations whatsoever."[11] In essence, Japan's leaders would remain aware that foreign countries existed yet choose to ignore them as long as possible.

The shogun's officials initially believed that they could maintain sovereign control simply by telling those whom they defined as "barbaric" to go away. By 1825, however, these advisers revealed anxiety about the success of their strategy by issuing the famous exclusion orders to fire on any ship approaching Japan's shores (though most of the guns and cannons in the country dated from the late 1500s and early 1600s). As Michael Auslin explains, "China's hegemonic position in East Asia and Japan's isolation preserved these [China's and Japan's] cultures until both were confronted with the technological insistence of the Western maritime powers. While they functioned, however, the two countries' strategic cultures were a closed system, subsuming all knowledge of and action in the world within their boundaries."[12] The biggest shock to Japan's intentionally sheltered system

---

[9] The best history of Japan by a Japanese historian available in English is Amino Yoshiko, *Rethinking Japanese History* (Ann Arbor: University of Michigan, 2012).

[10] Between 1998 and 2001, the Japan Forum on International Relations sponsored a multiyear project to examine Japan's place in the century ahead, including the role of the sea in understanding Japan's identify. For quick reference, see Ito Kenichi, Okazaki Hisahiko, and Ota Hiroshi, "The Vision of the Maritime Nation of Japan," Japan Forum on International Relations, February 2001, http://www.jfir.or.jp/e/special_study/seminar3/conver_puro.htm.

[11] George Alexander Lensen's 1950 article remains a *tour de force*. See George Alexander Lensen, "Early Russo-Japanese Relations," *Far Eastern Quarterly* 10, no. 1 (1950): 2–37.

[12] Michael R. Auslin, *Negotiating with Imperialism: The Unequal Treaties and the Culture of Japanese Diplomacy* (Cambridge: Harvard University Press, 2004).

came in 1853 following the arrival of U.S. Navy commodore Matthew C. Perry. Long disgruntled anti-shogunal forces in the southwest aligned with those just north of the capital to use this crisis to overthrow the Tokugawa regime. In 1867, they connived to spirit the emperor out of his Kyoto-defined shadows and place him on the throne at the center of power in Edo, renaming it Tokyo in 1868. The Meiji era (1868–1912) thus witnessed at its inception a political cocktail elemental to the formation of Japan's modern strategic culture. Warriors loyal to the emperor were extremely well rewarded in financial terms when they turned over their vassal estates to the newly defined nation of imperial Japan, the early conceptualization of which remained mediated in regional terms—one was from Satsuma or Mito Province, for example—while the military took on an increasingly active role in creating national identity.

Leading policymakers in the Meiji government determined that for Japan to avoid falling prey to the imperializing policies of the European powers and the United States it had to reverse centuries of closed borders and embark on a great exploration of the modern world. The government sponsored scholarships for thousands of the most talented Japanese students, writers, artists, and scientists to travel around the world and return to Japan with the best of what they encountered. As one historian observes, "their real goal was to master the inner 'spirit' of the civilization—the principles that Westerners used to invent those products."[13]

Among the intrepid early Meiji-era world travelers was Hirobumi Ito, who came to be known as the George Washington of Japan. Ito greatly influenced Japan's Meiji constitution in 1889—Asia's first experiment in constitutional governance—and was the first Japanese prime minister. He nonetheless profoundly distrusted political parties and also the growing number of voices clamoring for "people's rights" (in the tradition of Locke and Rousseau, whose works were wildly popular at the time among opposition politicians). Moreover, Ito determined that Western modernity was primarily the result of industrialization. Facing these popular movements, he argued that a strong emperor (or imperial system) was the only way that Japan could navigate the internal and external contradictions of the times: "The one institution which can become the cornerstone of our constitution is the Imperial House" (i.e., the emperor, divinely defined).[14] The Meiji constitution would rest on Japan's "national essence and polity" (*kokutai*), and the emperor was this body's sovereign, "sacred and inviolable."[15] Until Japan's catastrophic

---

[13] Bob Tadashi Wakabayashi, ed., *Modern Japanese Thought* (Cambridge: Cambridge University Press, 1998), 4.

[14] Quoted in ibid.

[15] Ibid.

collapse in 1945, the emperor was defined as the divine fountainhead of the Japanese people, shaped by "a moral, religious, almost mythical entity. Japanese society was founded not on a social contract but, rather, on racial unity" under this supreme being.[16]

In the meantime, Japan's growing military prowess impressed the world powers, beginning in the wake of the country's defeat of Russia in 1905. Indeed, China had learned of Japan's deadly strength a decade earlier during the first Sino-Japanese War (1894–95), while Taiwanese, Koreans, Ryukyuans (Okinawans), and the indigenous Ainu population within Japan had also come to understand Japanese power via the brutal strategies of colonial control already in play.

Fast forward to the 1920s and 1930s: Japan witnessed a period of unprecedented population growth and rapid industrialization. In the mix, some politicians fanned virulent nationalism and demanded new privileges for the military's place in Japanese society, creating a highly combustive atmosphere in which seeking involvement in a peaceful, liberal order became defined as "un-Japanese." At this juncture, strong racial essentialism buoyed religious zealots, who rallied their cause in the emperor's holy name. Those who fell outside their rigid definitions—especially colonials—were regarded as less than human and thus expendable. At the time, the United States' hotly contested racial exclusion laws specifically targeted Japanese immigrants and only further fueled extremist flames back in Japan.

Noticeably, when most Americans consider the history of modern Japan, they skip much of this and think first of the attack on Pearl Harbor on December 7, 1941. Without doubt, Admiral Isoroku Yamamoto stunned Americans—and the world—with his early morning raid against a U.S. naval base on a U.S.-held territory in the Pacific Ocean. His complete victory against the United States at Pearl Harbor displayed the more expansive strain in the strategic thinking of his nation's empire builders, as well as fully demonstrating Japanese naval and air capabilities.

It is important, therefore, to recall Admiral Yamamoto's understanding of Japan's strategic realities at the time—not least because he was himself so well-versed in the international conditions of the day. In 1939, he famously opined: "For the first six months of the conflict, I will run like a wild boar, and for the first two years we will prevail; but after that, I am not at all sure of events."[17] The self-awareness of Japan's greatest admiral of that period is noteworthy not simply for its candor and foresight but also for the simmering divisions it reveals within the nation's strategic outlook at

---

[16] Kenneth B. Pyle, "Meiji Conservatism," in Wakabayashi, *Modern Japanese Thought*, 125, 126.

[17] Quoted in Mark D. Roehrs and William A. Renzi, *World War II in the Pacific* (New York: M.E. Sharpe, 2004), 45.

the dawn of World War II. The main debate then revolved around whether Japanese forces would be victorious in the ways that the more rapacious policy planners desired. Yamamoto knew that he would win battles in the short term, yet he also understood that the nature of the war that Japan's planners then envisioned—a total war stretching from the interior of northern China southward into the Pacific to northern Australia at the expense of the inhabitants therein—would ultimately eviscerate the nation.

Yamamoto's realization stemmed in no small part from his knowledge of Japan's history as a growing population that for thousands of years remained largely within the contours of its island borders (consisting of Kyushu, Shikoku, and Honshu, with Hokkaido becoming part of Japan in 1869 and the Ryukyu Islands in 1871). Over time, the Japanese people—as they would eventually consider themselves—diversified their government and economy as different rulers allowed, but the configuration of the archipelago's borders by early modern strategists remained very important, including in the 1930s when what we know now as Japan became commonly understood as "the homeland" or "the mainland" (different from the new parts of the empire, which were known as the "outer" territories). These earlier contours of Japan are significant today, considering policymakers' current debates over the country's place in the world.

Throughout Japanese history, fluid understandings of how Japan would engage openly with the world beyond have yielded periods of economic and cultural growth. When leaders have attempted to shore up their own power by countering these trends, the system becomes too inflexible, which is in large part what the world witnessed with imperial Japan's total defeat in 1945. Starvation rations for both Japanese troops abroad and civilians in the homeland were costing the nation its future as much as the fire bombings and ill-fated campaigns; nonetheless, military expansionists kept increasing the empire's claim to new territory while rigidly imposing a hierarchy on those it ruled at the cost of all who could be called Japanese. In the end, the collapse of Japan's empire at once returned the nation from its octopus-like sprawl from north Asia to the South Pacific back to the seahorse-shaped borders of Japan today—largely the same shape it had been in 1868.

Equally important, Japan's defeat in World War II introduced the current constitution, which endures and remains a powerful and deeply realized social contract, despite—or because of—its U.S. imprimatur or the fact that it went into effect in 1947 under U.S. occupation. For these reasons, it is critical to understand that Japanese strategic culture during the past 70 years has taken seriously the rights embedded in this constitution. What Japan at the time may have agreed to out of compulsion is now for the broad majority of

Japanese essential to their view of Japan's role in the world—not something to be manipulated for expedient gain.

Occupation-era prime minister Shigeru Yoshida readily exchanged Japan's right to wage war (as defined in Article 9) for U.S. security guarantees and economic stimulus. He thus can be credited with ushering the so-called peace constitution into play.[18] The historian John Dower has pithily summed up the myriad contradictions created then that last to this day:

> No modern nation ever has rested on a more alien constitution—or a more unique wedding of monarchism, democratic idealism, and pacifism; and few, if any, alien documents have ever been as thoroughly internalized and vigorously defended as this national charter would come to be. Although it bore the unmistakable imprint of the conqueror and shocked Japan's conservative elites…it tapped into popular aspirations for peace and democracy in quite remarkable ways.[19]

For many outside Japan, these "remarkable ways" at times may make the country appear out of step with other nations of similar importance. As a result, popular views about Japan's pacifist posture in the world—as a strong nation that eschews waging war—are deeply felt and manifested in the writings and aims of Japanese thinkers and policymakers who espouse this strategic outlook for their nation.

The Abe administration is working hard to counter this position by overturning Article 9 to realize its particular vision of Japan's role in the world (i.e., by regaining the right to wage war abroad). Thus, repeated polls demonstrating that a majority of citizens wants to hold onto Article 9 collide with this minority view of Japanese strategic culture.[20] Today Japan stands at this historical crossroads, with many on both sides of the debate rightfully taking pride in the fact that Japan has not waged war since 1945. In this vein, China and South Korea's collective charges of renewed Japanese militarism do not simply fall on deaf ears; rather, they cause bewilderment all around, which boils down to Japanese wondering why their country continues to be singled out and whether these societies look within themselves. That said,

---

[18] Based on his post-1945 understanding that anything short of a first-rate military would be useless, many credit one of Yoshida's predecessors and mentors, Prime Minister Kijuro Shidehara, with initially proposing Article 9 in the 1947 constitution. See, for example, Klaus Schlichtmann, "The Ethics of Peace: Shidehara Kijuro and Article 9 of the Constitution," *Japan Forum* 7, no. 1 (1995): 43–67. Interestingly, some of Japan's more conservative supporters of retaining Article 9 today—oil executives and bankers, among others—summon Shidehara's views when arguing that Japan should not change its military strategy beyond its borders. See "Japan's Pacifist Constitution: Keeping the Peace," *Economist*, May 14, 2014, http://www.economist.com/blogs/banyan/2014/05/japans-pacifist-constitution.

[19] John W. Dower, *Embracing Defeat: Japan in the Wake of World War II* (New York: W.W. Norton, 1999), 347.

[20] Blair, "What Abe's Stunning Win Means for Japan's Pacifist Constitution."

within Japan the nature and value of Article 9 remain definitional for a majority of Japanese to describe the nation they wish to embody in the world.

The Broader Context of Maritime Japan

The March 11, 2011, trifecta of an earthquake, tsunami, and nuclear meltdown in northeast Japan reminded everyone that the archipelago is an inherently unstable place, surrounded by a formidable sea. This awful and ongoing event coincided with Japanese leaders' efforts to redefine their country anew as a maritime state, bringing the moment's contingencies into stark relief. On the one hand, Japan's islands present very obviously perceived boundaries as the land itself ends at shoreline; yet on the other hand, there is daily debate over how rigidly to fix the nation's borders, all of which are in the sea (essentially lines strung from one outer island to the next, drawn in the ocean encircling Japan). One of the biggest questions in Japanese governance today—whether there should be more or less state centralization—guides much of the discussion. Differences aside, the country's leaders appear committed to again orienting Japan to the sea, as it was positioned during the first half of the twentieth century. Collectively they have worked across political lines to connect domestic and foreign policies with recently developed international laws of the sea and ocean standards.

At first glance, this issue may seem nonsensical: Japan is an island after all. Of the roughly 127 million Japanese people, only about half a million live on the nation's habitable offshore islands (roughly 430 out of the 6,852 islands that make up the archipelago). In addition, 25,000 of the 50,000 U.S. servicemen and servicewomen in Japan (and scores of other Americans and foreigners working for the U.S. military) live on the most hotly contested outer island, Okinawa.

Yet the tensions involved in reorienting Japan to the sea are deeply fraught and reveal what is at stake. As one security analyst observes, legacies of imperial Japan's naval might and total defeat continue to inform policy planning for Japan's Maritime Self-Defense Force today.[21] For decades after World War II, a social consensus held that the country's island nature caused its defeat in 1945. Against this backdrop, over the past twenty years a renewed commitment to Japan's maritime disposition as elemental to the nation's future strength has gained traction, with members of the Japan Coast Guard and Maritime Self-Defense Force emerging as new cultural heroes. The issue of claiming national space in the seas around Japan is critical. There is pride in the fact that the addition of Japan's territorial oceans to its

---

[21] Alessio Patalano, "Post-war Japan as a Sea Power: Imperial Legacy," *Wartime Experience and the Making of a Navy* (New York: Bloomsbury Academic, 2015).

land mass would make Japan the world's sixth- or seventh-largest country, and many are pleased that a stretched out measurement of the nation's coastline would make it one and a half times as large as the coastline of the United States and twice as large as that of China.[22] (Proponents of this view, moreover, use baselines drawn in the sea to connect outer islands that encircle the main islands more commonly recognized as Japan, creating a starkly defined, lopsided shape.)[23] Moreover, in April 2014 the Japanese government issued a foreign policy that for the first time tied each of its tiny disputed territories—in the East China Sea, the Sea of Japan/East Sea, and the Sea of Okhotsk—into a single policy as "inherent territory" of Japan. Tensions remain extremely high over these issues, which is of substantial concern to the United States because of its security obligations to defend Japanese territory when attacked. The problem is not the U.S. commitment to Japan but rather what the country's government claims as Japanese territory.

Some prioritize securing solid definitions and historical visions to shore up this view of maritime Japan, while others favor agreements centered on joint resource development, requiring more nuanced claims in the sea. Taken in a broad context, the reasons are clear. A new era of ocean imperialism has begun. Its codes are transforming islands into objects that contain the surrounding seas rather than the other way around, as long has been the case. Many coastal states—archipelagoes like Japan and the Philippines as well as those with partial ocean borders such as Italy and the United States—now define their distant offshore islands as outer baselines in order to lay exclusive claim to their nearby waters.

Consequently, the value of islands in terms of national interests has shifted from what is seen above the waterline to the bathometrics surrounding islands and radiating outward onto the earth's crust far below the surface—areas that could contain energy reserves on the ocean floor for immediate and future consumption. Part and parcel of this change is reconceiving the ocean itself, which is the planet's only remaining area over which it is possible to name exclusive control. International laws now allow governments to claim up to 350 nautical miles in exclusive territorial seas beyond the baselines marked by islands. Nations make discrete but occasionally overlapping claims to exclusive economic zones for fishing privileges and to extended continental shelf areas for access to resources in the ocean floor.

---

[22] As Kenichi Matsumoto suggests, if one were to lay a piece of string alongside Japan's coastline and do the same with China and the United States, Japan becomes perceived on a much bigger scale. See Kenichi Matsumoto, *Kaigansen no rekishi* [Coastline History] (Tokyo: Mishimasha, 2009).

[23] Ibid.

Japan lies at the center of this monumental shift, even if many within the country (and most outside it, for that matter) are not aware of its role. Japanese leaders, however, demonstrate a profound understanding of what is happening, having made significant policy changes during the first decade of the 21st century to align the nation with the new realities of maritime law. In 2007 the Basic Act on Ocean Policy went into effect, and its main lobbying group, the Nippon Foundation, declared that "sixty-two years after the end of World War 2, the maritime nation of Japan has finally set sail on a voyage to protect the sea."[24] With this recent policy push, Japanese leaders have again set forging a maritime state as their unifying goal, even if they are divided in their strategic views of how best to accomplish it.

With regard to today's strategic outlook, as far as Japan's maritime orientation is concerned, the debate over Article 9 of the constitution harkens back to the Tokugawa period during which the idea of the nation as rigidly bordered engendered Japan's collapse. Then, as now, the debate centered on how the country's island nature defines its strategic culture: as inward-looking and tightly defined or as open-ended and engaged with the world. The Tokugawa shogunate's determination to regulate everything involved with going out to sea helped speed along its own demise in no small part because these strict limits attempted to force the Japanese people to remain within a tightly drawn perimeter around the country's islands. Those who today overwhelmingly support scrapping Article 9 favor sending Japanese troops into the world yet equally demand a rigidly drawn maritime perimeter around Japan. On the one hand, this strategic outlook argues that Japanese troops should be able to fight alongside allies globally; on the other hand, it claims rigid boundaries that only Japan upholds as its sovereign territory.

Japan's strategic outlook has been shifting for roughly two decades from one of rather clear-cut dependence on the U.S. protective shield to one of increasing autonomy. In the wake of the renewed 1997 U.S.-Japan Defense Guidelines, it became clear, moreover, that this shift would entail a domestic political transfer of power among factions within the same ruling LDP. According to Samuels, "a reinstitutionalization of Japanese grand strategy [was] under way in full public view: fifteen new security-related laws were enacted between 1991 and 2003, and a Defense Ministry was created in 2007....The resulting transformation will seem as epochal as what

---

[24] For more information on the Nippon Foundation and its extensive efforts to promote Japan's maritime nature (including through the establishment of a national holiday called Ocean Day, as well as substantial financial support for domestic and international fellowships to analyze all sorts of aspects of Japanese and global interests in oceans), see the organization's website at http://www.nippon-foundation.or.jp/en.

transpired after the Pacific War."[25] Invoking a metaphor of "salami slicing," Samuels demonstrates that "rather than groping to define" a strategic vision, Japanese leaders who wanted to overturn postwar restrictions on the nation's military capabilities engaged in serious policy study and planning during the 1990s. As the Cold War's bipolarities evaporated, military and political thinkers who had long chafed under the weight of what they viewed as an outdated, formal agreement that was disconnected from current conditions began to slice away at Article 9 without actually confronting the difficulties of constitutional amendment. Most observers determine that the first major "slice" of Article 9 occurred in 1992 on the heels of the first Gulf War. The international community—failing to note Japan's enormous financial contributions—roundly criticized the country for not sending troops to support allies.[26] Those in the Japanese government who wanted to rebuild a proactive force structure began to sense the opportunity to renew their quest in earnest. Japan's International Peace Cooperation Law was passed in 1992 despite opposition parties challenging the constitutionality of dispatching Japanese troops abroad. Although these voices mostly acquiesced to the idea of Japanese troops being involved in UN peacekeeping operations, they did not budge on the issue of allowing Japan to participate in peacekeeping force maneuvers.

At this point, a faction within the ruling LDP realized its potential to overtake the long dominant "Yoshida faction" (named for Prime Minister Shigeru Yoshida, a strong advocate of accepting permanent U.S. basing structures in Japan). As a result, the so-called hawkish branch of the LDP emerged and worked to realize its specific vision of Japan's strategic culture. It had already begun laying the groundwork for translating this vision into practice with Prime Minister Junichiro Koizumi's April 2001 declaration that he would review collective self-defense. Thus, after the September 11 terrorist attacks, Koizumi pushed ahead with this plan and immediately stood before his fellow citizens, famously promising to "show the flag" alongside the United States.[27]

That Japan could not send ground troops to Afghanistan and Iraq because of its constitutional ban against doing so did not deter Koizumi's quest to make Japan a "normal nation" in the eyes of the world, as he

---

[25] Samuels, *Securing Japan*, 86.

[26] The infamous manifestation of this was the March 1, 1991, "Thank You" full page advertisement in the *New York Times* by the Kuwaiti government that failed to include Japan despite Japan's payment of $13 billion toward the war effort. For a discussion of how this continues to rankle some in Japan, see Nakanishi Hiroshi, "The Gulf War and Japanese Diplomacy," Nippon.com, December 6, 2011, http://www.nippon.com/en/features/c00202.

[27] See Yu Uchiyama, *Koizumi and Japanese Politics: Reform Strategies and Leadership Style* (London: Routledge, 2010), 83–86.

regularly said. Moreover, Koizumi authorized countless measures that quietly and increasingly snipped away at Article 9. Changes included dispatching oil tankers from the Maritime Self-Defense Force to Diego Garcia in the Indian Ocean to assist in refueling U.S. and British ships, marking the first time since 1945 that Japanese military vessels had been involved in military operations beyond Japan's borders. Equally monumental was the passage in 2003 of so-called emergency laws, which delineated newly specific roles for the Self-Defense Forces during disasters and other contingencies. Notably, none of these measures were overturned under the Democratic Party of Japan (DPJ) administrations between 2009 and 2012. This is further evidence that while two competing visions exist for how best to use Japanese military capabilities abroad, both sides agree that Japan is very much part of the international community, and especially so as a maritime state.

Recent policy shifts by the current administration demonstrate a firm conviction to ratchet up public interest in the issue of Japan's control over the nation's collective territorial disputes with China, Taiwan, South Korea, and Russia. Together, these boil down to sovereignty contests over tiny islands between Japan and each of its neighboring countries. For years, Japanese geography textbooks for middle and high school students have featured maps that include these tiny islands as Japanese territory, yet only recently has Tokyo so emphatically advertised rigid claims in both Ministry of Foreign Affairs and Ministry of Defense publications—aimed at audiences well beyond domestic consumers of schoolbooks.[28] This push would seem to require the international community to accede to Japan's claims, which arguably is most problematic in the case of the dispute with South Korea. The U.S. position, though supportive of Japan in dealing with Russia and ready to apply treaty obligations in handling Japan's administrative control of the Senkaku/Diaoyu Islands in the dispute with China, is not welcoming to Tokyo stirring up territorial sentiments opposed to Seoul's claims. It is in U.S. interests to encourage Japanese policy planners to reduce tensions by working collaboratively with neighboring states as they continue to broaden the stakes for Japan in the world as a maritime nation.

The Current State of Play

Relatedly and against the long-building shift described in the last section, a number of unforeseen events have occurred during the past several years that have prompted a true awakening of social consciousness among a broad

---

[28] Ministry of Foreign Affairs (Japan), "Japanese Territory," April 4, 2014, http://www.mofa.go.jp/territory/index.html; and Ministry of Defense (Japan), "Defense of Japan 2016," 2016, http://www.mod.go.jp/e/publ/w_paper/2016.html.

cross section of the Japanese society. As a result, a surge of vocal popular opposition has emerged on a scale unseen in Japan since the major antiwar protests of 1960. Japanese policymakers and the public are confronting this reality and thus have exhibited a bifurcated strategic outlook that is now more evident than at any point during the post–World War II era.

Without question, the March 2011 disasters changed the face of the Japan Self-Defense Forces for many Japanese because of troops' dedicated response to helping those in incredible need during the catastrophes. Japanese citizens overwhelmingly and openly displayed their gratitude to troops who offered humanitarian assistance. This held true for U.S. soldiers assisting in Japanese communities, too, as part of what is commonly known as Operation Tomodachi (Operation Friendship).

The ongoing nightmare of the Fukushima Daiichi nuclear power plant meltdowns jarred many Japanese into interrogating received information in new ways, including through social media, the foreign press, and other venues.[29] Thus, when the security legislation debates began in earnest during summer 2014 and continued through 2015, many Japanese transformed their surprise into action and openly challenged such potentially profound changes to national identity.[30]

Since 2014, a growing number of citizens have taken to the streets to protest the security legislation, reaching 100,000 in September 2015 and resuming in spring 2016. In addition, numerous lawsuits have been filed against the legislation, and tens of thousands of academics, lawyers, journalists, former politicians and bureaucrats, and others have signed mass letters contesting the reforms. Therefore, to understand Japan's bifurcated strategic culture it is critical to understand this alternative view of Japan. Some naturally decry such a position as naive, misguided, or, worse, a free ride on the United States, yet proponents of this view stand firm in their opposition to the ruling party's mandates to dispatch Japanese troops to wage war overseas. As such, this position is just as Japanese as the ruling party's view, which is more widely reported outside the country.

For quite some time, the focus on the reinterpretation of collective self-defense obfuscated the fact that the current administration's policies toward constitutional change would not simply transform Japan's military

---

[29] For a recent assessment of the Fukushima crisis published in a truly international venue—the kind to which many Japanese continue to turn—see Andrew R. Marks, "The Fukushima Nuclear Disaster Is Ongoing," *Journal of Clinical Investigation* 126, no. 7 (2016): 2,385–87, https://www.jci.org/articles/view/88434.

[30] The most prominent challenge came from the Students Emergency Action for Liberal Democracy (SEALD), whose articulate and intelligent young leaders captured the nation's attention during the group's short-lived existence (2014–16). See Linda Sieg and Teppei Kasai, "SEALDs Student Group Re-invigorates Japan's Anti-War Protest Movement," *Japan Times*, August 29, 2015.

posture but introduce a number of other major social and governmental changes as well: returning the emperor to a position of power, rewriting the status of women, and relaxing laws separating religion and the state, among other measures. Popular concern with the current administration's amendment of Article 9, however, brought into relief these other issues. Theoretically, tensions with North Korea and China could boost public support for changing Article 9, yet popular opposition continues to make clear that the majority of Japanese do not want to revise the constitution and has also drawn increasing scrutiny to many of the other proposed revisions. Even the ruling party's coalition partner, New Komeito, openly opposes the revised version.

In this light, it is useful to remember that from the end of World War II through the transformation that occurred in the wake of September 11 to allow more contingent alliances, the United States consistently maintained a foreign policy of formal alliance structures—beginning with Japan—that sought to spread democratic governance and access to markets in exchange for mutual security cooperation. Post-2001 shifts to "coalitions of the willing" notwithstanding, in this long-held view of U.S. foreign policy, Japan is the United States' greatest success. Thus, when thinking about Japan's strategic culture today and into the near future, it is vital to remove lenses that view Japan the way the United States might want to see the country. It is imperative to take seriously how the Japanese people continue to see their country, if only because the United States' original license to demilitarize Japan remains deeply felt among those who advocate humanitarian uses alone for their country's military.

Importantly, however, the effort to reconfigure Japan's military is not only driven by the current administration. As Richard Samuels, Kenneth Pyle, and others have so well described, the main opposition party in existence prior to the new DPJ has also supported such measures, provided that first there is open constitutional debate and a national referendum. Unique to the recent hard-line push to revise Article 9 is the view that Japan's twentieth-century history of violence is settled and therefore not part of the conversation.

Without becoming bogged down in the region's so-called history wars, it is significant that in the course of Japan's recent debates about security legislation, a renewed determination to reclaim a meaningful democracy has arisen within Japan. Much of this dovetails with thinking about Japan's place in Asia moving forward against the backdrop of the multiple histories of violence that Japanese troops perpetrated throughout Asia and the Pacific during World War II. Sociologist Akiko Hashimoto explains this phenomenon on a broader comparative scale:

> Over time, [a] kind of emotional socialization that taps into instincts for self-preservation turns into "feeling rules," with which children learn to internalize how they are *supposed* to feel about war in a pacifist country. Clearly, this choice of strategy is not geared toward raising nascent critical thinkers who would assume responsibility for past atrocious deeds of their forefathers as in a culture of contrition like Germany, but focused instead on *not* raising the type of Japanese people who could perpetrate another abhorrent war in the future.[31]

Beginning in early 2014, a steadily expanding number of Japanese citizens began publicly protesting Abe's vision for Japan, while opposition parties worked to stymie his increasing reliance on strong-arm political tactics. One increasingly popular approach to countering the prime minister's security legislation built on a growing trend of letter-writing campaigns focused on related issues. The one letter that garnered the most international media attention, an "Open Letter in Support of Historians in Japan," appeared in May 2015 and was signed by nearly five hundred scholars of Japan studies around the world. It drew attention to the Abe administration's efforts to stifle academic and press freedoms, including overt and documented attempts at censorship of textbooks and broadcast content. The May 2015 letter—together with several others—encouraged further activism. Many Japanese academics, artists, and ordinary citizens continue to write or sign statements expressing concern about the nation's present and future trajectory.[32]

On the streets, opposition to Japan's new security legislation grew in conjunction with the parliamentary deliberation that began in earnest early in June 2015. Most memorably—and the moment that palpably awakened society at large—three prominent constitutional law scholars testified on live television and unanimously asserted that the bills were unconstitutional. One of the three experts, Yasuo Hasebe had been invited by the LDP to testify on the presumption that he would support the measures. Hasebe not only denounced the legislation but in an interview with Reuters said of Abe, "I think he hates the concept of modern constitutionalism, the concept that the powers of government should be restricted by the constitution."[33]

Together with polls that repeatedly show that Japanese want to "protect" the constitution—using the same word (*mamore*) that Abe and his supporters use to justify their desire for Japanese troops to fight abroad in order to "protect" Japan—these letters reveal a deep commitment to containing troops inside Japan's borders. Beyond facilitating signature-gathering efforts, the

---

[31] Akiko Hashimoto, *The Long Defeat: Cultural Trauma, Memory, and Identity in Japan* (New York: Oxford University Press, 2015). Emphasis is in the original.

[32] Jordan Sand, "A Year of Memory Politics in East Asia: Looking Back on the 'Open Letter in Support of Historians in Japan,'" *Asia-Pacific Journal: Japan Focus*, May 1, 2016.

[33] Linda Sieg, "Japan Security Debate Masks Clash of Views on Pacifist Constitution," Reuters, July 15, 2015.

Internet has also helped opponents of the security legislation withstand the vitriol routinely hurled by its supporters at those who would raise even basic questions about the meaning of "self-defense" as defined in Article 9. It has also served as a refuge for bloggers who are apprehensive in the wake of recently enacted secrecy laws that grant far greater surveillance capability to police.

Over the years, the salami-slicing process has suited many in Japan who agree that Japanese soldiers should, for example, assist with UN peacekeeping operations in Cambodia and South Sudan or participate in humanitarian relief efforts in Afghanistan, Rwanda, and other places. Never, though, has the debate been as intense as it is now over the question of Japanese troops acting militarily in conjunction with specific allies.

The current government regularly campaigns on promises of economic reform and social stability, yet would appear to undermine both of these important goals through insistence on foreign policy reforms that are out of sync with the broad majority of Japanese people. Nowhere was this clearer than during the lead-up to the July 2016 upper house elections. Prime Minister Abe repeatedly assured voters that the election would solely reflect his aims to reinvigorate the economy, yet following his party's overwhelming victory he immediately announced that he would "seek advice from Diet committees on constitutional revision."[34] Examples include expanding the military budget, ending proscriptions against domestic arms development, divisive security legislation, and targeting the constitution in ways that define Japan and the Japanese people more rigidly than ever while also urging a much more assertive and expeditionary military. Equally noticeable, Abe regularly explains these reforms in terms of his "duty" to rid Japan of its postwar "masochistic" existence (that is, its inability to wage war abroad).[35]

Although most Japanese do not reject the idea of their nation's troops playing a humanitarian role in war, they do reject the notion of Japan waging war to support interests beyond its borders. Parliamentarians such as Hiroyuki Konishi suggest instead that Japan offer the world assistance: Japanese troops should be the world's rescue force following natural disasters, among other humanitarian operations. Konishi and his colleagues emphasize that climate change poses a common threat to humanity, and Japan could shoulder that burden in keeping with its constitution and strategic culture.

---

[34] Jeff Kingston, "Empire of the Setting Sun," *Foreign Policy*, August 15, 2016.

[35] Abe regularly uses these terms during television interviews in Japan. One interview with Fuji TV in April 2015 caught international attention. See "Enough with WWII Apologies: Japan PM Sees No Need to Reinforce Remorse," RT, April 21, 2015, https://www.rt.com/news/251505-japan-abe-wartime-apologies.

In many ways, the security legislation would obviate the need for amending the constitution. The Abe administration has upheld the constitutionality of collective self-defense, allowing for the possibility of dispatching troops abroad to engage in military maneuvers alongside allies. Supporters of the legislation have attempted to steer the debate toward a hypothetical attack on a U.S.-flagged ship in Japan's territorial waters. A majority of Japanese reject even that scenario as constituting an attack on Japan, though some are willing to consider the possibility, not least because of China's overt bellicosity in the region. (The dispute over possession of the uninhabited Senkaku/Diaoyu Islands in the East China Sea has intensified since 2012, leading to repeated confrontations between Chinese and Japanese ships and aircraft, and the escalating standoff in the South China Sea draws much attention as well.) But there is nearly universal opposition in Japan to the prospect of Japanese troops providing front-line assistance to U.S.-backed campaigns against the Islamic State of Iraq and Syria (ISIS). According to an *Asahi Shimbun* poll published on May 2, 2015, 95% of Japanese opposed the idea of such action.[36]

More so than for any other Japanese leader in 70 years, therefore, a widening opinion gap has emerged during Abe's tenure over the nature and legitimacy of Japan's postwar constitution. The majority of Japanese remain attached to Article 9. Keigo Komamura, an expert on constitutional law at Keio University, articulates the underlying view that fuels the pro-constitution majority: The United States imposed the constitution during the occupation, but just like women's right to vote, which it includes, the constitution is elemental to Japanese society today and was a "legitimate imposition."[37] Those determined to maintain Article 9 are thus expressing an understanding of Japanese strategic culture that is held by a majority of Japanese citizens and presents a vision for the future that is radically different from what the current administration insists is the only way forward.

Moving Forward

Although two competing visions exist for how Japan should move forward, it is not possible to divide these camps along simple lines. Regardless of how the debate proceeds in the coming months and years over reshaping its military posture, Japan will be a maritime nation. There are fundamental issues with the hard-line vision for Japan's future, not in the least that the United States and Japan have renewed their security obligations, with Washington

---

[36] *Asahi Shimbun*, May 2, 2015.

[37] Keigo Komamura, "Destroying 'The Rule of Law,'" *Asahi Shinbun*, June 12, 2015.

continuing its long-standing commitment to defend "territories under the administration of Japan." While the United States has repeatedly clarified that it upholds Japan's administration of islands in the East China Sea, it does not make similar assertions about islands that Japan contests with South Korea in the Sea of Japan/East Sea or with Russia in the Sea of Okhotsk. Nonetheless, the Abe administration makes increasingly provocative assertions of control over these contested islands, as well as Okinotori Reef in the south, in part to claim the most rigidly defined space possible as Japanese territory. Because these assertions directly implicate U.S. assurances of security protection, they raise the question of this policy's broader aims.

Backed up even by the current ruling party's 2012 proposal for constitutional revision, such spatial claims are a first in modern Japanese history.[38] Neither the 1889 nor 1947 Japanese constitution so clearly articulated the idea of national territory, instead choosing to leave matters more open-ended. Many proponents of the hard-line view do not appear to be aware that the last time Japanese leaders so rigidly defined their nation in the sea—for example, when rulers over two hundred years ago tried to circumscribe a tight perimeter around the island nation—it collapsed from within under the weight of their demands.

There are abundant reasons that the United States might welcome a greater military commitment from Japan to aid in U.S.-led wars. However, Washington must take seriously the depth of commitment that Japanese citizens have to the constitutional proscription against waging war beyond Japan's borders. While a more proactive view of Japanese strategic culture would mesh well with current U.S. priorities, many Japanese have a very different understanding of their nation's place in the world. For any reordering of Japanese strategic culture to be a productive and positive force for Japan, the region, and the world, U.S. planners must thoughtfully weigh both of these strategic visions as equally pertinent. Sheila Smith described this state of affairs in a prescient essay penned prior to the passage of security legislation and long before the recent elections:

> The United States is largely seen as an advocate for greater action by the Japanese military, both in terms of its radius of operations and the latitude it has to cooperate with U.S. forces on shared missions. But the U.S. stake in Japan's constitution extends far beyond this narrow debate over how the Self-Defense Force operates. It is in the interest of the United States to ensure that any changes Abe makes are fully supported by the Japanese people. Otherwise, any decision on collective self-defense would undermine confidence in the alliance if it was perceived as appeasing Washington rather than serving Japan's own interests.

---

[38] These claims are tied directly to the Ministry of Foreign Affairs' 2014 definition of the territory of Japan—also a first. See Ministry of Foreign Affairs (Japan), "Japanese Territory." An English translation of the LDP's proposed 2012 constitutional amendment is available at http://www.voyce-jpn.com/#!ldp-draft-constitution/px2wu.

> The Japanese people must support this evolving role for their military and remain confident that their government will only use military force for the purpose of self-defense.[39]

With Japan's strategic planners determined to reorient the country again toward becoming a strong maritime state, U.S. policymakers need to understand the deep divisions that exist among Japanese planners and in Japanese society more broadly regarding how best to shape the country's presence in the sea and role in the world at large. U.S. resources may increasingly shift to addressing concerns in the South China Sea, and Washington may count on Japan's assistance. Is Tokyo prepared for this? And what about Japanese society at large?

A paramount concern is that most Japanese view their nation's nonmilitary outlook as essential to its strategic culture. This includes a majority of Japanese legal experts—including professional organizations such as the Japanese Bar Association—who regard the nation's new laws as unconstitutional and oppose them. In March 2016, in response to the laws going into effect, a new political party called Minshinto (Democratic Party) appeared through the merger of the nation's two largest opposition groups with the primary purpose of rescinding the bills.[40] The new party failed to surmount the ruling coalition in the July 2016 parliamentary elections due to a lack of a broader message and voters' general unease about the economy. Yet in the meantime, a host of lawsuits against the Japanese government are underway that challenge the constitutionality of the new security provisions.[41] Together these lawsuits—and others in the works—manifest a profound social understanding shared by politicians and policy planners in the opposition party that the right not to wage war is axiomatic for Japanese strategic culture.

In the broader context of Asian security concerns, it has never been more important to take seriously the profound gap between these opposing positions. Japan remains one of the United States' strongest allies and Asia's most vibrant open society.[42] As Keigo Komamura has argued, the ruling party's proposed changes to the principles underlying Japan's post-1945 understanding of itself likely could make it increasingly difficult for Japan to peacefully challenge the counterproductive stances that China and

---

[39] Smith, "Reinterpreting Japan's Constitution."

[40] For more on the Minshinto party, see Michael Cucek, "Some Nice Things about the Minshinto," *Shisaku*, April 1, 2016, http://shisaku.blogspot.com/2016/04/some-nice-things-about-minshinto.html.

[41] "Over 700 People Sue State over Japan's Security Laws," *Mainichi Shimbun*, April 27, 2016; and "Over 800 Citizens, A-Bomb Survivors Sue Government over Security Laws," Kyodo News, June 8, 2016.

[42] Of serious recent concern are active threats to freedoms of the press within Japan. For elaboration, see UN Human Rights Office of the High Commissioner, "Japan."

North Korea take in the region: "Why should Japan go this way?" Komamura asks. "Why should we shut down channels of communication? Only our *existing* legal principles go beyond borders and make it possible for [those] in conflict with one another to stand on common ground."[43]

The multiple valences of the internal divide over Japanese strategic culture could lead, moreover, to outcomes contrary to U.S. security interests. Results could range from the unintentional encouragement of unwarranted, regionally destabilizing militarist impulses at one end of the spectrum to an equally unintentional encouragement of anti-American sentiment at the other. These strategic considerations are raised against the backdrop of the potential negative economic impact, both regionally and worldwide, that is engendered by Japan's potential re-entry into the cadre of normal nations. Japan would have to pay for a larger share of its own self-defense at the expense of its nonmilitary economy. Since 1945, it has become one of the world's strongest economies in part due to the protection and cost-savings provided by U.S. military power. Those who favor a makeover of Japanese strategic culture thus need to consider the impact of such a dramatic change not only on the identity of modern Japan but also on its long-term economic stability.

---

[43] Keigo Komamura, "Constitution and Narrative in the Age of Crisis in Japanese Politics" (paper presented at the Association for Asian Studies in Asia, Kyoto, June 25, 2016). Emphasis is in the original.

EXECUTIVE SUMMARY

This chapter argues that South Korea exhibits a relatively undisputed and enduring strategic culture based on autonomy that only partially corresponds to its relative power, economic wealth, and political system.

MAIN ARGUMENT

South Korea's strategic culture centers on notions of a proud, influential, and autonomous nation—the sources of which trace back to the premodern tributary system. Given the emphasis on charting its own course and being as independent as possible in its foreign policy, South Korea believes that choosing sides between the U.S. and China goes against its national interests. Furthermore, Seoul is more comfortable with a strong China than is often believed and more skeptical of Japan than is often expected. This strategic culture stems from differing past experiences with the two countries. Whereas South Korea enjoyed years of stability as a Chinese tributary, its cataclysmic experiences during Japanese occupation left a deep impression that Japan is not to be trusted.

POLICY IMPLICATIONS

- South Korea does not view its choices about grand strategy as mutually exclusive, especially between its alliance with the U.S. and engagement with China. Thus, pressure on South Korea to choose will be perceived as undermining Seoul's priorities of relative autonomy and independence.

- Given the heightened tension between the U.S. and China, the South Korean government will have to pay particular attention to ensuring that its interests—particularly those regarding North Korea—do not increasingly become hijacked by Sino-U.S. rivalry.

- South Korea views its position in Asia and the world as much through an economic as a political or security lens. Its policies emphasize trade and investment as much as political or diplomatic relations, and are designed to advance its domestic economic priorities.

The Pursuit of Autonomy and South Korea's Atypical Strategic Culture

David C. Kang and Jiun Bang

The Republic of Korea (ROK) has confounded several expectations. Despite warnings about a rapidly growing China and calls for greater security cooperation with Japan,[1] South Korea has become China's largest trade partner, while diplomatic relations are more tense with Japan than they are with China. This has led to claims that Seoul may be misguidedly accommodating Beijing or that it is "tilting" toward China and has entered the latter's orbit or sphere of influence.[2] South Korea's willingness to have good relations with China partly arises from a desire to affect the foreign policy of North Korea's closest supporter. After all, North Korea has been South Korea's main external threat since 1945. Yet this pragmatism does not change the reality that South Korea has drawn closer to China over the past two decades, not moved farther away.

David C. Kang is a Professor of International Relations and Business at the University of Southern California, where he is also Director of the Korean Studies Institute and the Center for International Studies. He can be reached at <kangdc@usc.edu>.

Jiun Bang is a Postdoctoral Fellow at the University of Michigan. She can be reached at <jiunbang@umich.edu>.

---

[1] For a discussion of ROK-China relations, see Chung Min Lee, "Recalibrating the Rebalance: A View from South Korea," Asan Forum, April 9, 2015, http://www.theasanforum.org/recalibrating-the-rebalance-a-view-from-south-korea; and Yoshihide Soeya, "The Future of U.S.-Japan-ROK Trilateral Cooperation: A Japanese Perspective," National Bureau of Asian Research (NBR), Brief, March 25, 2016, http://nbr.org/research/activity.aspx?id=659. For a discussion of ROK-Japan cooperation, see McDaniel Wicker, "America's Next Move in Asia: A Japan-Korea Alliance," *National Interest*, February 24, 2016.

[2] For instance, see Evans Revere, "Trilateral Development in Northeast Asia: South Korea, Japan, and China," interview by Julia Oh, NBR, December 15, 2015, http://nbr.org/downloads/pdfs/psa/Revere_interview_121515.pdf.

In contrast, South Korea has had endemic friction with Japan, even though Japan shares with South Korea the traits of a capitalist market economy, a democratic political regime, and an alliance with the United States. Indeed, there are voices in South Korea that appear to be more worried about Japanese remilitarization than fearful of growing Chinese power.[3] This has led to a flourishing academic discourse about why the two states seemingly cannot get along. Popular arguments to explain South Korea's behavior are that the country is hedging or that it is employing a variant of "soft balancing."[4]

This atypicality on the part of South Korea vis-à-vis its relationships with China and Japan, and its subsequent reluctance to fully embrace its position in a tripartite U.S.-Japan-ROK alliance, has often vexed U.S. observers. For example, in 2015 Wendy Sherman—then the U.S. undersecretary of state for political affairs—stated that such issues as South Koreans and Chinese being "sensitive to changes in Japan's defense policy," along with the fact that the two have "quarreled" with Japan over the "comfort women" issue, are all "understandable" but "can also be frustrating."[5] Implying that South Koreans did not understand their own strategic interests as well as she did, Sherman went on to add that "nationalist feelings can still be exploited, and it's not hard for a political leader anywhere to earn cheap applause by vilifying a former enemy." This statement prompted immediate repudiation by South Koreans, who took Sherman to be blaming the ROK for its behavior toward Japan (its "former enemy").[6]

Yet these enduring traits are not simply superficial nationalist feelings exploited by cynical politicians, as Sherman claims. Rather, they reflect a deeper, stable, and fundamental South Korean strategic culture. As Alastair Iain Johnston writes, strategic culture "is an integrated system of symbols that acts to establish pervasive and long-lasting grand strategic

---

[3] Seok-min Oh, "Japan's Greater Military Role Double-Edged Sword for S. Korea," Yonhap, April 28, 2015, http://english.yonhapnews.co.kr/national/2015/04/28/92/0301000000AEN20150428008400 315F.html.

[4] For a discussion of hedging, see Sukhee Han, "From Engagement to Hedging: South Korea's New China Policy," *Korean Journal of Defense Analysis* 20, no. 4 (2008): 335–51; and Cheng-Chwee Kuik, "Introduction: Decomposing and Assessing South Korea's Hedging Options," Asan Forum, June 11, 2015, http://www.theasanforum.org/introduction-decomposing-and-assessing-south-koreas-foreign-policy-options. For a discussion of soft balancing, see T. J. Pempel, "Soft Balancing, Hedging, and Institutional Darwinism: The Economic-Security Nexus and East Asian Regionalism," *Journal of East Asian Studies* 10, no. 2 (2010): 209–38.

[5] The speech commemorated the 70th anniversary of the end of World War II. See Wendy R. Sherman, "Remarks on Northeast Asia" (speech given at the Carnegie Endowment for International Peace, Washington, D.C., February 27, 2015), http://www.state.gov/p/us/rm/2015/238035.htm.

[6] For instance, see "Toeing Japan's Line," *Korea Herald*, March 4, 2015, http://www.koreaherald.com/view.php?ud=20150304000752&mod=skb; and "Japanese PM Needs to Show Courage to Admit Japan's Past Wrongdoings," *Dong-A Ilbo*, March 2, 2015, http://english.donga.com/List/3/all/26/410196/1.

preferences by formulating concepts of the role and efficacy of military force in interstate political affairs, and by clothing these conceptions with such an aura of factuality that the strategic preferences seem uniquely realistic and efficacious."[7] This chapter seeks to explore the perhaps puzzling nature of South Korea's foreign policy choices by tracing the sources of the country's strategic culture. In doing so, it bridges the historical and external foundations of this strategic culture with more contemporary and internal sources. While the former greatly influence South Korea's assumptions about its adversaries and overall threat perception, the latter facilitate its confidence about its ability to manage such threats. In addition to discussing the enduring impacts of Japanese colonialism and the Korean War, this analysis will trace the sources of South Korean strategic culture much further back to the premodern tributary system of international relations. Examining Korea's relations and its position in that particular context is critical for understanding why a proud South Korea may be less worried about an assertive China than it is about an assertive Japan. Meanwhile, the complications that come with a compressed process of modernization and democratization have seriously tested South Korea's mettle and self-confidence, reinforcing the value and appeal of a relatively autonomous and independent foreign policy. Furthermore, although the United States is its chief ally and most important security partner, South Korea has always had a more complicated and independent relationship with its patron than has Japan.

This chapter begins by pinpointing the key sources of South Korea's strategic culture. It then assesses the impact of that culture on the country's foreign policy choices. The assessment begins with a general discussion about how strategic culture has shaped South Korea's conception of power and next considers a few specific ongoing and perhaps controversial initiatives and priorities to demonstrate the influence of strategic culture on actual foreign policy outcomes. This section also discusses how South Korea has cultivated its own way of interpreting, analyzing, and reacting to the environment by tracing some of its most important strategic relations involving China, Japan, and the United States. The chapter concludes by summarizing key elements of this analysis and reinforcing the notion that South Korea is perhaps the best example to show why taking strategic culture seriously is important for understanding international relations and particularly regional security dynamics in East Asia.

---

[7] Alastair Iain Johnston, *Cultural Realism: Strategic Culture and Grand Strategy in Chinese History* (Princeton: Princeton University Press, 1998), 37.

The Key Sources of South Korea's Strategic Culture

Strategic culture has both internal and external sources as well as both historical roots and contemporary causes. The question of whether history affects the present comes with asking whether there is anything culturally unique or distinctive about East Asia. That is, we might assume that all people and states are essentially the same, and because of modernization, globalization, and industrialization, all East Asian states and peoples want, perceive, and act essentially the same as Western states and peoples. On the other hand, are East Asian states so completely Westernized that they can be thought of as participating in a "shared culture [that] is a precondition for the formation of a society of states"?[8] That question is harder to answer. But we also might ask whether history, culture, language, religion, and context have any bearing on how East Asian leaders and peoples view and interact with one another and the rest of the world. It might be that distinctive cultures, memories, patterns, or beliefs shape contemporary East Asian international relations, and acknowledging this influence may force us to consider whether we can truly explain contemporary East Asia without reference to its own culture and history.

Western, Westphalian values are normative around the globe, and South Korea is no different in this regard. It accepts unquestioningly the basic rules of the international game, and sees no alternative approach to this. South Koreans accept the principle of the sovereign equality of nation-states, for example. However, although Westphalian values and norms have penetrated deeply into South Korean society, they have not thoroughly erased other values and norms. The two coexist, sometimes uncomfortably, and manifest themselves in contemporary South Korean attitudes, views, and indeed conflicts over issues such as history and territory.

External Factors: History

Premodern. As is the case for many countries, actual Korean history is not the same as the story about Korean history that emerged in the twentieth century. Nonetheless, this more recent narrative is a nationalist historiography that enjoys wide consensus in South Korea, indeed approaching a strategic culture of conventional wisdom. Those widely accepted historical facts are demonstrably wrong, although the enduring traits of South Korean strategic culture fit—however roughly—the actual cause of events. For example, contemporary South Koreans do not question that during its ancient history Korea suffered serial invasions, mostly from

---

[8] Barry Buzan, "Culture and International Society," *International Affairs* 86, no. 1 (2010): 1.

Japan but also from the north, to the point that the statement that "Korea has endured over 900 invasions throughout its history" is repeated often and without qualification.[9] John Duncan notes that a dominant strand of Korean identity consists of a "master narrative" depicting the Korean experience as "one of almost incessant foreign incursions."[10] This meme is, however, a recent perspective and arose during the twentieth-century great-power land grab over Korea. Indeed, the key point of that meme is not that Korea suffered invasions, but that it suffered invasions from Japan. South Koreans do not view Chinese relations the same way.

More important for today's strategic culture are enduring patterns in the Korean history of regional relations. Historically, Korea has possessed a confident view of itself as one of the most civilized countries in the known world. Korea was ranked more highly by China than Japan by virtue of its stable relations with China and its more thorough adoption of Chinese ideas.[11] Korea was unquestionably near the top of the hierarchy of the international system at the time and was seen as a model tributary state. Relations between the Choson and Ming Dynasties were close, with Korea annually dispatching three embassies to China during the fifteenth century and Korean elites "eagerly importing Chinese books and ideas."[12] Ki-baek Lee concludes that the Choson Dynasty's "relationship with Ming China on the whole proceed[ed] satisfactorily."[13] This stable relationship continued under the Qing Dynasty. As one scholar notes, "Korea emerges in Qing court records as the loyal domain par excellence. In the *Comprehensive Rites*, Korea appears first among the other domains, and imperial envoys dispatched to the Korean court are always of a higher rank."[14]

Just as important for contemporary South Korean strategic culture is the enduring idea that China, while a civilizational influence, was not the threat that Japan was. The extraordinary longevity of the Choson Dynasty (1392–1910) is

[9] For more discussion about the twentieth-century invention of history by nationalist states throughout East Asia, see David C. Kang, *East Asia Before the West: Five Centuries of Trade and Tribute* (New York: Columbia University Press, 2010), chap. 8.

[10] John B. Duncan, "The Uses of Confucianism in Modern Korea," in *Rethinking Confucianism: Past and Present in China, Japan, Korea, and Vietnam*, ed. Benjamin A. Elman, John B. Duncan, and Herman Ooms (Los Angeles: Asia Institute, 2002), 431–62, 432.

[11] So-ja Choi, *Myeongchong sidae Chunghan kwanggyesa yeongu* [Study on Sino-Korean Relations during the Ming-Qing Periods] (Seoul: Ewha Womans University Press, 1997).

[12] John E. Wills Jr., "South and Southeast Asia, Near East, Japan, and Korea," in *The Chinese Civilization from Its Origins to Contemporary Times*, vol. 1, ed. Grandi Opere Einaudi and Maurizio Scarpari (forthcoming), 18.

[13] Ki-baek Lee, *A New History of Korea*, trans. Edward W. Wagner (Cambridge: Harvard University Press, 1984), 189.

[14] James Louis Hevia, *Cherishing Men from Afar: Qing Guest Ritual and the Macartney Embassy of 1793* (Durham: Duke University Press, 1995), 50.

itself prima facie evidence of Korea's stable international environment. Indeed, contrary to the account of "incessant invasions" between 1368 and 1895—a period of over 500 years—Korea experienced pirate raids in only 19 years, skirmishes along its northern border in only 25 years, and actual wars in only 16 years.[15] In short, it experienced astonishing stability during five centuries of existence as a single political entity. While Choson Korea clearly needed to manage its relations with China, relations with China did not involve much loss of independence. Instead, the country was largely free to run domestic affairs as it saw fit and could also conduct foreign policy independently from China.[16] One scholar notes the following:

> While the Koreans had to play the hand they were dealt, they repeatedly prevailed in diplomacy and argument…and convinced China to retreat from an aggressive position. In other words, the tributary system did provide for effective communication, and Chinese and Korean officialdom spoke from a common Confucian vocabulary. In that front, the relationship was equal, if not at times actually in Korea's favor.[17]

In practical terms, the Chinese Song and Korean Koryo Dynasties formally demarcated their border at the Amnok River (known as the Yalu River in Chinese) in 1034, and that border has remained essentially unchanged to the present day. Although South Korea does not necessarily like dealing with China, it has no choice, and indeed it has lived with China for centuries. The result of this long-standing and stable relationship between Korea and China is that Koreans have less fear of China than many expect.

In contrast, premodern relations between Korea and Japan were distant at best and singularly marked by the Japanese invasion of Korea in 1592. That war, lasting six years and involving Ming Chinese troops, Jurchens, and Korean and Japanese soldiers, was a vicious conflict that devastated the Korean Peninsula and reinforced an image of Japan as violent, untrustworthy, and uncivilized. In the centuries both before and after the invasion, Japan conducted limited and only sporadic diplomatic interactions with Korea, and indeed the rest of East Asia. Vibrant trade relations existed between the two countries throughout the entire premodern era, but trade was heavily regulated and never widened to become the foundation of a true

---

[15] David C. Kang, Ronan Tse-min Fu, and Meredith Shaw, "Measuring War in Early Modern East Asia: Introducing Chinese and Korean Language Sources," *International Studies Quarterly* (forthcoming).

[16] Son Seung-chol, ed., *Kangjwa Hanilgwangye-sa* [Lectures on Korea-Japan Relations] (Seoul: Hyonumsa, 1994); and Etsuko Kang, *Diplomacy and Ideology in Japanese-Korean Relations: From the Fifteenth to the Eighteenth Century* (New York: St. Martin's Press, 1997), 6–9.

[17] Gari Ledyard, "Chinese 'Control' over Choson," Korea Web, March 21, 2006, http://koreanstudies. com/pipermail/koreanstudies_koreanstudies.com/2006-March/017808.html.

cultural relationship.[18] Yet although Japan only invaded Korea once before the modern era, it was the unpredictability and intensity of that invasion that most framed Korean views of Japan.

Twentieth century. Events of the twentieth century reinforced, albeit with some significant modifications, this premodern Korean strategic culture. If China was the immovable mountain under whose shadow one must live, Japan was the unpredictable and dangerous neighbor that seemed superficially placid but could snap at any time. Thus, when Japan responded to the arrival of Western imperial powers in the late nineteenth century, the results for Korea were disastrous. If stability and a focus on China had characterized the previous five hundred years, chaos and Japan dominated the twentieth century. In short, South Korea's strategic culture has historically viewed China as a major power to be dealt with and Japan as a threat to be defended against. That basic interpretation of the world holds today.

The two most important events of the twentieth century that affected South Korea's enduring strategic views of itself and the world were Japanese colonization and the Korean War.[19] Japanese colonization in the twentieth century was not only harsh but particularly galling for Koreans. By the 1930s, Japan had officially outlawed the Korean language and prohibited the use of Korean names. The 35 years of increasingly oppressive colonization left a deep imprint on South Korean strategic culture that Japan was not to be trusted. Two invasions, spaced three hundred years apart, reinforced a historical lesson that Japan was a barbarous and violent country to be feared, contained, and ignored as much as possible.

The humiliation of colonization by Japan also led Korean historians to emphasize how masculine and strong Korea had been in the past. In this modern context, the centuries in which Korea had been a close subordinate of China were reinterpreted as weakness and toadying. To counteract this perception, historians reached back fifteen centuries to claim a relationship with the Koguryo kingdom (37 BCE–668 CE), which straddled present-day China and the Korean Peninsula. This new nationalist historiography downplayed the centuries of stability and close relations with China in favor of a tenuous relationship to the Koguryo kingdom, which was actually crushed by combined Chinese (Tang) and Korean (Silla) forces.[20]

---

[18] James B. Lewis, *Frontier Contact between Choson Korea and Tokugawa Japan* (New York: Routledge, 2003).

[19] On Japanese colonialism in Korea, see Gi-wook Shin and Michael Robinson, eds., *Colonial Modernity in Korea* (Cambridge: Harvard University Press, 2001). On the division of the Korean Peninsula and the Korean War, see Bruce Cumings, *The Origins of the Korean War*, vol. 1 and 2 (Princeton: Princeton University Press, 1981).

[20] Andre Schmid, "Rediscovering Manchuria: Shin Chae-ho," *Journal of Asian Studies* 56, no. 1 (1997): 26–46.

Just as searing was the division of Korea into two parts after over eleven centuries as a unified country. With independence from Japan came the immediate U.S. and Soviet military occupation of the peninsula; brief bickering between the two superpowers resulted in the creation of two governments, both claiming to be the only legitimate Korean state and to represent the entire Korean people. The focus of South Korea instantly turned inward to the peninsula. Every external relationship was viewed through the lens of how it would affect North-South relations. The North Korean invasion of South Korea in June 1950 resulted in a horrific three-year war that resolved nothing, left the demilitarized zone between the sides in almost the exact same place it had started, devastated the peninsula from Busan to the Yalu River, and left an estimated two million Korean soldiers and civilians dead. The impact of the war and division continues to this day, with North Korea being the most salient security threat to South Korea. Yet North Korea also has become an important domestic political issue as well—many South Koreans have relatives on the other side of the border, with over 130,000 people on the register to be selected for the inter-Korean family reunions as of December 31, 2015.[21]

South Korea began to focus on the United States for its survival, and more deeply for its intellectual and strategic leadership. The country's leaders came to regard the United States as critical for national security and economic development. And yet Korea remained far from a reliable ally—during the 1950s, Syngman Rhee was so difficult to work with that U.S. advisers frequently voiced frustration with him.[22] Victor Cha notes that the U.S. alliance was structured in part to restrain Rhee from starting another war and dragging the United States along with him. He writes that the United States' fear of entrapment "especially applied to the South Korean authoritarian state under Syngman Rhee, who harnessed rabid anti-communism both to legitimize his rule and to try to embroil the U.S. in further conflict on the Korean peninsula."[23]

The interpretation and historical memory of the Korean War in South Korea demonstrate how differently the ROK views its own strategic situation. China was directly implicated in the continuing division of the peninsula through its immense military support of the northern Kim Il-sung regime. Mao Zedong's own son was killed in action in Korea, and it is estimated that

---

[21] Ministry of Unification (ROK), *2016 tongil baekseo* [2016 Unification White Paper] (Seoul, 2016), http://www.unikorea.go.kr/content.do?cmsid=1493.

[22] Jung-en Woo, *Race to the Swift: State and Finance in Korean Industrialization* (New York: Columbia University Press, 1991), especially chap. 4.

[23] Victor D. Cha, "'Rhee-straint': The Origins of the U.S.-ROK Alliance," *International Journal of Korean Studies* 15, no. 1 (2011): 5.

the People's Liberation Army suffered 150,000–180,000 fatalities in battle. Yet despite being a major cause of the survival of North Korea, China does not figure prominently in South Korea's memorial about the war, nor does the war play into contemporary South Korean views of Chinese intentions. South Koreans do not blame China nearly as much as they blame the United States and Russia for the division. In short, historical memory is born out of strategic culture: the way in which the Korean War is remembered and portrayed in contemporary South Korea shows again how enduring are the country's conceptions of its neighbors.

Perhaps most intriguingly, although the division of the peninsula has affected the conduct of both Koreas' foreign policies, it did not fundamentally alter the larger strategic culture of either side. Both Koreas claim to be the true Korea, both claim to be the most noble expression of the Korean identity, and both strive for independence and have proved to be somewhat difficult, or at least unconventional, allies for their more powerful patrons.

In sum, there are clearly long-enduring strands of Korean strategic culture that have roots deep in history. Confidence, a desire for independence, the ability to deal with a powerful China, and suspicion of a less Confucianized Japan—all these traits were intensified during the twentieth century. The United States' arrival and South Korea's focus on the West modified but did not fundamentally alter these traits.

Internal Factors

History is important because it explains the context for how South Korea has come to view itself, especially vis-à-vis neighboring China and Japan. In fact, the collective sense of injustice arising from history is also reinforced by social discontent at the domestic level. This is attributable in part to the highly compressed and incomplete nature of democratization and the resultant perception of an inability to control one's own fate, which charges the South Korean elites to maximize the ROK's self-confidence and autonomy at the foreign-policy level.

While South Korea is often proud of its quick success at becoming a beacon of democracy, it is more accurate to distinguish between formal democracy—the institution and its components on paper—and effective democracy—how democracy is actually run on an everyday basis.[24] South Korea has clearly achieved the former but is still struggling with the latter. In fact, there are ongoing concerns about the government backsliding on freedoms and increasing state centralization, with the most classic

---

[24] See Ronald Inglehart and Christian Welzel, *Modernization, Cultural Change, and Democracy: The Human Development Sequence* (Cambridge: Cambridge University Press, 2005), 149.

contemporary illustration of this public perception of a "broken system" being the *Sewol* incident of 2014.[25] Since the sinking of the ferry, three documentaries have been made about the incident—*The Truth Shall Not Sink with Sewol* (2014), *Cruel State* (2015), and *Upside Down* (2016)—and there is now a mark on the South Korean psyche so deep that the National Institute of Korean Language designated the "*Sewol* generation" as one of Korea's neologisms in 2014.[26] From the perspective of the public, the elites are clearly not beholden to the democratic norms of accountability and representation, further reinforcing the popular belief in the hypocrisy of South Korean democracy. From the perspective of the elites, constant domestic pressure to resolve this tension between democracy as an ideal and democracy in practice has tested their self-confidence and increased their desire to recharge South Korea's autonomy and strength abroad.

Further evidence of this domestic frustration and anxiety is the lack of public trust in the government. For example, one survey found that only 2.6% of South Korean college students trust politicians, ranking them last, even below complete strangers (at 8.4%).[27] The findings of a joint survey of 1,051 high school students (belonging to the *Sewol* generation) conducted in August 2014 by the Hankyoreh Economy and Society Research Institute and Chamgyoyook Research Institute were similarly grim. Trust in the president and the executive leadership fell from 23.7% before the incident to 6.8% afterward, while trust in the National Assembly dropped from 18.9% to 5.4%. The percentage of respondents who felt a sense of pride as citizens of South Korea also fell dramatically from 61.9% to 24.9% after the *Sewol* incident.[28] Justifiably so, many South Koreans saw the incident as humiliating, as it exposed the failure of South Korean society to protect its own citizens in their homeland. The pride factor is particularly interesting because it challenges

[25] For a discussion of state centralization, see Simon Mundy, "Strength of South Korea's Democracy Faces Stern Test," *Financial Times*, April 27, 2014, http://www.ft.com/cms/s/0/22d819ac-cca6-11e3-ab99-00144feabdc0.html#axzz40jJRQKTQ; and Lee Se-young, "A Time of Regression: S. Korea's Democratic Rankings Slide," *Hankyoreh*, December 16, 2015, http://english.hani.co.kr/arti/english_edition/e_national/722173.html. For a comprehensive timeline of the *Sewol* incident, see "Ferry Disaster in South Korea: A Year Later," *New York Times*, April 11, 2015, http://www.nytimes.com/interactive/2015/04/12/world/asia/12ferry-timeline.html.

[26] The *Sewol* generation refers to South Koreans of a similar age to the victims of the *Sewol* ferry sinking, who were mostly high school students. "2014 shineo" [Neologisms of 2014], National Institute of Korean Language (ROK), December 2014, 61, http://www.korean.go.kr/front/reportData/reportDataView.do?report_seq=801&mn_id=45.

[27] Kwanwoo Jun, "In South Korea, Strangers More Trusted Than Companies or Politicians," *Wall Street Journal*, Korea Real Time, January 19, 2015, http://blogs.wsj.com/korearealtime/2015/01/19/in-south-korea-strangers-more-trusted-than-companies-or-politicians.

[28] Choi Hae-jung, "Sewolho saedae kook-kaga nareul jikyeojungeot, 7.7 bboon" [*Sewol* Generation: Only 7.7% Believes That the Country Can Ensure Their Safety], *Hankyoreh*, August 20, 2014, http://www.hani.co.kr/arti/society/society_general/652076.html.

South Korea's self-confidence but also reinforces the need to be competent at the regional and global levels.

One implication of domestic anger and anxiety is heightened pressure on the government to perform internationally and position South Korea vis-à-vis other states to stave off some of its insecurities. To that end, having a strong executive has been relatively useful—numerous presidential decrees and executive orders have allowed the executive to bypass a gridlocked legislature.[29] Even former president Kim Dae-jung, who was credited with the success of the first inter-Korean summit in 2000, was accused of not consulting the legislative branch on key decisions regarding the Sunshine Policy toward the North, and hence was vulnerable to charges of an "imperial presidency."[30] There is also swift action against any political sympathies toward South Korea's neighbor to the north and at least a rough semblance of consensus or bipartisanship that Japan is a threat and that China can be managed.[31] In fact, even though policies have waxed and waned with incoming administrations as a result of their need to decouple themselves from the identity of prior regimes, the idea of engagement with China has survived the test of time, as has the unrelenting resentment against Japan.

Further evidence of the South Korean elites' efforts to make sure that a proactive South Korea has control over its fate—and in the process earn esteem and recognition—is to be active about proposing roles for South Korea that would make it a pivotal shaper of events in the region. In the last two decades, South Korea has put forth multiple ideas that indicate a yearning for some type of regional leadership, or at least recognition. Former president Roh Moo-hyun attracted much attention for his speeches in March 2005 that described South Korea's "balancing" role for peace and prosperity on the Korean Peninsula and in Northeast Asia more broadly. Former president Lee Myung-bak made a clear push to place the ROK at the forefront of the Global Green Growth Initiative with his vision for "low-carbon, green growth" in August 2008. Most recently, current president Park Geun-hye proposed the Northeast Asia Peace and Cooperation Initiative in 2013, which entails "a process for the building of an order of multilateral cooperation and

---

[29] For a discussion on presidential powers, including empirical examples, see Byung-kook Kim, "Party Politics in South Korea's Democracy: The Crisis of Success," in *Consolidating Democracy in South Korea*, ed. Larry Diamond and Byung-kook Kim (Boulder: Lynn Rienner Publishers, 2000), 53–86.

[30] For more on this example, see Young Whan Kihl, *Transforming Korean Politics: Democracy, Reform, and Culture* (New York: Routledge, 2015), 289.

[31] In the first verdict of its kind, the Constitutional Court of Korea ordered in December 2014 the disbandment of the United Progressive Party after finding it to be in violation of South Korea's constitution and a threat to national security, given the party's proclivities toward North Korea. See Sang-hun Choe, "South Korea Disbands Party Sympathetic to North," *New York Times*, December 19, 2014, http://www.nytimes.com/2014/12/20/world/asia/south-korea-disbands-united-progressive-party-sympathetic-to-north-korea.html.

trust," or "trustpolitik," to promote peace in the region.[32] Despite subsequent questions and skepticism about the details of each of these policy platforms, there has been continuity in elite aspirations for South Korea to play a more assertive role in international affairs, with little to no apprehension about the country taking on leadership roles. This may explain why one of the formal objectives of the ROK Ministry of Foreign Affairs is to contribute to international society by consolidating South Korea's status as a "middle power" and earning "prestige."[33]

Thus, while a strong executive has come to lead the collective discourse about South Korea's approach to its neighbors and simultaneously reinforced the national attitude that has been shaped by history, the general lack of real or perceived freedom at the domestic level has solidified the country's commitment to maintaining autonomy at the international level. Just as a considerable segment of the domestic population feels like the system is broken and there is no viable way out, South Korea as a state has often been frustrated by the overbearing force of the regional structure and its incapacitating influence on agency. A prime example is Seoul's lack of leverage or options in negotiations with North Korea. Pyongyang may be more resistant to external influences than many hope. Rather than understanding South Korea in sheer material terms by viewing it as the classic "shrimp among whales," it is more instructive to also recognize the internal sources of South Korea's strategic culture that have shaped its preference for a proactive over a reactive foreign policy, one that accentuates autonomy. This emphasis reflects the need to compensate for the helplessness that comes with not having much agency or control at the societal level.

Again, the contrast with Japan is instructive, in that generations of observers have described Japan as a "reactive" state (with the Shinzo Abe government being a recent exception).[34] In that sense, it may be more accurate to describe South Korea as a country that fears that the ocean and its currents, rather than any whales out at sea, may swallow it whole. The country's elites have clearly been aware of the importance of succeeding in the foreign policy sphere in order to mitigate growing domestic discontent. An assertive South Korea that has a voice in shaping its own surroundings is one way to guarantee that the country does not once again become irrelevant, or worse become trapped in a geopolitical structure that it had no hand in making.

---

[32] Ministry of Foreign Affairs (ROK), "Northeast Asia Peace and Cooperation Initiative," 2015, http://www.mofa.go.kr/ENG/North_Asia/res/eng.pdf.

[33] Ministry of Foreign Affairs (ROK), "Woori waegyo jeongchaek-e gijowa mokpyo" [Platform and Objectives of Our Foreign Policy], http://www.mofa.go.kr/trade/purpose/keynote/index.jsp?menu=m_30_10_10.

[34] For more on this perception, see, for example, Kent E. Calder, "Japanese Foreign Economic Policy Formation: Explaining the Reactive State," World Politics 40, no. 4 (1988): 517–41.

The Impact of Strategic Culture on South Korea's Foreign Policy Choices

Both the external and internal sources of South Korea's strategic culture have revealed why the ROK places such a high premium on being able to chart its own course and pursue a relatively independent foreign policy. Thus, while it may seem banal to claim that countries strive for independence, in South Korea's case this principle has deep roots. For example, South Korea has taken actions that defy its key ally, the United States, and at times it has cozied up to its main existential threat, North Korea. Without a basic understanding of this feature of South Korean strategic culture, observers may be puzzled by the country. This section will first focus on Seoul's conception of power and how this has been informed by its relations with Pyongyang. South Korea's efforts to reinforce its security while retaining some level of autonomy have produced apparent inconsistencies in its foreign policy choices, such as in the transfer of operational control (OPCON) from the United States. The section will also discuss several contemporary foreign policy debates in South Korea, such as those surrounding the Terminal High Altitude Air Defense (THAAD) system and the Asian Infrastructure Investment Bank (AIIB), as well as the general state of political interaction with China and Japan. These examples demonstrate the complex process through which the ROK's strategic culture is translated into actual foreign policy outcomes.

South Korea's Conception of Power

South Korea's understanding of power is still largely informed by material capabilities. Security is not an abstract concept but rather something that is practiced directly or indirectly on an everyday basis. The slogan released by the Ministry of Patriots and Veterans Affairs for the commemoration of the Korean War on June 25, 2016—"There is neither country nor citizen without security"—captures just how pervasive the consciousness toward traditional security is for South Korea.[35] Similarly, a 2015 nationwide survey by the Ministry of Public Safety and Security found that 69.1% of citizens said they felt "insecure," including 73.5% of college students.[36] Security, then, is not something that is taken lightly by either the elites or the public.

---

[35] Ministry of Patriots and Veterans Affairs (ROK), "Bohun-e-shik 1% jeungkaneun sahwae galdeung yoin gamsowa 11 jo 9 choneokwon-e kyungjae seongjang jeunga hyokwa" [1% Increase in Consciousness for Veterans Affairs Decreases Societal Tensions and Leads to 11.9 Trillion Worth in Economic Growth], May 31, 2016, http://www.mpva.go.kr/open/open210_view.asp?id=40382.

[36] Ministry of Public Safety and Security (ROK), "2015 nyeon kookmin ahnbo-e-shik josa kyeolgwa bogoseo" [2015 Report on Survey Results of Security Consciousness of Citizens], June 2015.

A part of that consciousness can be traced to North Korea. The way that South Korea has thought about power is inevitably shaped by the presence of its neighbor, which among other things has been a continuous military provocateur on the Korean Peninsula. As the sinking of the corvette *Cheonan* in March 2010 and the artillery shelling of Yeonpyeong Island later that year demonstrate, North Korea is integral to South Korea's calculus, particularly its military posture and the exercise of power. It will be almost impossible to completely detach the concept of power from material capabilities so long as North Korea continues to pose an existential security threat. This reality has produced a complex situation for Seoul: on the one hand, it recognizes the value of an effective military alliance with the United States, but, on the other hand, it must also keep the notions of autonomy and sovereignty intact.

This dilemma between greater autonomy and greater security is clear from the ongoing debates about the transfer of wartime OPCON over South Korean combat forces from the United States. The two countries have enjoyed a close alliance for over a half century. During that time, the United States has stationed military forces in South Korea to prevent a second North Korean invasion. The United States transferred peacetime OPCON to South Korea in 1994. This decision coincided not only with greater awareness of the importance of autonomy on the part of the ROK but also with recognition by the United States that it needed to share some of its responsibilities (or "burdens") abroad with its key allies. During the Roh Moo-hyun administration (2003–8), the issue of wartime OPCON became central to Roh's general platform of greater independence and sovereignty. The two countries subsequently agreed to transfer wartime OPCON to South Korea's Joint Chiefs of Staff by 2012. However, the sinking of the *Cheonan* by North Korea created a more amenable atmosphere in which to argue against the transfer. Thus, Presidents Lee Myung-bak and Barack Obama agreed to postpone the transfer until December 2015. Most recently, in 2014 President Park Geun-hye requested another delay, a decision that led to domestic criticism, given her initial campaign pledge to retake wartime control by 2015.[37] Now the target date for the transfer is somewhere around 2020, but there are still lingering doubts about whether this process will actually occur according to schedule.

As the OPCON issue demonstrates, Seoul's attempt to achieve a balance between autonomy and security while managing its relations with Pyongyang has produced apparently inconsistent or even contradictory policies. A similar challenge complicates relations between South Korea and the United States

---

[37] For more on the delay of the transfer, see Sang-hun Choe, "U.S. and South Korea Agree to Delay Shift in Wartime Command," *New York Times*, October 24, 2014, http://www.nytimes.com/2014/10/25/international-home/us-and-south-korea-agree-to-delay-shift-in-wartime-command.html.

in other areas. Although the U.S.-ROK alliance is currently very strong, it was considered by many to be in deep disarray only a decade ago, threatened by chronic anti-U.S. sentiment within South Korea. Hillary Clinton herself accused South Koreans of "historical amnesia" because they did not remember the U.S. support during the Korean War.[38] From the United States' support of dictator Chun Doo-hwan in the 1980s to Washington's tepid support for South Korea amid its economic troubles during the "IMF crisis" (International Monetary Fund crisis) of 1997–98 and disagreements about how best to deal with North Korea during the Roh years, there is a group of South Korean citizens and politicians who are deeply skeptical of U.S. influence and goals. In 2011, for example, a sizable percentage of South Koreans did not believe that the *Cheonan* was sunk by North Korea.[39]

What does this all mean for South Korea and its conception of power? On the one hand, there exists a compelling reason for power to be based on material capabilities, given the immutable realities of geography; on the other hand, power must be multidimensional to reflect South Korea's strategic culture and its desires for autonomy. The example of the OPCON transfer captures this very tension between needing to retain some sovereignty but also secure military capabilities. The resulting picture is a complex one that combines the ROK's need for an effective force as expressed by national capabilities—particularly of the military kind due to the threat from the North—with efforts to retain some semblance of independence. The country has always decided on its own path, which sometimes converges with the interests of allies such as the United States and other times does not.

The Contemporary Debates over THAAD and the AIIB

THAAD. The debate surrounding THAAD illustrates that issues about military capabilities cannot be reduced solely to an analysis of power in the material sense. Judging by the large proportion of the debate dedicated to talking about what it means to host such a system, rather than about the system's operational effectiveness, there is more to this debate than physical security. In fact, South Korea's decision in July 2016 to host THAAD technology supplied by the United States has quickly morphed into a debate about geopolitics and even domestic politics. One issue is whether the deployment of this system is simply focused on gaining leverage against China or is indeed meant to counter the threat of North Korea's

---

[38] "Hillary Clinton Bemoans 'Historical Amnesia' in Korea," *Chosun Ilbo*, October 26, 2005, http://english.chosun.com/site/data/html_dir/2005/10/26/2005102661015.html.

[39] Cho Jong Ik, "3 in 10 Don't Trust Cheonan Result," Daily NK, March 24, 2011, http://dailynk.com/english/read_print.php?cataId=nk03700&num=7496.

missile program. A second issue is whether the Blue House deliberated enough before reaching a decision, especially in light of opposition from the legislature, such as by the Justice Party, and by the public, particularly in Seongju, which was chosen as the host site for THAAD. (This echoes both the foreign and domestic sources of South Korea's strategic culture.)

Some in the ROK are baffled at why China is not more annoyed at the North, which after all is the provocateur and should feel the brunt of any repercussions from its missile tests. The fact is that even before the critical test in February 2016, Korea watchers in the United States were proposing that Seoul "exercise its sovereign right to defend the country and its citizens against the North Korean threat brought on, in part, by Beijing's unwillingness to confront its belligerent ally."[40] The problem—at least from where South Korea stands—is that the North Korean issue has increasingly become tied to the larger U.S.-China strategic rivalry. Instead of seeing THAAD as offering the opportunity for greater co-leadership, Seoul fears the loss of agency and control in its foreign policy. As evidence, some such as Seo Hyung-soo, a lawmaker in the Minjoo Party of Korea, have proposed the indigenous platform of the Korea Air and Missile Defense as an alternative to THAAD.[41] The point is that a seemingly obvious decision—to some outside observers—provoked such an extensive round of introspection in South Korea itself.

This is not the first time that South Korean leaders have felt the need to carve out their own independent path. Back in February 2001, then president Kim Dae-jung hosted a bilateral summit with Russian president Vladimir Putin, which resulted in a joint communiqué that was interpreted as Seoul criticizing U.S. plans for a national missile defense system (on the grounds that such a system would potentially require a modification of or U.S. withdrawal from the 1972 Anti-Ballistic Missile Treaty). Washington viewed this move as a "Russia tilt" on the part of South Korea.[42] Putin had visited North Korea in July 2000—the first visit of its kind by a Russian leader—and there was hope that Seoul could enlist Moscow's help in dealing with the North Korean threat. Immediately after the announcement, U.S. officials pressed Seoul for a clarification of the joint statement, at which

---

[40] Bruce Klingner, "South Korea Needs THAAD Missile Defense," Heritage Foundation, Backgrounder, no. 3024, June 12, 2015, http://www.heritage.org/research/reports/2015/06/south-korea-needs-thaad-missile-defense.

[41] Byong-gil Choi, "The Minjoo Seo Hyung-soo 'THAAD Bandae Dangron-e-ro Jeonghara'" [Seo Hyung-soo of the Minjoo Party Argues for "Anti-THAAD" to Be Overall Party Platform], Yonhap, August 8, 2016, http://www.yonhapnews.co.kr/bulletin/2016/08/08/0200000000A KR20160808109700052.HTML?input=1195m.

[42] Patrick E. Tyler, "South Korea's New Best Friend?" *New York Times*, March 1, 2001, http://www.nytimes.com/2001/03/01/world/south-korea-s-new-best-friend.html.

point the ROK Ministry of Foreign Affairs made a semantic distinction between endorsing the Anti-Ballistic Missile Treaty as a "cornerstone of strategic stability" and necessarily opposing national missile defense on grounds of violating the treaty.[43] Seoul had meant to communicate the former rather than the latter message. Soon thereafter, in March 2001, Kim met with President George W. Bush in Washington, D.C., where the main item on the agenda was North Korea.

Thus, the process of crafting a policy toward the North has often become subsumed under a larger geopolitical rivalry. This leaves South Korea in the rather tricky predicament of having to manage any fallout as a result of pursuing national interests that give off the semblance of "taking sides."

AIIB. A prima facie reading of the debate around THAAD may lead one to mistakenly conclude that South Korea has somehow opted to embrace the United States as its partner at the expense of its relations with China. The AIIB demonstrates the utility of recognizing that South Korea's calculus is often motivated by a much larger mindset rooted in its strategic culture and its aspirations to gain proactive control of the environment of which it is a part.

The AIIB officially opened for business on January 16, 2016, with Jin Liqun as its head (a former vice minister of finance in China) to address, among other things, the shortage of infrastructural capital in Asia. Even before its launch, the AIIB had attracted considerable media attention. The very provenance of the bank was viewed to be a blow to U.S. economic leadership and influence in the Asia-Pacific, given the decision by many of its key trans-Atlantic and trans-Pacific allies to join the institution.[44] The continued narrative about U.S. hostility to this Chinese-led initiative elicited a response by Obama, who had to explain that the United States was not opposed to the idea, but that "our simple point to everybody in these conversations around the Asian infrastructure bank is, let's just make sure that we're running it based on best practices."[45]

A clear example of how South Korea's participation in the AIIB is focused less on China (or the United States) and based more on the ROK's own interests as directed by its strategic culture is the fallout from the scandal concerning

---

[43] Don Kirk, "South Korea Now Pulls Back from Russia on Missile Shield," *New York Times*, March 2, 2001, http://www.nytimes.com/2001/03/02/world/south-korea-now-pulls-back-from-russia-on-missile-shield.html.

[44] For instance, see Nicholas Watt, Paul Lewis, and Tania Branigan, "U.S. Anger at Britain Joining Chinese-Led Investment Bank AIIB," *Guardian*, March 13, 2015, http://www.theguardian.com/us-news/2015/mar/13/white-house-pointedly-asks-uk-to-use-its-voice-as-part-of-chinese-led-bank.

[45] Ian Talley, "Obama: We're All for the Asian Infrastructure Investment Bank," *Wall Street Journal*, April 28, 2015, http://blogs.wsj.com/economics/2015/04/28/obama-were-all-for-the-asian-infrastructure-investment-bank.

the AIIB's vice president and chief risk officer Hong Kyttack. He was initially appointed as one of the bank's five vice presidents but was recently replaced due to his mismanagement of the Korea Development Bank, where he served as head. Since Hong's exit, the South Korean media has been acutely aware of the decreasing influence that South Korea may have within the AIIB and has expressed concerns that other major powers in the organization, such as India, Russia, and France, are "waiting for their opportunity to absorb Korea's stake" in the institution.[46] Hence, there is no reason to view the decision to join the AIIB as siding with China (or against the United States). Instead, changes in economic and trade relations highlight that South Korea has continued to evolve and morph over the past two decades in ways that make it more focused on itself and less focused simply on the United States. South Korea is more interested in its ability to assume a direct stake in the institutions that affect it; the recent reports in July 2016 that South Korean finance experts had applied for senior positions at the AIIB confirm this aspiration to be an active shaper of events rather than a passive bystander.[47] This tracks with South Korea's own strategic culture, which is characterized by a commitment to be autonomous and is pro-ROK rather than pro-China or pro-U.S.

South Korea's Relations with China and Japan

China. On the whole, South Korea has defied expectations for how China's closest neighbors would react to its increasing capabilities. Although there has been enough debate to have dislodged any serious notion that countries in East Asia would attempt to contain China militarily, there is still an expectation by the United States for more initiatives on the part of such countries to at least aid the United States in offsetting China's growing might.[48] The above discussion of the AIIB shows that this outcome is unlikely in the case of South Korea. Indeed, ROK military expenditures have steadily contracted over the past two decades as a proportion of South Korea's overall economy (see **Figure 1**). While South Korea devoted around 4.5% of its GDP to the military in the late 1980s, by the late 1990s that percentage had dropped

---

[46] Koon-deuk Bae, "AIIB-ae mugwanshim-han jeongbu: Naenyeon Hankook Chonghwae yoochi-do eryeopda" [Government Disinterested in AIIB: Hosting Next Year's General Assembly Will Be Difficult], *Aju News*, August 8, 2016, http://www.ajunews.com/view/20160808145544091.

[47] Joo-wan Kim, "AIIB goweejik chuga gongmo-ae Hankook-in 2–3 myung jiwon" [2–3 South Koreans Apply for Additional Opening for Senior Positions at AIIB], *Hankook Kyungjae*, July 30, 2016, http://www.hankyung.com/news/app/newsview.php?aid=2016073060721.

[48] Although there is no explicit targeting of China, the Heritage Foundation does recommend that "the U.S. should urge the most capable of its alliance partners to augment their contributions to their defense and to aid in addressing international security challenges." See "Solutions 2016: Alliances and International Organizations," Heritage Foundation, http://solutions.heritage.org/foreign-affairs/alliances-and-international-organizations.

FIGURE 1   Military expenditures, 1989–2014

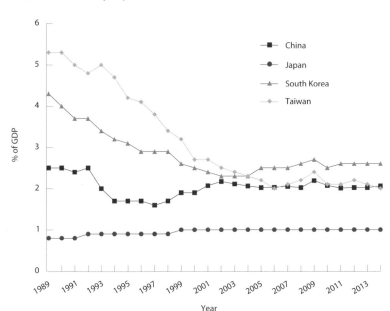

SOURCE: Stockholm International Peace Research Institute (SIPRI), SIPRI Military Expenditure Database, http://www.sipri.org/research/armaments/milex/milex_database.

to under 3% of GDP, and it appears unlikely to increase anytime soon. In short, South Korea has not responded to China's rise with any measurable increase in its own military capabilities.

At the same time, South Korea, similar to all regional countries, is rapidly expanding its economic relations with China. China overtook the United States as the top destination for South Korean exports in 2003, and in 2007 China also overtook Japan as the number one market for South Korean imports (see **Figure 2**). Needless to say, the speed with which China outpaced other major partners—particularly as South Korea's destination for exports—is significant. Although the net value of imports and exports started off roughly similar in 2000, by 2014 there was a clear divergence in the dominance of China as South Korea's major trading partner. Moreover, the ROK government announced in March 2016 that roughly nine out of ten foreigners who had obtained residency visas through investing in public

FIGURE 2 Major origins and destinations of South Korea's imports and exports, 2000–2014

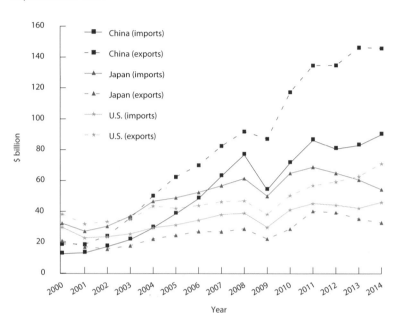

SOURCE: IMF, Direction of Trade Statistics, http://data.imf.org/?sk=9D6028D4-F14A-464C-A2F2-59B2CD424B85.

development projects in South Korea (the "immigrant investor program") originated from China.[49]

The movement of people is also illuminating. The number of South Korean students traveling to China to study purportedly increased nearly fourfold during 2001–12 from 16,372 in 2001 to 62,855 in 2012, which made China the second most popular destination after the United States, with a comparable figure of 73,351.[50] Likewise, the ROK Ministry of Justice announced that, as of February 2016, not only did the highest percentage of registered foreigners in South Korea come from China—at 946,895 (51%), followed by the United States at 139,868 (7.5%)—but also the number of

[49] "9 out of 10 Immigrant Investors in Public Business Are from China," Yonhap, March 28, 2016, http://english.yonhapnews.co.kr/news/2016/03/28/0200000000AEN20160328002600315.html.

[50] "S. Korean Students in China Quadruple in 11 Years," Yonhap, October 2, 2013, http://english.yonhapnews.co.kr/national/2013/10/02/25/0302000000AEN20131002002500315F.html.

foreign students studying in South Korea reached 105,193, with 62,318 of those coming from China (59.2%).[51] To some extent, then, considering the basic asymmetry between the ROK and China in sheer human capital, there seems to be relative reciprocity in the way that the two publics are becoming enmeshed into each other's society.

The South Korean public holds views about China that put it squarely within the mainstream of East Asian countries. In 2015 the Pew Research Center found that more South Koreans think that China will eventually replace the United States as the world's greatest superpower than think China will never replace the United States (59% and 40%, respectively). In terms of favorable and unfavorable views of China, South Koreans were also well within the Asian mainstream (61% favorable, 37% unfavorable).[52] It is for this reason that South Korea and its strategic culture can provide such insights about the complexity of regional relations in general, not just about the Korean Peninsula.[53] More specifically, while comprehensive engagement with China has been a stable component of South Korean foreign policy (as it has been for many other countries in the region), Seoul has also exhibited seemingly contradictory behavior, such as agreeing to host THAAD despite disapproval from Beijing. The interaction between the two countries makes the most sense once we acknowledge that while South Korea may be less wary of an assertive China based on its past relations with the country, it is also not willing to let that dictate its core national interests of autonomy and independence.

Japan. In contrast to the generally stable relations between China and South Korea, ROK-Japan relations have almost never been smooth. This is the case despite the fact that there are several shared features between South Korea and Japan that should theoretically encourage cooperation. Both countries are liberal democracies and highly interconnected in terms of trade.[54] Moreover, they are treaty allies with a common great-power patron (the United States), which, according to network analysis, should be a key

---

[51] "Chool-ip-guk, waegukin jeongchaek tongae wolbo" [Policy and Monthly Statistics on Immigration and Foreigners], Ministry of Justice (ROK), Korea Immigration Service, February 2016, 4.

[52] Richard Wike, Bruce Stokes, and Jacob Poushter, "Views of China and the Global Balance of Power," Pew Research Center, June 23, 2015, http://www.pewglobal.org/2015/06/23/2-views-of-china-and-the-global-balance-of-power.

[53] For more on these views, see Tom Switzer, "Asia's Confidence in America Is Fraying," *Wall Street Journal*, June 9, 2016.

[54] For more on their trade connections, see Charles A. Kupchan, *How Enemies Become Friends: The Sources of Stable Peace* (Princeton: Princeton University Press, 2010); John M. Owen, "How Liberalism Produces Democratic Peace," *International Security* 19, no. 2 (1994): 87–125; and Bruce Russett, *Grasping the Democratic Peace: Principles for a Post–Cold War Peace* (Princeton: Princeton University Press, 1993).

element in catalyzing cooperative ties between otherwise distant actors.[55] To a third party, the antagonism that exists between Japan and South Korea is rather confusing, especially given that North Korea provides a clear common threat, which should serve as glue rather than a wedge for bilateral ties.

Relations worsened during the first three years of the Park Geun-hye administration, with the first formal meeting between President Park and Prime Minister Abe not occurring until a November 2015 summit. This coolness between the countries is not new. The Japanese newspaper *Asahi Shimbun* and the South Korean newspaper *Dong-A Ilbo* have conducted joint public opinion surveys in both countries since the 1980s, which provide telling insights on how sentiments between the two publics have shifted over time (see **Figures 3** and **4**). Most notably, the polling data reveals that

FIGURE 3 Survey results of South Korean sentiments toward Japan, 1984–2015

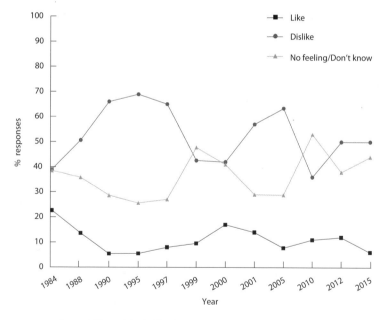

SOURCE: *Dong-A Ilbo* and *Asahi Shimbun,* 1984–2015.

---

[55] See Duncan J. Watts, "Networks, Dynamics, and the Small-World Phenomenon," *American Journal of Sociology* 105, no. 2 (1999): 493–527; Zeev Maoz, "Preferential Attachment, Homophily, and the Structure of International Networks, 1,816–2,003," *Conflict Management and Peace Science* 29, no. 3 (2012): 341–69; and Brandon J. Kinne, "Network Dynamics and the Evolution of International Cooperation," *American Political Science Review* 107, no. 4 (2013): 766–85.

FIGURE 4 Survey results of Japanese sentiments toward South Korea, 1984–2015

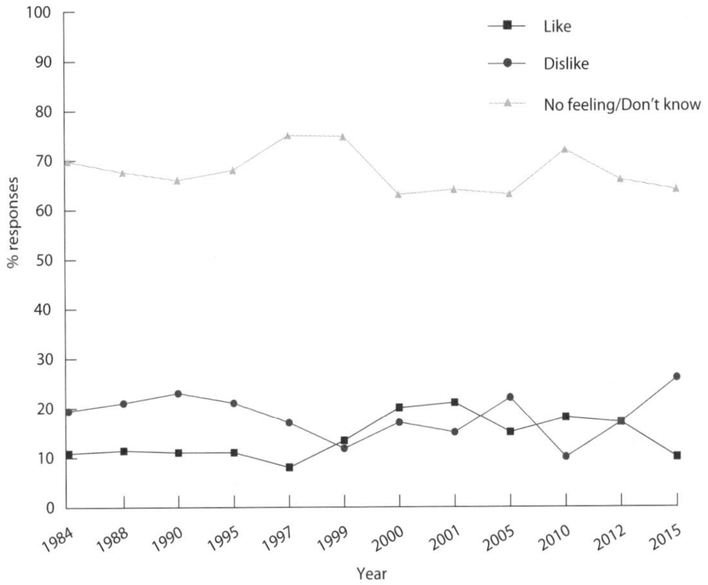

SOURCE: *Dong-A Ilbo* and *Asahi Shimbun*, 1984–2015.

South Koreans have consistently disliked Japan. In 1984, around 39% of South Koreans "disliked" Japan, while a historical high of 22% "liked Japan." The percentage of South Koreans who like Japan fell to a low of nearly 5% in 1990 and registered only 6% in 2015. Dislike for Japan peaked in 1995 at 69% and in 2015 was 50%. As for Japan, the predominant feeling is one of apathy or uncertainty, with a large percentage of Japanese since the 1980s responding that they have no particular feelings toward South Korea one way or the other. The percentage of Japanese who like South Korea peaked in 2001 at 21% but by 2015 was only 10%, while the percentage of those who are uncertain peaked in 1997 at 75% and in 2015 was 64%. The negative sentiments thus seem to flow more strongly in one direction, from South Korea to Japan, although neither country particularly likes the other.

To place ROK-Japan relations in perspective, however, fairly strong and deeply rooted institutional structures still weave the two states together. For instance, the existing parliamentarians' unions in Japan and South Korea have been active since the early 1970s, and have since managed to hold a total of 39 annual general assemblies from 1972 to 2015.[56] Even though issues of high politics, such as forging the General Security of Military Information Agreement, are still quite challenging, it was only in December 2015 that South Korea and China started operating a hotline between their top defense officials,[57] whereas a similar direct telephone channel linking South Korea and Japan was established back in 1999. In this context, relations have improved significantly, even in the 1980s when Japan, rather than China, was widely perceived as a threat. In short, while it is true that protracted tensions and lingering animosity will make it unlikely that the ROK-Japan relationship will be one of cooperation in the near future, as is perhaps hoped for by many in the United States, tensions are mostly political rather than military. The two countries' economic relations are quite deep, and the overall relationship is not insurmountably tumultuous.

Conclusion

Historical and external sources have shaped the threat perception of South Korea and its enduring strategic culture: specifically, its relative ease in dealing with China and its resentment and distrust toward Japan. Meanwhile, the more contemporary and internal sources that have shaped South Korean strategic culture come from the country's experience with a highly compressed and incomplete process of modernization and democratization that has generated a structure with little to no perceived room for agency and choice. This has come to inform South Korea's foreign policy stance and reinforce such values as autonomy and independence. The ROK's conception of power and the continued role that North Korea has played in shaping South Korea's commitment to expressing power as national capabilities exhibit strong military and security undertones.

South Korea's pursuit of its own national interests is increasingly being co-opted into the larger U.S.-China strategic rivalry, thereby generating a misinterpretation about the country's behavior and the likelihood of it taking sides. Perhaps the most important lesson is that the ROK will probably never have the strategic priorities that the United States may expect or desire. Yet Seoul has embraced the U.S.-ROK alliance, and even more so it has embraced the contemporary U.S.-led international order and its institutions. South Korean and U.S. observers widely agree that the alliance is stronger than ever; all of this is true. Leaders in Seoul, as well as the South Korean public more

---

[56] Jiun Bang, "Parliamentarians' Unions in Japan and South Korea: Parliamentary Diplomacy in Northeast Asia," in *Diplomatic Studies*, ed. Stelios Stavridis and Davor Jancic (forthcoming).

[57] "S. Korea, China Establish Military Hotline," Yonhap, December 31, 2015, http://english.yonhapnews.co.kr/news/2015/12/31/0200000000AEN20151231006500315.html?3985eca0.

generally, view close relations with the United States as a key element of the ROK's grand strategy and foreign policy.

But South Korea has just as often chosen to make decisions that avoid cleaving too closely to the United States, and this pattern is unlikely to change in the future. South Korea has an enduring and close relationship with the United States, but it also desires good relations with its regional neighbors, particularly China. The evidence is consistent and broad that Koreans do not view China with the same skepticism that either Japanese or Americans do. This is not simply a recent function of a few incidents but rather an enduring element of South Korean strategic culture. It is unlikely that one or two negative incidents will swing Korean attitudes and approaches to China away from a generally positive view. South Koreans frame many foreign relations with China in commercial rather than strategic terms. South Korea has pushed back against a massive China for centuries while retaining its own independent national identity, and that is unlikely to change. Perhaps most importantly, the South Korean public feels far less threatened by China than perhaps people in other countries do. In this context, Park Geun-hye's attendance at the 70th anniversary of the end of World War II in Beijing, also attended by Xi Jinping and Vladimir Putin, was not a mistake or a miscalculation on her part. Nor was it an instrumental strategic visit, made with hopes of gaining Chinese support on North Korea. Rather, Park attended the event because South Korea and China share many similar views about the war, its consequences, and its impact on their two countries. The only foreseeable developments that may severely dislodge the two are if China's unconditional support of North Korea increases exponentially to the point that it neutralizes South Korea's own efforts at pressuring the North, or if Seoul's relations with Tokyo progress enough that this bilateral component makes the U.S.-Japan-ROK trilateral framework that much more functional and lucrative at the expense of some discord with China. Both scenarios, however, are unlikely.

Similarly, South Korea's decision to finally deploy THAAD and the muted Chinese reaction to it are further evidence of a complex and relatively mature relationship between the two sides. South Korea and China might not be close, but they know how to deal with each other. Beijing largely knew and accepted that South Korea would deploy THAAD, although the timing was perhaps sooner than Beijing had expected. And despite rhetorical denunciation of the deployment, deep down Seoul knows that China would also prefer to disaggregate politics and economics and limit any spillover from the former to the latter. This does not, of course, stop Beijing from doing its best to express its displeasure with the deal on a diplomatic level: efforts in August 2016 by the UN Security Council to adopt a statement that denounced North Korea's ballistic missile tests were apparently thwarted by Beijing's demand to include in the statement its opposition to South Korea's decision to host THAAD.[58]

More directly, often overlooked as Western observers try to make sense of South Korea's relatively workmanlike relations with China is that both countries share very similar viewpoints on a number of key issues. Both China and South Korea interpret the first half of the twentieth century the same way—as a time of victimhood. Both see Japan as the key cause of the tumult of the twentieth century. Both see Japan's ostensible intransigence on issues of history as the key obstacle to better regional relations, and both have enduring maritime disputes with Japan that date from the Japanese imperial period. In short, on many issues, China and South Korea see the world similarly. It is no surprise then that an event commemorating the end of the Pacific War might have a South Korean attendee but not a Japanese one.

In contrast, ROK-Japan relations will probably never be as warm as the United States wishes, and the cause is not myopia or naiveté on the part of South Koreans but rather arises from a deep and enduring worldview. A recent example was the appointment of Tomomi Inada as Japanese defense minister in August 2016. She openly denies the Nanjing massacre and visits the Yasukuni Shrine. Inada was once barred from entering South Korea because she had plans to visit Dokdo, and she made removal of the "comfort women" statue a key issue in the recently concluded accords between the two sides.[59] The U.S. press has emphasized the significance of the appointment of Inada as the first female defense minister in Japan, while yet again completely overlooking the South Korean concerns as trivial. But these concerns are a result of a deeply held understanding about the causes of war, imperialism, and the peninsular division in which Korea is still caught. Japan is implicated in the events of the twentieth century in Korea, and continued intransigence by key Japanese officials provokes disapprobation in South Korea across the political spectrum. This situation will not change simply because the United States views the issues differently. While South Korea and Japan can cooperate on some issues, Korean skepticism of Japanese motives and intentions is unlikely to change significantly in the short run.

Given these deeply rooted principles of South Korean strategic culture, the task for the United States may be to work within the contours of this culture rather than trying to convince South Koreans to view

---

[58] "China's THAAD Objection Thwarts UNSC's Push to Denounce N. Korea's Missile Launches," Yonhap, August 10, 2016, http://english.yonhapnews.co.kr/news/2016/08/10/0200000000A EN20160810005651315.html.

[59] Eric Johnston, "Abe's Defense Minister Pick Sparks Concern over Relations with South Korea," *Japan Times*, August 3, 2016, http://www.japantimes.co.jp/news/2016/08/03/national/politics-diplomacy/ abes-defense-minister-pick-sparks-concern-relations-south-korea.

the world differently. The implications for the United States are fairly clear. The ROK desires a close relationship with the United States but is unlikely to significantly alter its stance toward either Japan or China just because Washington wants it to. There will always be attempts at trilateral cooperation among Japan, South Korea, and the United States, but gains will likely be harder to achieve than expected. The United States' understanding of South Korea's attempts to avoid being caught in U.S.-China rivalry will also help relations remain smooth.

South Korea as a case study has larger implications for the future of regional security: although some countries clearly wish to choose between the United States and China, most East Asian countries want good relations with both great powers. Accurately understanding East Asian regional perceptions and grand strategies is central to U.S. policy in East Asia. The key debate over U.S. policy in the region is whether priority should be given to diplomatic and economic or military concerns. The Obama administration's "rebalance" to Asia is often seen simply as a military response to China's rise. However, if East Asian states have limited defense spending because they see few direct threats to their survival and prefer to use multilateral institutions and diplomacy to deal with issues that arise, then the U.S. rebalance should emphasize diplomatic and economic engagement. Asia is in sync with the United States' desire to share burdens—the result of fiscal constraints in the United States and a desire to strengthen regional architecture. This study of South Korean strategic culture reveals that the region may be more stable than is popularly believed, and that the U.S. rebalance to Asia should remain focused on diplomatic and economic initiatives and not be sidetracked too much by military concerns. If there is no incipient containment coalition in East Asia, then worries about war and the need for a muscular U.S. military presence are perhaps overstated.

EXECUTIVE SUMMARY

This chapter analyzes India's strategic culture in terms of the cultural resources on which its strategic elite draws, the main traditions of strategic thought, and their influence on India's behavior.

MAIN ARGUMENT

India's strategic culture is informed by ideas taken from Hindu texts, nineteenth- and twentieth-century religious revivalists, and modernist thinkers. These ideas shape three traditions of strategic thought: Nehruvianism, realpolitik, and Hindu nationalism. The Nehruvian tradition has been dominant since independence in 1947, underpinning a commitment to strategic restraint; the other two traditions are less influential on policy but important because of the potential alternatives they offer to Nehruvianism. Moreover, if the Hindu nationalist tradition did begin to assert greater influence over India's strategic culture, Indian behavior would likely remain restrained, as that tradition emphasizes achieving domestic social unity as a precondition for the international recognition of Indian greatness.

POLICY IMPLICATIONS

- Although India continues to grow in economic and military power, it remains wedded to strategic restraint, underpinned by the Nehruvian tradition of strategic thought and practice, which will continue to shape its approach not just to South Asia but also to China and the U.S.

- Given that India's strategic elite remains concerned with status-seeking and recognition of civilizational greatness, and remains skeptical about elements of the contemporary liberal international order, India is unlikely to align itself fully with Western policy agendas.

- The U.S. and other states will need to allow India time to further modernize its economy, develop its military capabilities, and finesse its approach to regional security. Policy and behavioral consistency will also be required to entrench the perception in the minds of India's strategic elite that the U.S. is a credible and reliable long-term strategic partner for India.

The Persistence of Nehruvianism in India's Strategic Culture

Ian Hall

India's elite is convinced that the modern state of India is the inheritor of a great and long-lived civilization, which should be accorded particular respect and status, regardless of modern India's economic or military power.[1] At the same time, this elite recognizes that the present international system is both hierarchical and anarchical, composed of a few rich and strong states and a larger group of poorer and weaker states, without an executive authority to enforce international law and deliver a modicum of international justice. It views the United Nations and the UN Charter as imperfect means of mitigating both the exploitation of the weak and the worse effects of anarchy. Yet it also looks forward to a "polycentric order" of a number of strong states, both Western and non-Western, that would boost the autonomy and lessen the dependence of all.[2]

Ian Hall is a Professor of International Relations at Griffith University in Brisbane, Australia, and the Acting Director of the Griffith Asia Institute. He can be reached at <i.hall@griffith.edu.au>.

The author thanks Manjari Chatterjee Miller for detailed comments on a draft of the chapter, Devesh Kapur for his invitation to present that draft at a Center for the Advanced Study of India workshop at the University of Pennsylvania, and all the participants at that workshop for their helpful input. He is also grateful to two anonymous reviewers for their suggestions for improvement. Any errors of fact or judgment are the author's own.

[1] For more on India's civilizational mindset, see Shrikant Paranjpe, *India's Strategic Culture: The Making of National Security Policy* (New Delhi: Routledge, 2013), 15; Rohan Mukherjee, "Statuspolitik as Foreign Policy: Strategic Culture and India's Nuclear Behavior" (unpublished manuscript), 6–7; and Baldev Raj Nayar and T.V. Paul, *India in the World Order: Searching for Major-Power Status* (Cambridge: Cambridge University Press, 2003).

[2] The phrase "polycentric order" is frequently encountered. See its use, for example, in Krishnaswamy Subramanyam's introduction in Jaswant Singh, *Defending India* (Basingstoke: Macmillan, 1999), viii.

Since independence in 1947, India's elite has held conflicting attitudes about the acquisition and use of military power in international relations. On the one hand, it generally considers acquiring and using military power regrettable or even straightforwardly immoral; on the other hand, it argues that both are necessary for India's national security, within certain limits. Most of the elite also deprecate military alliances as means of managing security challenges and—at least until recently—deprecate regional institutions as alternative means. Both methods are considered contrary to the spirit of the UN Charter and risky in themselves, potentially entangling states in the conflicts of others. Slowly, however, these elite beliefs about alliances and regionalism appear to be changing as the influence of the postcolonial generation fades and a new one emerges with a different set of strategic concepts and approaches.[3]

To what extent these beliefs and arguments are functions of India's strategic culture is a question that has been hotly disputed by scholars and practitioners for 25 years. In 1992, in a seminal paper produced for the U.S. Department of Defense, George K. Tanham argued that India's strategic thought and practice were shaped by cultural influences and elite interpretations of the country's geography and history, especially the experience of British rule. Together, these factors shaped elite preferences for "strategic independence and autonomy," Tanham suggested, but also—along with severe resource constraints—limited India's capacity to construct a coherent plan to achieve these objectives.[4]

This argument prompted a number of other assessments of India's strategic culture, notably by Kanti Bajpai, Rajesh Basrur, Rodney W. Jones, Bharat Karnad, Subrata K. Misra, Shrikant Paranjpe, Rahul Sagar, and Jaswant Singh. These analysts are divided about Tanham's account, some arguing that it was "crude," and others endorsing or at least tacitly agreeing with his conclusion that India's elite struggles to think and act strategically as a result of the distinct set of ideas and practices that shape the culture of policymaking.[5] In particular, some worry that deep-seated and wrongheaded ideological convictions, as well the habits of *jugaad* (last-minute improvisation) and excessive secrecy, continue to prevent the emergence of sound strategy.[6]

---

[3] Ian Hall, "Multialignment and Indian Foreign Policy under Narendra Modi," *Round Table: The Commonwealth Journal of International Affairs* 105, no. 3 (2016): 271–86.

[4] George K. Tanham, *Indian Strategic Thought: An Interpretive Essay* (Santa Monica: RAND Corporation, 1992). The paper was summarized in George K. Tanham, "Indian Strategic Culture," *Washington Quarterly* 15, no. 1 (1992): 129–42.

[5] Rajesh Basrur, "Nuclear Weapons and Indian Strategic Culture," *Journal of Peace Research* 38, no. 2 (2001): 183. Among those in tacit agreement are Bharat Karnad and Jaswant Singh.

[6] On ideology, see Bharat Karnad, *Why India Is Not a Great Power (Yet)* (New Delhi: Oxford University Press, 2015). On *jugaad*, see Sandy Gordon, *India's Rise to Power* (Basingstoke: Macmillan, 1995), 5–6.

This chapter draws on, criticizes, and extends this literature. To assess the extent and nature of the influence of strategic culture over India's strategic thought and behavior, the chapter is divided into three sections. The first explores the sources of India's strategic culture, especially the texts, concepts, and arguments that India's elite has inherited from the country's ancient past and the anti-imperial struggle against British rule. The second section examines the three dominant traditions of thought about strategy that have emerged in India since independence. Each tradition is composed of sets of beliefs about international relations and India's role in the world, accounts of its national interests, and assessments of the threats that the country faces and the best means of countering those threats. The third section analyzes the impact of India's strategic culture on its strategic behavior, in particular the country's policies and practices regarding the acquisition and use of military power to further its interests or enhance its security. The conclusion argues that, since independence, India has seen shifts in foreign policy but consistency in strategic culture. This strategic culture emphasizes a desire for status and autonomy, on the one hand, and a perceived need for relative restraint concerning the acquisition and use of force in international relations, on the other.

Sources of Indian Strategic Culture

Indian strategic culture is shaped—as other states' strategic cultures are shaped—by the interpretations of India's geography and history of various scholars, sages, analysts, and practitioners, each making use of concepts and arguments derived from the country's extraordinarily rich and varied intellectual inheritance.[7] These interpretations generally acknowledge the unusual geographic context of South Asia, bounded by the Himalayas to the north, the Indian Ocean to the south, and hills and jungle to the east, which ought to provide security. They also highlight its historical experience of successive invasions, mainly from the northwest, via what is now Afghanistan and Pakistan, but also from the sea, that led to the conquest and domination of large parts of the subcontinent by outsiders.[8] They note that these successive

---

[7] Alastair Iain Johnston rightly argues that explanations of strategic behavior that depend on strategic culture should describe the process of socialization in which an elite is acquainted with key ideas and dominant interpretations. See Alastair Iain Johnston, "Thinking about Strategic Culture," *International Security* 19, no. 4 (1995): 32–64. In the Indian case, sadly, we do not yet have systematic accounts of the ideas taught to members of the Indian Foreign Service, Indian Administrative Service, or higher ranks of the military. For this reason, this chapter must infer the ideas that inform Indian strategic culture from texts produced by the strategic elite.

[8] It should be noted that France and Portugal also ruled significant territories in India. France held various towns, including Pondicherry (now Puducherry), Karaikal, Yanam, and Mahe, between 1668 and 1954; Portugal held Goa between 1510 and its forcible return to India in 1961.

migrations of peoples have transformed South Asia, including Indo-Aryan migrations in the Iron Age, later Persian and Greek invasions, various movements of Muslim peoples from the eighth to the twelfth centuries, the Mughal supremacy from 1526 to 1857, and modern European intrusions into the subcontinent from the sixteenth century onward. These interpretations also observe the deleterious effects of the partition of British India into the modern states of Myanmar, India, and Pakistan (with the latter itself splitting into Pakistan and Bangladesh in 1971), and the post-imperial estrangement of these states from others in the region that were once tied to the British Empire and to earlier South Asian polities, including Afghanistan, Bhutan, Myanmar, Nepal, and Sri Lanka.

Moreover, the interpretations of South Asian geography and history that inform India's strategic culture grapple with issues that are not at the forefront of the minds of Western strategic elites: with intercivilizational and religious conflict and accommodation; with the social and political implications of significant differences of religious and philosophical belief; with legacies of imperial rule by autochthonous and foreign elites; with issues, in other words, of cultural as well as political and economic unity and disunity.

Last, the intellectual resources that inform these interpretations are diffuse. They represent a range of views about social life in general, the best ways to approach strategic policymaking and practice, and justifications for different strategic decisions. These resources can be crudely divided into two sets: classic Hindu texts and texts produced in the modern period by various thinkers, including Hindu revivalists, modernists, and politicians informed by both broad intellectual traditions.[9]

Classic Hindu Texts

The first set of intellectual resources consists of the very large collection of Hindu texts that have accumulated since the so-called Vedic period, commonly dated to around 1500–500 BCE. These comprise prescriptions and justifications of religious practices, which include the so-called Vedas;

---

[9] These resources do not, of course, exhaust the intellectual resources that India's strategic elite could use. Modern India is the inheritor of substantial bodies of strategic thought and practice from the Mughal period and the Raj. These are rarely referenced by India's elite after 1947, however, except as foils; instead, the elite sought to establish a new strategic approach for postcolonial India. On Mughal strategy, see Jayashree Vivekanandan, "Strategy, Legitimacy and the Imperium: Framing the Mughal Strategic Discourse," in *India's Grand Strategy: History, Theory, Cases*, ed. Kanti Bajpai, Saira Basit, and V. Krishnappa (New Delhi: Routledge, 2014), 63–85. On British strategy, see Lawrence James, *Raj: The Making and Unmaking of British India* (London: Abacus, 1998), 63–78. Contemporary accounts and later historical studies of the strategies of various ancient, medieval, and early modern Hindu, Muslim, and Sikh kingdoms, including those of the Marathas and Nizam of Hyderabad, are also significant in themselves but not influential on modern Indian strategic thought. See Paranjpe, *India's Strategic Culture*, 11–42.

philosophical meditations, such as the Upanishads; epic stories with moral lessons, such as the *Mahabharata* or *Ramayana*; and collections of knowledge about various subjects. The latter are divided into two main categories: the *sutras*, which are compendia of aphorisms, and the *shastras*, which are more systematic treatises. The latter group includes a major text on the science of government, the *Arthashastra*.

These texts advance a series of different accounts of human relations with the gods, the nature of the universe, and the correct path to knowledge, among other issues. Indeed, scholars identify at least six major philosophical traditions originating in ancient India, some central to Hinduism and some to Buddhism and Jainism, which both trace their origins to the era of social turmoil at the end of the Vedic period.[10] The sheer complexity of Hindu thought and practice thus provides Indian analysts and practitioners with a wide range of textual authorities from which to draw in their strategic analyses. It also makes it difficult for both Indians and outsiders to credibly describe a single Hindu tradition of strategic thought, though scholars have identified three philosophical dispositions derived from Hindu thinking that likely shape Indian strategic culture: fatalism, moralism, and activism.

In his RAND paper, Tanham argued that fatalism and moralism best characterize Indian strategic culture. For evidence, he pointed to the *Bhagavad Gita*, part of the epic *Mahabharata*, the well-known story of a great war between two families.[11] The *Bhagavad Gita* supposedly relates Krishna's advice to a protagonist, Arjuna, who is wavering about whether he should fight in that war, risk his life, and kill others. Krishna's advice is that Arjuna must fulfill the *dharma* (roughly, duty) that his *varna* (roughly, caste) prescribes: as a *kshatriya* (warrior), he has a binding obligation to fight, regardless of his reservations about that path of action.[12] Tanham argued that this story illustrates a blend of the fatalism (one should accept one's lot in life) and moralism (one should do one's duty, according to one's lot) that are characteristic of Hinduism and Indian strategic culture.

Other analysts of Indian strategic culture point to an activist disposition in Hindu texts that they think is influential, locating it especially in the *Arthashastra*, the ancient manual of statecraft attributed to Kautilya,

---

[10] For a careful account of the historical evolution of Hinduism, see Andrew J. Nicholson, *Unifying Hinduism: Philosophy and Identity in Indian Intellectual History* (New York: Columbia University Press, 2014). For a primer on ancient and medieval Indian philosophy, see Sue Hamilton, *Indian Philosophy: A Very Short Introduction* (Oxford: Oxford University Press, 2001).

[11] Tanham, *Indian Strategic Thought*, 15. The text of the *Bhagavad Gita* (Song of the Lord) was composed, along with the rest of the *Mahabharata*, somewhere between the fourth century BCE and fourth century CE from earlier oral sources. See *Mahabharata*, John D. Smith, trans. (London: Penguin, 2009), xvii.

[12] *Mahabharata*, 353–66.

which dates to the time of the Mauryan empire in the fourth century BCE.[13] Although consistent with the religious injunction that individuals should perform their dharma according to their varna, the *Arthashastra* is neither fatalistic nor moralistic. It focuses on what Kautilya called the practical "science of wealth and welfare" (*artha*) in this world rather than on the salvation of souls. It represents, in other words, a tradition of action-oriented thought in ancient South Asia. The *Arthashastra* assumes that events can be manipulated to the advantage of those who study them methodically and act in accordance with the right philosophical maxims about good and bad policies and, crucially for strategists, the "distinction between good and bad use of force."[14] To that end, the *Arthashastra* provides frank, pragmatic advice on the punishment of crime and rebellion, covert operations in foreign policy, and the conduct of war.

Modern Texts and Ideas

The second set of resources used by India's postcolonial elite includes works by the various religious thinkers, philosophers, and practitioners who emerged from the early nineteenth century onward and shaped the nationalist struggle against British rule. These thinkers provided new and influential interpretations of classic Buddhist, Hindu, and Jain texts, as well as influential interpretations of India's experience of Mughal and British imperial rule. They also supplied accounts of how Hindus and Indians should act in the modern world—how they should regain their confidence, rebuild their nation and construct a state, and interact with other societies.

These thinkers include the Bengali intellectual Swami Vivekananda (1863–1902), who was educated in the Western liberal tradition but became a devotee of the mystic Ramakrishna Paramahamsa. Vivekananda was one of a number of Hindu intellectuals who tried to reground Hinduism to better resist criticisms from Western rationalists and Christians, restore confidence to Hindus, and provide a template for a future postcolonial Hindu nation.[15] According to Vivekananda, Hinduism teaches that God and all creations are

---

[13] Kautilya, *Arthashastra*, ed. and trans. L.N. Rangarajan (New Delhi: Penguin, 1992). On Kautilya's supposed influence on Indian strategic culture, see Lucian W. Pye, *Asian Power and Politics: The Cultural Dimensions of Authority* (Cambridge: Belknap Press, 1985), 138–39; and George J. Gilboy and Eric Heginbotham, *Chinese and Indian Strategic Behavior: Growing Power and Alarm* (Cambridge: Cambridge University Press, 2012), 25–32. On Kautilya's ideas more broadly, see George Modelski, "Kautilya: Foreign Policy and International System in the Ancient Hindu World," *American Political Science Review* 58, no. 3 (1964): 549–60; and Roger Boesche, *The First Great Political Realist: Kautilya and His Arthashastra* (Lanham: Lexington Books, 2003).

[14] Kautilya, *Arthashastra*, 84.

[15] On Vivekananda and his influence on Hindu nationalism, see especially Jyotimaya Sharma, *A Restatement of Religion: Swami Vivekananda and the Making of Hindu Nationalism* (New Haven: Yale University Press, 2013).

one in the world and that there are many valid paths to God. The mission of Indians and Hindus is to spread this message, which would help end "fanaticism and religious wars," which "mar the life of man and the progress of civilisation."[16]

Vivekananda rejected fatalism and embraced activism. He argued that Hindus needed to engage in what he called *karma-yoga* (loosely, social work) for the betterment of society, using modern ideas and techniques appropriated from the West. Vivekananda desired a "European society with India's religion," believing that as India mastered modern science and technology, it would rise to conquer its former imperial masters—both Muslim and Western—with the superior spiritual power of Hinduism.[17]

By contrast, Mohandas Gandhi (1869–1948) taught that to restore India to its former standing in the world and shape its future, Hindus should reject these elements of modern Western culture and instead embrace Buddhist and Jain ideas, notably *ahimsa* (loosely, nonviolence).[18] Gandhi argued that by embracing nonviolence and using what he called *satyagraha* (soul force or truth force)—speaking truth to imperial power regardless of the consequences—Indians could end British rule and restore their independence. In contrast to Hindu revivalists like Vivekananda, however, Gandhi argued that, once independent, Indians should eschew the pursuit of power and instead return to traditional forms of life, centered on the village and underpinned by a commitment to *swadeshi* (economic self-reliance).

India's anticolonial movement and the postcolonial state were also influenced by the ideas of secular modernists, above all Jawaharlal Nehru (1889–1964), who became India's first prime minister in 1947 and governed until his death in 1964. Nehru's thought drew together a liberal tradition that included figures such as G.K. Gokhale (1866–1915) with a socialist perspective that emerged in the interwar period, which Nehru encountered as a student at Cambridge and then in London.

The modernists were moralists and activists, not fatalists. Nehru described his philosophy as "scientific humanism," laying out a progressive, modernizing vision, which contrasted with Hindu revivalism and Gandhi's idealization of India as a collection of self-sufficient villages.[19] Nehru agreed with Gandhi that satyagraha could be an effective mode of bringing about

---

[16] Swami Vivekananda, *The Nationalistic and Religious Lectures of Swami Vivekananda* (Calcutta: Advaita Ashrama, 1990), 13, 17.

[17] Quoted in Sharma, *Restatement of Religion,* 117–18.

[18] There are many excellent studies of Gandhi's life and thought. See especially the controversial but insightful Kathryn Tidrick, *Gandhi: A Political and Spiritual Life,* rev. ed. (London: Verso, 2013).

[19] Rodney W. Jones, "India's Strategic Culture," U.S. Defense Threat Reduction Agency, October 31, 2006, 12, http://fas.org/irp/agency/dod/dtra/india.pdf.

social change. However, he believed that other methods, including the use of military power, could sometimes be used, and that swadeshi should be pursued at a national level to give India the independence and autonomy it needed in the world. Like Gandhi, he also admired the moral leadership of ancient and modern Indians, especially the Buddhist king Ashoka, who embraced ahimsa after forging his empire.[20] Nehru's aim was to build and reform the country into a wealthy and modern society conscious of its religious and cultural inheritance but governed by a secular state that mixed British constitutionalism and parliamentarianism with new techniques of economic planning, informed by the most up-to-date scientific knowledge.[21]

Modernist nationalists like Nehru shared with the Hindu revivalists and other religious thinkers like Gandhi the desire to remove the British from India, the conviction that India has some kind of essential unity, the idea that dependence on other states must be avoided, and the belief that the greatness of Indian civilization must and will eventually be recognized by others. Partition, therefore, came as a severe blow to their sense of what India is and should be: a blow to modernists who believed that the aspirations and interests of Indian Hindus and Muslims (and others) could be accommodated within a properly constituted modern state, and a blow to Hindu revivalists who believed (and still believe) that an essentially Hindu South Asian *Akhand Bharat* (undivided India) had a primal unity that must be realized in some political form after independence.

Traditions of Strategic Culture

Since 1947, three traditions of thought and practice have vied for preeminence among India's strategic elite, each drawing in different ways on the intellectual resources outlined above.[22] By far the most dominant is the Nehruvian tradition, which has a broadly instrumental view of the utility of military force, overlaid by a set of moral arguments derived from both Indian and Western sources about the limits that ought to be imposed on its use and the detrimental political and economic effects of investing too heavily in a state's armed forces.[23] Alongside this tradition sit two others, both critical of the Nehruvian orthodoxy. The first is what might be best termed amoral realpolitik, also derived from both Western and Indian sources. The second

---

[20] For more on this admiration, see Jawaharlal Nehru, *The Discovery of India* (New Delhi: Penguin, 2004).

[21] Judith M. Brown, *Nehru: A Political Life* (New Haven: Yale University Press, 2002), 189, 196–97, 204–9, 224–36.

[22] Jones, "India's Strategic Culture," 20–21.

[23] Kanti Bajpai, "Through a Looking Glass: Strategic Prisms and the Pakistan Problem," *India International Centre Quarterly* 28, no. 2 (2001): 121–24.

is an assertive Hindu nationalist tradition that has a conception of the value of military force and its utility in international relations that is distinct from both the Nehruvian and the realpolitik traditions. The realpolitik tradition sees the threat and use of force in essentially instrumental and amoral terms, arguing that India ought to build and wield as much power as is necessary to secure and extend its interests in an anarchical international system. Hindu nationalism expresses a more conflicted view: it sees the need for military power in today's world but also looks beyond this world to one in which, once the spiritual truths of the *sanatana dharma* (loosely, eternal religion) are recognized by all, it no longer will be necessary to possess or use such power.

The Nehruvian Tradition

The Nehruvian tradition has been the mainstream tradition of Indian strategic thought since independence and has done the most to shape India's strategic culture. It blends moralism derived from Hindu, Buddhist, and Jain sources via the thought of Gandhi and others with Nehru's activist disposition, while emphasizing the limited capacity that a relatively poor and weak state has to shape the international system to better fit its interests and aspirations. It holds that dependence must be avoided and self-reliance pursued if India is to act autonomously in the world. This tradition also conceives of military power as a necessary instrument of states in a world of power politics but recognizes it as a tool of oppression and regrets the diversion of funds from projects addressing social needs to the building and maintaining of military forces. It asserts that, because of both moral and pragmatic considerations, military power should be accumulated cautiously and wielded with the utmost restraint.

For Nehruvians, the relationship between India's greatness as a civilization and its material weakness is—and should be—at the center of Indian strategic calculation. Elevating status-seeking to become a policy priority,[24] they make the recognition of India's civilizational inheritance, moral wisdom, and past suffering at the hands of successive invaders core aims for Indian politicians and diplomats, alongside the pursuit of more prosaic national interests.[25] But at the same time, Nehruvians argue that India lacks the material power to exercise decisive influence on the international system by economic or

---

[24] Mukherjee, "Statuspolitik as Foreign Policy," 6–7; Nayar and Paul, *India in the World Order*; and Deepa Ollapally, "Mixed Motives in India's Search for Nuclear Status," *Asian Survey* 41, no. 6 (2001): 925–42.

[25] On demands for recognition of past suffering in Indian foreign policy, see especially Manjari Chatterjee Miller, *Wronged by Empire: Post-Imperial Ideology and Foreign Policy in India and China* (Stanford: Stanford University Press, 2013).

military means. Until it acquires these means, India must rely instead on moral appeals and careful diplomacy.

Nehruvians recognize the reality that power politics persist in contemporary international relations. To that extent, they are realists, though their realism is tempered by the belief in moral progress: power politics will, they argue, come to an end when the world (especially the Western world) realizes the error of its ways.[26] Nehruvians also treat military power with caution, conscious that armies can be tools of oppression, as the Indian Army was under the British, as well as defenders of society.[27] For these reasons, Nehruvians recognize the need to keep military forces, given the present state of the world, but insist that these forces must be kept under strict civilian control, limited in size, and used sparingly and only with restraint.

At the same time, Nehruvians conceive of India's national interests in ways that arguably generate greater need for military forces than others might. They see the whole of South Asia as India's particular and exclusive sphere of influence, a space bound together by geography, given the lack of natural barriers between the Hindu Kush in the west and the mountains of the Myanmar-Thai border to the east and between the Himalayas and the Indian Ocean. Nehruvians are generally convinced that India must retain its control over this sphere of influence and ensure that buffer states exist to help it manage the potential threat from the north from China. These perceptions generate the need for military forces capable of not just defending India but also intervening where necessary in its immediate neighborhood.

The Realpolitik Tradition

The realpolitik tradition, which some call "hyperrealist,"[28] derives inspiration from both Indian and Western thought. Realpolitikers might be characterized as fatalists insofar as they argue that India should accept the international system as it is, but they are activists insofar as they argue that India can and should improve its relative position within that system. They reject moralism as detrimental to clear thinking. Realpolitikers generally perceive that India's postcolonial political elite has shown itself to be unable to engage in the robust strategic analysis required for effective strategic policymaking and incapable of building the military force that India needs

---

[26] Nehru, *Discovery of India*, 597–610; and Stephen P. Cohen, *India: Emerging Power* (Washington, D.C.: Brookings Institution Press, 2002), 39.

[27] Nehruvians also recognize that at no point—at least after 1857—did the British Indian Army fight for independence. See Stephen Peter Rosen, *Societies and Military Power: India and Its Armies* (Ithaca: Cornell University Press, 1996), 198.

[28] Bajpai, "Through a Looking Glass," 127–29.

to maintain its national security and pursue its national interests.[29] Instead, the realpolitikers complain that Nehruvian-influenced India has settled for "inexpensive, low-risk prestige."[30]

A few—but by no means all—Indian realpolitikers draw on Hindu texts to construct their arguments. Bharat Karnad, for example, peppers his most recent book with references to the *Rig Veda* and Kautilya.[31] In the main, however, they take their inspiration from both classical and structural realist work originating in the West and are best seen as modernists in the vein of Gokhale and Nehru rather than that of Vivekananda or Gandhi.[32] Realpolitikers conceive of the international system as anarchical and argue that states should seek power to ensure their national security and advance their national interests. They argue that India must eschew its historical obsessions with status and moral causes and become a "normal" state, building and utilizing military power in the same way as other major powers.[33] Some also take a significant interest in geopolitics, including the work of Alfred Thayer Mahan, Halford Mackinder, and Nicholas Spykman.[34]

In particular, the realpolitikers argue that India must build capabilities that will allow it to deter potential threats, proactively and effectively defend itself when attacked, and project military power in support of India's wider regional and international interests. They are advocates of a "firm India" akin to the United States or Israel.[35] To that end, some Indian realpolitikers have long advocated that India acquire a credible nuclear capability with sufficient warheads and reliable delivery systems to deter possible Chinese aggression, as well as intervention from other great powers.[36]

Like many realists in the West, Indian realpolitikers are often "small l" liberals in domestic politics, though some have sympathy with Hindu

---

[29] "The state," Verghese Koithara argues, "has been consistently incapable of assessing objectively what needed to be done, and also what could be done if a determined effort were to be made." See Verghese Koithara, *Society, State and Security: The Indian Experience* (New Delhi: Sage Publications, 1999), 97.

[30] Ibid., 98.

[31] Karnad, *Why India Is Not a Great Power (Yet)*, 62, 75, 167.

[32] See, for example, the work of Harsh V. Pant (such as "A Rising India's Search for a Foreign Policy," *Orbis* 53, no. 2 (2009): 250–64), who draws on American classical realism, and compare with the work of Rajesh Basrur (such as "Theory for Strategy: Emerging India in a Changing World," *South Asian Survey* 16, no. 1 (2009): 5–21), who draws on structural realism.

[33] For more on pursuing India's modern interests, see especially C. Raja Mohan, *Crossing the Rubicon: The Shaping of India's New Foreign Policy* (New York: Palgrave, 2003).

[34] For more on this criticism, see Karnad, *Why India Is Not a Great Power (Yet)*, 106–7.

[35] Subrata Mitra, "The Reluctant Hegemon: India's Self-Perception and the South Asian Strategic Environment," *Contemporary South Asia* 12, no. 3 (2003): 413.

[36] For more on these nuclear aspirations, see, for example, the introduction of Bharat Karnad, ed., *Future Imperilled: India's Security in the 1990s and Beyond* (New Delhi: Viking, 1994), 10–11; and Bharat Karnad, *Nuclear Weapons and Indian Security: The Realist Foundations of Strategy*, 4th ed. (New Delhi: Macmillan, 2005).

nationalism or at least with the Bharatiya Janata Party (BJP), and some of the latter do borrow and adapt their ideas.[37] Unlike Hindu nationalists, however, who are ambivalent and split on this issue, Indian realpolitikers seek social and economic modernization to lay the foundation for national power. They accept that this may involve greater liberalization, but unlike liberals they do not believe that greater engagement and interdependence in the global economy will diminish the possibility of conflict or mitigate the threats that India faces. Rather, they look to modernization and liberalization as the means required to build the necessary resources to strengthen the military and give politicians the capacity to use force to secure India's national interests when needed.[38]

The Hindu Nationalist Tradition

Like the Nehruvians and realpolitikers, Hindu nationalists conceive of military power as a means to an end, but that end is the general recognition of the greatness of Hinduism and the truth of the sanatana dharma. In that sense, they are moralists above all. Unlike the realpolitikers, Hindu nationalists do not see an anarchical international system as a permanent feature of world politics, do not reduce national power to military power, and do not believe that all policy priorities should be subordinated—at least in the long run—to the building of military power. Instead, they argue that power politics will ultimately be replaced by more peaceful forms of interaction between states, that national power is a function of the unity and strength of civil society rather than just of the quantity and quality of military forces, and that globalization and liberalization should be moderated to protect Hindu values, even at the expense of faster or more effective military modernization. Like Nehruvians, Hindu nationalists are convinced that Hindus are fundamentally peaceful people, or at least that when the rest of the world acknowledges the truths that Hinduism offers, the world will become more peaceful.

Indeed, Hindu nationalists generally assume that the anarchical international system will be superseded by a less conflictual alternative. As Rahul Sagar observes, prominent nationalists like V.D. Savarkar looked forward to a federal world state, while M.S. Golwalkar believed that a world state giving political expression to human unity will be realized

---

[37] Sreeram S. Chaulia, "BJP, India's Foreign Policy and the 'Realist Alternative' to the Nehruvian Tradition," *International Politics* 39, no. 2 (2002): 213–34.

[38] Rahul Sagar, "State of Mind: What Kind of Power Will India Become?" *International Affairs* 85, no. 4 (2009): 810.

by transcendentalism.[39] Golwalkar argued that Hinduism will play a crucial role in bringing about a world state, as its teachings brought about a general realization of the "inner bond of harmony" between all peoples.[40] But this could only occur when Hindus had recovered their strength: "In order to be able to live and strive for the unity and welfare of the world," Golwalkar argued, "we [must] stand before the world as a self-confident, resurgent and mighty nation."[41]

For Hindu nationalists, then, the pursuit and use of military force is a regrettable but temporary necessity imposed on India by a divided world rather than a perpetual challenge, as it is for realpolitikers. Moreover, they see military power as just one expression of national power, and importantly see national power as a function of the condition of Indian civil society. Without a unified society that displays the correct degree of manliness and muscularity with regard to both domestic and international politics, they argue, a state's military forces will never be able to fulfill their true potential.[42] The priority of Hindu nationalists is the creation of a confident Hindu *rashtra* (very loosely, state) that is respectful to national minorities (Muslims, Christians, and others) but which instills in all citizens the belief that "service to the nation is the supreme end," trains Hindus "to be strong and robust," and aims to restore Akhand Bharat (undivided India) "from the Himalayas to Kanyakumari."[43]

To that end, Hindu nationalists focus first on what Golwalkar called "internal threats"—a category in which he included Muslims, both inside India and from Pakistan; Christians; and Communists—and only secondarily on external threats, with the latter considered less in terms of nation-states and more in terms of civilizations.[44] For most 19th- and 20th-century Hindu nationalists, the civilizations of concern were the West and Islam; their 21st-century successors add China to this list. To address these threats, Hindu nationalists argue that India should limit its citizens' exposure to Western materialism, Christianity, and foreign forms of Islam, as well as Chinese influence. In terms of domestic politics, this implies strict control over foreign-funded NGOs and missionaries. In foreign relations, it implies

---

[39] Rahul Sagar, "'Jiski Lathi, Uski Bhains': The Hindu Nationalist View of International Politics," in Bajpai et al., *India's Grand Strategy,* 238–44.

[40] M.S. Golwalkar, *Bunch of Thoughts,* 3rd ed. (Bangalore: Sahitya Sindhu Prakashana, 2000), 10–17.

[41] Ibid., 9.

[42] On the overt emphasis on masculinity in Hindu nationalist thought, see especially Golwalkar's "Be Men with a Capital 'M,'" in ibid., 435–48.

[43] Ibid., 172.

[44] Ibid., 177–201.

careful calibration of India's engagement with great powers, especially the United States and China, and with the global economy.

Unlike contemporary Nehruvians and realpolitikers, many Hindu nationalists continue to aspire to "strategic autonomy" underpinned by a version of swadeshi in economic policy.[45] Although BJP governments have pursued or pledged some liberalization of the Indian economy, including lowering certain barriers to trade and investment, arguments about the need for maintaining controls on foreign economic entities and ideas persist in Hindu nationalist thought. For example, Subramanian Swamy, an economist and member of the Rajya Sabha (the upper house of India's parliament), argues that "unbridled globalization" undermines Indian values. Instead, he favors a more controlled, state-led model of economic development that builds autonomy and avoids dependence.[46]

Strategic Culture, Capabilities, and Behavior

After independence, Nehru crafted a strategic policy designed for a relatively weak state to build and maintain a measure of autonomy, secure itself against internal security challenges and proximate threats from regional neighbors, and reform elements of the international system.[47] This policy had three components:

- Avoiding alliances and binding entanglements with the U.S. and Soviet superpowers and their respective blocs in a policy that came to be known as "nonalignment"

- Maintaining significant civilly controlled military forces, especially the army, to deal with internal security threats and threats from the immediate region

- Using diplomacy, especially within the UN system, and moral suasion targeted at global public opinion to bring about normative change in the international system, particularly regarding decolonization, racism, and disarmament

Together, these measures were designed to attain a sufficient measure of internal and external security at a minimal cost so that India might devote the greatest possible proportion of its resources to economic and social development.

---

[45] For more on strategic autonomy, see especially Subramanian Swamy, *Hindus Under Siege: The Way Out* (New Delhi: Har Anand, 2007).

[46] Ibid., 76–92.

[47] Jones, "India's Strategic Culture," 12.

This strategic policy meshed with the main elements of the emerging strategic culture that Nehru helped generate, including the conviction that great-power conflict would persist in the medium term due to ideological and economic competition, a pragmatic attitude toward the possession and use of force, reservations about the dangers of possessing too large or too influential a military, and a belief that India was a great civilization with an intellectual and cultural inheritance sufficiently rich for it to play the role of moral exemplar.[48] Nonalignment mixed idealistic hopes about a future international order with realistic calculations about the risks inherent in allying with one bloc or another. Maintaining a large military force, albeit with a carefully constrained budget of less than 2% of GDP,[49] and using it only when India's national interests were threatened, also reflected a Nehruvian mix of idealism and pragmatism.[50] Finally, Nehruvian faith in diplomacy reflected (in part, at least) the belief that India's intellectual and cultural inheritance, especially Buddhist and Hindu ideas about peace and coexistence, could help mitigate international conflict.[51]

Nehruvianism after Nehru

For critics, India's defeat in the 1962 border war with China demonstrated failures not just in Nehru's handling of the bilateral relationship with Beijing but also in his government's management of the armed forces, which were seen to be poorly equipped and badly led. Perhaps surprisingly, however, these criticisms did not lead to the displacement of the Nehruvian strategic culture that had emerged in the 1950s.

Instead, it persisted for a number of key reasons. Above all, India remained relatively poor and weak. Its economy struggled during the 1960s and 1970s to attain growth rates much higher than the rate of population

---

[48] For more on these beliefs, see Jawaharlal Nehru, *India's Foreign Policy: Selected Speeches, September 1946–April 1961* (New Delhi: Ministry of Information and Broadcasting, 1961). The best analysis of Nehru's thought on international relations remains A.P. Rana, "The Intellectual Dimensions of India's Nonalignment," *Journal of Asian Studies* 28, no. 2 (1969): 299–312.

[49] K. Subrahmanyam, "Indian Defence Expenditure in Global Perspective," *Economic and Political Weekly*, June 30, 1973, 1,155.

[50] See especially Srinath Raghavan, *War and Peace in Modern India* (New York: Palgrave Macmillan, 2010). Until the 1962 border war with China, India's military fought Pakistani-backed militants in Kashmir in 1947–48, engaged in a counterinsurgency operation in support of the civil power against separatist Nagas from 1956, and invaded Portuguese-run Goa in 1961. During the late 1950s and early 1960s, India was also involved in a covert effort to destabilize Chinese-ruled Tibet. On the latter, see Bruce Riedel, *JFK's Forgotten Crisis: Tibet, the CIA, and the Sino-Indian War* (Washington, D.C.: Brookings Institution Press, 2015).

[51] For more on this belief, see especially A.P. Rana, *The Imperatives of Nonalignment: A Conceptual Study of India's Foreign Policy Strategy in the Nehru Period* (New Delhi: Macmillan, 1976); and Ollapally, "Mixed Motives in India's Search for Nuclear Status," 926–27.

growth, limiting Indian ambition and assertiveness.[52] Second, the Congress Party remained in power for most of the 1960s, 1970s, and 1980s, and given Nehru's stature, it was in the interests of Congress Party leaders to identify their national security policies with his.[53] Third, most of the major political and bureaucratic figures who dominated Indian strategic policymaking in this period were appointed, mentored, or strongly influenced by Nehru in the immediate postcolonial years.[54] Fourth, endemic internal security challenges diverted much-needed resources and distracted attention from external security threats.[55] Last, India's elite became more inclined to socialist interpretations of international relations during this period, reinforcing postcolonial worries about the threats to autonomy that might result from economic dependency, as well as concerns about U.S. behavior in Southeast Asia and its alliance commitments to Pakistan.

Incremental changes to policy did, however, occur within the Nehruvian framework. Nonalignment was modified when the United States halted arms supplies to both India and Pakistan during the 1965 war, and India, still bereft of a reliable domestic defense industry, turned to the Soviet Union to ensure a reliable supply of defense technology and economic assistance. The two signed the Indo-Soviet Treaty of Friendship and Cooperation in August 1971.

After 1962, India also expanded and modernized its armed forces, which doubled in size to close to one million personnel by the middle of that decade.[56] Defense expenditures rose above 4.0% of GDP, then settled at around 3.5% in the mid to late 1960s, which was higher than the previous decade but still markedly lower than the global average.[57] These efforts to build India's forces paid off when Pakistan's attempt to reclaim Jammu and Kashmir in mid-1965 led to a swift war between the two. Following China's first nuclear test in 1964, India also initiated its own nuclear weapons

---

[52] Kaushik Basu and Annemie Maartens, "The Pattern and Causes of Economic Growth in India," *Oxford Review of Economic Policy* 23, no. 2 (2007): 143–67.

[53] For emphasis on the continuities in India's approach to foreign policy in the immediate aftermath of the 1971 treaty with the Soviet Union, see Indira Gandhi, "India and the World," *Foreign Affairs*, October 1972, 65–77.

[54] For an anecdotal account of Nehru's influence over this generation, see Jagat S. Mehta, *The Tryst Betrayed: Reflections on Diplomacy and Development* (New Delhi: Penguin, 2010).

[55] K.P.S. Gill, "The Dangers Within: Internal Security Threats," in Karnad, *Future Imperilled*, 116–31. On fears of foreign interference in internal conflicts, see Surjit Mansingh, "Indira Gandhi's Foreign Policy: Hard Realism?" in *Oxford Handbook of Indian Foreign Policy*, ed. David M. Malone, C. Raja Mohan, and Srinath Raghavan (Oxford: Oxford University Press, 2015), 111.

[56] K. Subrahmanyam, "Five Years of Indian Defence Effort in Perspective," *International Studies Quarterly* 13, no. 2 (1969): 162. See also Stephen P. Cohen and Sunil Dasgupta, *Arming without Aiming: India's Military Modernization* (Washington, D.C.: Brookings Institution Press, 2010), 8.

[57] Subrahmanyam, "Indian Defence Expenditure in Global Perspective," 1,155. Subrahmanyam also observed that Indian defense expenditures rose by an average of 5.4% per annum in the two decades between 1950 and 1970.

program, which culminated in a test in 1974, but it made no subsequent move to build or deploy a nuclear deterrent.

India also became more assertive in South Asia, particularly in the 1970s and 1980s. In December 1971, India decisively intervened in what was then East Pakistan, helping create the new state of Bangladesh. Under Indira Gandhi, it advanced a South Asian and Indian Ocean Monroe Doctrine, seeking to prevent the two superpowers from having meaningful influence in the region. In the mid-1980s, Rajiv Gandhi initiated another round of military modernization.[58] The new confidence that program helped generate was manifest in the scale of the Brasstacks exercise in 1986–87, which demonstrated India's conventional military superiority over Pakistan and caused alarm in Islamabad, as well as in Indian military interventions in Maldives and Sri Lanka in the late 1980s.

During the 1970s and 1980s, then, essential elements of the Nehruvian strategic policy, underpinning a Nehruvian strategic culture, remained in place. India continued to be formally nonaligned, albeit closer to the Soviet Union than before. It took an essentially pragmatic approach to its armed forces, sustaining and building the army, in particular, and using it assertively within South Asia when Indian interests were perceived to be under threat. India also tried periodically to bring about systemic reform in international relations through moral suasion, as Rajiv Gandhi did in the mid-1980s, for example, with his call for universal nuclear disarmament.[59]

New Expedients

Indian foreign and security policy changed significantly during and after 1991, as it used a series of tactical expedients to try to shore up India's deteriorating economic position and international standing. First, in 1991, Narasimha Rao's Congress-led government pushed through a package of reforms that partially liberalized the economy. These reforms helped generate GDP growth rates of over 6% for almost every year between 1992 and 2005 and provided greater resources for the Indian state. Second, India began a process of diplomatic re-engagement with states and institutions in East Asia—the so-called Look East policy, now called Act East under Narendra Modi. This generated several different payoffs. India gained much higher levels of aid and development assistance and greater investment

---

[58] In this phase, emphasis was placed on the hitherto relatively neglected navy, which gained an aircraft carrier (the INS *Viraat*, formerly HMS *Hermes*), a leased Soviet nuclear-powered submarine, and thirteen more Soviet and German diesel submarines. In addition, India acquired T-90 tanks, Bofors artillery pieces, Mirage-2000s, and MiG-29s.

[59] For more on Rajiv Gandhi's policies, see Harish Kapur, "India's Foreign Policy under Rajiv Gandhi," *Round Table: The Commonwealth Journal of International Affairs* 76, no. 304 (1987): 469–80.

flows from Japan, and eventually a wide-ranging strategic partnership with Tokyo. It achieved a free trade agreement with the Association of South East Asian Nations (ASEAN), concluded in 2009, as well as admission to the ASEAN Regional Forum (1996) and East Asia Summit (2005). Third, in 1998, India tested five nuclear devices and then announced that it was building a full-fledged deterrent, which would eventually involve a triad of air-launched, land-based, and sea-based weapons.[60] Although these acts led to international condemnation, they prompted the United States to commence broad-based discussions that ultimately brought India significant prizes: a ten-year bilateral defense cooperation agreement in 2005 and a deal that would allow India access to civilian nuclear technology outside the Nuclear Non-Proliferation Treaty, finalized in 2008.[61]

In the 2000s, as these tactical expedients paid off, a new phase of military modernization began, mainly through imports from Russia, the United States, and elsewhere. Again, however, this process occurred comparatively slowly, as reflected in India's relatively modest defense budgets (which ranged from 2.5% to 3.2% over the period between 1990 and 2007) and reported shortfalls in capital spending during this period.[62] At the same time, India also began to explore the possibilities inherent in bilateral strategic partnerships with key states involving potential defense technology transfers and defense cooperation agreements. Between 1998 and 2015, India formed 28 strategic partnerships of varying types, with different levels of commitment—some focused on defense and security, and others focused on access to markets or raw materials.[63] Besides deepening its engagement with the United States, India also developed key strategic partnerships with Afghanistan, China, Iran, Japan, Russia, and Vietnam, suggesting that "multialignment" might finally be replacing "nonalignment."

---

[60] For details on the program as a whole, see Ashley J. Tellis, *India's Emerging Nuclear Posture: Between Recessed Deterrent and Ready Arsenal* (Santa Monica: RAND Corporation, 2001).

[61] S. Paul Kapur and Sumit Ganguly, "The Transformation of U.S.-India Relations: An Explanation for the Rapprochement and Prospects for the Future," *Asian Survey* 47, no. 4 (2007): 642–56.

[62] Cohen and Dasgupta, *Arming without Aiming*, 18. The original data is from the Stockholm International Peace Research Institute. In most of these years, and later, a significant proportion of funds earmarked for capital expenditure on new weapons systems were returned to the Ministry of Finance. In 2014–15, for example, more than $1 billion was returned unspent. See Gurmeet Kanwal, "India's Defense Budget Is Inadequate for Military Modernization," Center for Strategic and International Studies, March 12, 2005, http://csis.org/publication/indias-defense-budget-inadequate-military-modernization.

[63] Hall, "Multialignment and Indian Foreign Policy," 278.

After Nehruvianism?

Some interpreted these changes as signaling a shift away from Nehruvianism and toward a new realism that matched some of the recommendations of the realpolitikers.[64] Others attributed some of them, including the nuclear tests conducted by the BJP-led government of Atal Bihari Vajpayee and improved relations with the United States, to the emergence of Hindu nationalism as a significant influence in strategic policymaking.[65] There are good reasons to argue, however, that Nehruvianism remains dominant in Indian strategic culture, but that realpolitik and Hindu nationalism are attracting growing levels of support within the elite. These changes are occurring for several different reasons—partly because India is becoming richer and more confident, partly because of generational change within the elite, and partly because the country's external environment is changing, demanding new responses to questions that are arguably not easily answered with Nehruvian resources.

Four areas, in particular, illustrate both the tenacity of Nehruvianism and the indicators of change: nuclear weapons; the multifaceted challenges posed by Pakistan and China, respectively; and the changing role—and growing salience—of the Indian Navy.

Nuclear weapons. Although welcomed by some realpolitikers and celebrated by Hindu nationalists, the strategic logic of the tests and development program was essentially Nehruvian in form. In short, acquiring nuclear weapons allowed a relatively weak India to maintain a degree of strategic autonomy in a changing and uncertain post–Cold War context, to continue to focus most of its scarce resources on economic development, and to buy time in which to modernize its conventional military. India's strategic elite reasoned that crossing the nuclear threshold might cause a temporary uproar in the international community and make the relationship with Pakistan more complicated—specifically by introducing a so-called stability-instability paradox—but it would help manage the threat from a rapidly rising China and the more distant possibility of the United States intervening in India's affairs.[66]

India's weapons program is also Nehruvian in form. It has advanced more slowly than any other state's program, including that of Pakistan,

---

[64] For more on this shift, see especially Mohan, *Crossing the Rubicon.*

[65] See, for example, Stuart Corbridge, "'The Militarization of All Hindudom'? The Bharatiya Janata Party, the Bomb, and the Political Spaces of Hindu Nationalism," *Economy and Society* 28, no. 2 (1999): 222–55.

[66] Andrew B. Kennedy, "India's Nuclear Odyssey: Implicit Umbrellas, Diplomatic Disappointments, and the Bomb," *International Security* 36, no. 2 (2011): 120–53. The fact that a Congress-led government almost conducted a nuclear test in 1995 supports the view that the 1998 tests were less a function of Hindu nationalist chauvinism and more a result of a consensus view within the strategic community.

which struggles with similar or worse limits on financial resources, scientific know-how, and access to technology. The Indian program is characterized by strong emphases on "restraint, stability and minimalism," underpinned by the belief among the strategic elite that the use of nuclear weapons is "morally unacceptable," but that their possession is necessary to deter existential threats to India's security that might arise in an international system shaped by unequal power and few checks on great-power political behavior.[67] This moralism does not fit with either realpolitik or Hindu nationalist thought about Indian strategy and the role nuclear weapons might play. Realpolitikers argue that India's nuclear weapons arsenal should be much larger than it is, and apparently is envisaged to be; that nuclear testing should be resumed to ensure the weapons are reliable; and that India should move much faster to develop a complete triad of delivery systems.[68] Some Hindu nationalists, for their part, have called for India to revise its draft nuclear doctrine, though at present they remain committed to the mainstream goal of a "credible minimum deterrent."[69]

The Pakistan challenge. Pakistan tested six nuclear weapons after India's tests in 1998 and moved to develop its own deterrent. In 1999, it infiltrated troops across the Line of Control (LoC) in Kashmir into the Kargil region. Once India detected the infiltration, it responded with force, using the army, with limited air support, to expel the Pakistani troops back over the LoC. In subsequent years, India experienced no more large-scale military attacks from Pakistan but suffered a string of terrorist attacks attributed to Pakistani-backed groups.[70] India did not, however, respond to these attacks with military action. It did mobilize some forces in 2001, after the attack on the Parliament building, but this process took time and created a window for domestic and international voices to urge restraint. In the mid-2000s, India also toyed with developing a force structure and a doctrine that might give it the means to engage in such action. The Indian Army advanced the so-called Cold Start concept, which envisaged the rapid mobilization of

---

[67] Basrur, "Nuclear Weapons and Indian Strategic Culture," 181, 184. Basrur's conclusions were based on interviews with a number of significant figures in the strategic elite with a direct concern with India's nuclear program. For more on this issue, see Jones, "India's Strategic Culture," 26.

[68] For more on India's nuclear arsenal, see, for example, Karnad's arguments in Karnad, *Why India Is Not a Great Power (Yet)*, 368–93; and Karnad, *Nuclear Weapons and Indian Security*.

[69] For more on the BJP's nuclear commitments, see, for example, BJP, "BJP Election Manifesto 2014," 2014, 39, http://www.bjp.org/images/pdf_2014/full_manifesto_english_07.04.2014.pdf. It should be noted that the BJP rapidly backed away from this commitment when it was criticized within and outside India.

[70] These included attacks on the Red Fort in Delhi (2000), the Indian parliament (2001), various targets in Mumbai (2003 and 2006) and New Delhi (2005), and finally Lashkar-e-Taiba's assault on Mumbai (2008).

armored forces that could be used for a swift punitive attack on Pakistan.[71] But this initiative was never implemented, and India likely lacks the capacity for such a response, and certainly lacks a publicly declared doctrine that might permit it. These gaps can be attributed to long-standing problems both within the army and in the coordination of ground forces with air forces in ways necessary to conduct a swift cross-border attack.[72]

That said, it should also be noted that neither the most prominent realpolitikers nor the Hindu nationalists argue for stronger responses, except in passing in the moment after terrorist attacks occur. Their reasons differ. While the realpolitikers argue that India should shed moral qualms about using force, they also argue that substantial investment in forces to counter Pakistani threats would be misplaced and is better spent addressing the much greater challenge posed by China. Moreover, some realpolitikers argue that as India's economy grows, Pakistan will eventually moderate its policies to take advantage of the trade and investment opportunities that will result.[73] Hindu nationalists, as we have seen, have a conflicted view of India's options. On the one hand, they see Muslim Pakistan as a grave threat to Hindu India; on the other, they see Pakistan as part of a greater Indian cultural whole in South Asia, to be treated as such even when the country is behaving badly. As a result, the capacity of Hindu nationalists to displace the Nehruvian approach is limited, compared to that of the realpolitikers. The latter seem to be gaining some ground in New Delhi, at least in making the case for greater economic engagement with Islamabad.[74]

The China challenge. China poses far more complex challenges for India. Its swift and sustained economic rise after 1978 has demonstrated the inadequacy of India's economic model and—for some—also highlighted the weaknesses in the country's political model. In the past twenty years, India's growth rate has only twice (in 1999 and 2015) exceeded China's. In 2015, China's nominal GDP was about three times the size of India's. In terms of India's security, China also poses major challenges. It has forged an "all-weather friendship" with Pakistan, which has involved the transfer of missile and other technologies to Islamabad.[75] As discussed above, China's acquisition of nuclear weapons in the mid-1960s prompted India to develop

---

[71] Walter C. Ladwig III, "A Cold Start for Hot Wars? The Indian Army's New Limited War Doctrine," *International Security* 32, no. 3 (2008): 158–90.

[72] For a useful discussion of Cold Start, see Cohen and Dasgupta, *Arming without Aiming*, 60–70.

[73] Shyam Saran, "What Can India Do about Pakistan?" *Wire*, August 28, 2015, http://thewire.in/9167/what-can-india-do-about-pakistan.

[74] Rahul Roy-Chaudhury, "Modi's Approach to China and Pakistan," in *What Does India Think?* ed. François Godement (Brussels: European Council on Foreign Relations, 2015), 96–101.

[75] Andrew Small, *The China-Pakistan Axis: Asia's New Geopolitics* (New York: Oxford University Press, 2015).

its own program, and the military threat posed to India across their hotly disputed border partly prompted New Delhi to cross the nuclear threshold in 1998. China's rule over Tibet continues to rankle Hindu nationalists and others, including realpolitikers like Brahma Chellaney who sympathize with Tibetan Buddhists and believe that Tibet ought to be an independent buffer state.[76] China's assertiveness in the East and South China Seas, aspirations to build a blue water navy capable of venturing into the Indian Ocean, and deals with Pakistan and Sri Lanka to build ports and resupply vessels are also of deep concern.[77]

India's approach to China has been consistent since the late 1990s, across governments led by both the Congress Party and Hindu nationalists. It involves four elements: relying on nuclear weapons to deter China from launching a major war across the border; cautiously engaging China economically to stimulate trade while also encouraging inward investment; acting with relative restraint, both in responding to incursions by the People's Liberation Army into disputed areas and in deploying improved forces on the border with China; and building strategic ties with the United States, Australia, Japan, Singapore, and Vietnam.

This approach is mostly consistent with a Nehruvian strategic culture insofar as it emphasizes restraint and autonomy, aiming to avoid costly conflicts that would sap India's limited resources and potentially costly commitments to other states that might be more keen on openly confronting China. It is designed to maintain the image of India, at least in China's mind, as a swing state capable of joining an anti-China coalition if one emerged in response to a serious threat from Beijing. At the same time, this approach is calculated to avoid creating the impression that India is "irrevocably committed to an anti-China containment ring" and thereby provoking Beijing into adopting "overtly hostile and negative policies" toward India.[78] It is also an approach based on a realistic assessment of China's broad-based support for Pakistan, which the Nehruvians recognize Beijing can and does use to pressure India indirectly.[79] Last but not least, this policy helps bridge the divide between old Nehruvians who are nostalgic for developing world solidarity against the West, including with China, and new Nehruvians who are more skeptical of Chinese intentions.

---

[76] See, for example, Brahma Chellaney, "India's Betrayal of Tibet," *Wall Street Journal*, July 28, 2003, http://www.wsj.com/articles/SB105934174617047500.

[77] For a critical assessment, see David Brewster, "Beyond the 'String of Pearls': Is There Really a Sino-Indian Security Dilemma in the Indian Ocean?" *Journal of the Indian Ocean Region* 10, no. 2 (2014): 133–49.

[78] Sunil Khilnani et al., *Nonalignment 2.0* (New Delhi: Center for Policy Research, 2012), 14.

[79] Ibid., 18.

Appeals from realpolitikers and Hindu nationalists to adopt a stronger approach to China have so far mostly failed. Some realpolitikers would like to see India adopt more assertive measures like rapidly developing nuclear-armed ballistic missile submarines to enhance deterrence; equipping Vietnam with nuclear warheads and BrahMos cruise missiles; deploying much better-equipped Indian Army units on the border; issuing stronger diplomatic protests and reprisals in response to Chinese provocations, such as cross-border incursions or visa denials to Indians from disputed territory; or simply developing much closer defense ties with the United States and its regional allies.[80] Some Hindu nationalists would like to see more assertive policies along similar lines. But both are stymied by the widespread perception that India simply lacks leverage over China, given the economic disparity between the two countries and the relative weakness of India's armed forces. This perception has helped the Nehruvian approach to persist even into Modi's term in office.

Indian Navy. Most analysts agree that India's strategic ambition, and therefore the reach of its armed forces, remains limited, even in its own region. Sandy Gordon argued in 1995 that India has a "fundamentally 'continental' strategic outlook" and lacks "the resources and confidence to play a full hand of sea-going capabilities and to range abroad," largely because its armed forces are tied down managing internal security challenges and South Asian regional instability.[81]

The persistence of a Nehruvian strategic culture, which tends to focus political and military attention on the security challenges to the north from where the majority of threats historically have emerged, exacerbates these problems. It contributes to the neglect of challenges such as the capacity of terrorist groups to smuggle personnel and arms into India by sea, as one did in Mumbai in 2008. This persistence of Nehruvianism also arguably contributes to the continued underfunding of the Indian Navy, which is allocated only 15% of the defense budget, and the relative overfunding of the Indian Army, which is mostly dedicated to defending northern India from Pakistan and China, as well as to maintaining internal security. This neglect has been repeatedly criticized by realpolitikers, but the bias toward the army, at least in the defense budget, remains.[82]

That said, the rise of China, and its growing political, economic and military presence in the Indian Ocean region, is convincing India to shift

---

[80] See Karnad, *Why India Is Not a Great Power (Yet)*; and Harsh V. Pant, *The China Syndrome: Grappling with an Uneasy Relationship* (New Delhi: HarperCollins India, 2010).

[81] Gordon, *India's Rise to Power*, 331.

[82] For a realpolitik critique, see C. Raja Mohan, *Samudra Manthan: Sino-Indian Rivalry in the Indo-Pacific* (Washington, D.C.: Carnegie Endowment for International Peace, 2012).

resources and attention from continental strategic challenges to maritime ones.[83] India's navy is being modernized—with Indian-built warships as well as through foreign acquisitions, including new Arihant-class nuclear missile submarines, aircraft carriers, destroyers, and frigates. The navy is also leading with regional defense diplomacy as a prominent player in the Indian Ocean Naval Symposium; in bilateral and multilateral exercises with the United States, Australia, and Japan, in particular; and in regional humanitarian and disaster relief provision.[84] Slowly, as India's navy becomes more salient in the country's strategic discourse, it will likely be able to gain a greater share of resources, especially given the fair degree of convergence between Nehruvians, realpolitikers, and Hindu nationalists about the importance of securing the Indian Ocean and playing a key role as a first responder in the region.[85]

A Modi Doctrine?

Given the rapidly changing circumstances India must confront, and given Modi's reputation as a decisive and hard-line politician, there was much speculation when he came to power in May 2014 that he would transform Indian foreign policy in his own image, despite the distinct lack of clarity in his campaign speeches and manifesto in this area.[86] The energy Modi brought to Indian diplomacy in his early months in office also gave rise to speculation about an emergent—and distinctive—"Modi doctrine."[87]

It is has since become clear, however, that Modi's foreign policy has largely followed lines laid down by his two predecessors, Vajpayee and Singh—policy shaped in a broadly Nehruvian strategic culture.[88] Modi has inched a little closer to the United States than Singh did, inviting President Barack Obama to Republic Day in 2015, signing a U.S.-India joint strategic vision, and renewing the Defense Framework Agreement for another ten years. But New Delhi has dragged its feet over further specific agreements on logistics and resupply and communications and navigation technologies. At the same time, India under

---

[83] David Brewster, *India's Ocean: The Story of India's Bid for Regional Leadership* (New York: Routledge, 2014).

[84] Dhruva Jaishankar, "India's Military Diplomacy," in "Defence Primer: India at 75," ed. Sushant Singh and Pushan Das, Observer Research Foundation, 2016, 18–24.

[85] Ankit Panda, "India: Indian Ocean First Responder?" *Diplomat*, December 30, 2014, http://thediplomat.com/2014/12/india-indian-ocean-first-responder.

[86] See, for example, Manjari Chatterjee Miller, "Foreign Policy a la Modi," *Foreign Affairs*, April 3, 2014, https://www.foreignaffairs.com/articles/india/2014-04-03/foreign-policy-la-modi.

[87] See, for example, Christophe Jaffrelot, "A Modi Doctrine?" *Indian Express*, November 20, 2014, http://indianexpress.com/article/opinion/columns/a-modi-doctrine.

[88] Ian Hall, "Is a 'Modi Doctrine' Emerging in Indian Foreign Policy?" *Australian Journal of International Affairs* 69, no. 3 (2015): 247–52.

Modi has re-engaged both China and Russia, and formally applied to join the Shanghai Cooperation Organisation (SCO), as well as the Beijing-led Asian Infrastructure Investment Bank (AIIB). Modi has also worked hard to boost ties with Japan—another cause close to Singh's heart—and with Southeast Asian partners like Singapore and Vietnam. Toward Pakistan, he has been firm, but hardly hard-line, continuing to talk to Islamabad through his foreign secretary and national security adviser, and occasionally in-person surprise meetings with Prime Minister Nawaz Sharif.

For all his undoubted energy, Modi's underlying strategy displays more continuity than change.[89] Securing India's economic interests remains paramount, displacing other strategic objectives. The knock-on effects of Modi's signature initiative, "Make in India," for military modernization make this clear: the Indian Air Force is desperate for modern combat aircraft, but the demands of "Make in India" have led to further delay and significant renegotiation of the agreement to buy French Rafale fighter aircraft. Initially interested in acquiring 126 units, India now apparently wants only 36, with the shortfall to be made up of Indian-manufactured planes.[90] Moreover, India still seems wedded to strategic restraint. In early January 2016, guerilla fighters likely originating from Pakistani territory attacked an Indian airbase at Pathankot, Punjab, killing eight Indians during a two-day gun battle. India's response was muted and arguably inconsistent with both realpolitik and Hindu nationalist principles: a suspension of bilateral talks and a call for a joint investigation. Overall, the Modi government has preferred to stick with Singh's strategy of multialignment to maximize both economic opportunity and strategic autonomy, rather than striking out along more ideological, Hindu nationalist lines.

Conclusion

India's strategic culture is shaped by different traditions of thought drawing on cultural resources that stretch back into the region's ancient past. Those cultural resources—Hindu texts, as well as the more recent writings of Hindu nationalists and modernists—advocate both moralism and amoralism with regard to military power and the use of force. And while both the religious revivalists and modernists agree that India ought to be recognized by other societies for its past greatness, cultural wealth, and spiritual wisdom, views vary on exactly how this might be achieved.

---

[89] Kanti Bajpai, "Continuity, but with Zeal," *Seminar,* April 2015, http://india-seminar.com/2015/668.htm.

[90] Sushant Singh, "Rafale Deal: France Rejects Bank Guarantee, Awaits India's Reply," *Indian Express,* May 25, 2016, http://indianexpress.com/article/india/india-news-india/rafale-deal-france-rejects-bank-guarantee-awaits-indias-reply-2817725.

Revivalists advocate enacting religious reform, forging social unity, building the muscularity of Hindus, and appropriating elements of Western science and technology and harnessing them to the sanatana dharma. Modernists look to more thoroughgoing political and social reform, allied to economic interventionism, and adopt a mostly pragmatic view of military power, at least in the present world.

The dominant tradition of strategic thought in India remains Nehruvian, with its belief in India's greatness, emphasis on the importance of attaining recognition of this status, and modernist instrumentalist view of the use of force balanced against the belief that the current phase of international relations in which military power is needed is temporary. The realpolitik and Hindu nationalist traditions mostly inform critical voices rather than strategic policymaking. Moreover, when Hindu nationalists have been in power, their ambivalence about military power and emphasis on the primacy of social unity—and therefore on domestic politics, not international relations—arguably undermine their capacity to reshape India's strategic priorities. The foreign policies of both Vajpayee's government and Modi's present one demonstrate the stickiness of Nehruvian strategic culture: neither has brought about a decisive change of direction in any area of policy, except perhaps in one: the BJP-led government's rapprochement with Washington in the early 2000s in the aftermath of the nuclear tests. But even here, it is debatable whether India's strategic elite played the more significant role in improving bilateral relations, given that Washington, rather than New Delhi, initiated dialogue.[91]

For interlocutors like the United States, India's strategic culture poses a number of challenges. Above all, there is the persistent desire for strategic autonomy, which is shared by Nehruvians, many realpolitikers, and Hindu nationalists and makes India deeply reluctant to enter into multilateral institutional obligations beyond those of the UN Charter and into substantive binding commitments in bilateral deals. India's recent reluctance under a Hindu nationalist government to move beyond the "in principle" agreement on defense logistics and military communication arrangements with the United States neatly illustrates this point and highlights the extent to which these concerns do not just emanate from the left wing of Indian politics. The desire for autonomy is also clear in India's recent attempts under Modi to balance closer defense ties with the United States with better diplomatic and economic relations with other states, including China and Russia, through the SCO and AIIB. As India shifts from nonalignment and the avoidance of ties to multialignment and greater enmeshment in a web of bilateral strategic

---

[91] See especially Strobe Talbott, *Engaging India: Diplomacy, Democracy, and the Bomb*, rev. ed. (Washington, D.C.: Brookings Institution Press, 2006).

partnerships and regional institutions, greater autonomy—to be achieved by accelerated development and widened opportunities for inward investment and technology transfer—is still the primary objective. India's simultaneous entreaties to the Arab world, Iran, and Israel also illustrate this tendency to put economic interests first and build better ties, while studiously avoiding entanglement in the quarrels of strategic partners.

The second challenge concerns status. All three traditions in Indian strategic culture maintain the idea that India is not a normal state but rather a "civilizational state" deserving a higher level of regard in international politics. For Nehruvians, this merely implies that interlocutors accord India respect and acknowledge its intellectual and cultural inheritance. But for Hindu nationalists, especially for hard-line adherents of Hindutva, this means something more: recognizing the superiority of Hinduism, the truth of the sanatana dharma, and the mission of both in bringing an end to civilizational conflict. Accommodating such views within the present international system will be challenging, especially if hard-line Hindu nationalists take control of the Modi-led government's foreign policy agenda and try to implement some of what the BJP promised in its 2014 manifesto in terms of securing greater international recognition of India's civilizational inheritance.[92]

Finally, it must be acknowledged that some elements of Indian strategic culture, especially Nehruvian strategic culture, should be reassuring for the United States, and indeed for other regional powers, including China and Pakistan. In particular, the tendency toward strategic restraint, even in the face of provocations such as major terrorist attacks on its cities, should generate more confidence in India than is often shown, especially since its acquisition of a nuclear deterrent. Despite the desire of some realpolitikers and hard-line Hindu nationalists for the country to be more assertive concerning China and Pakistan, India continues to display relatively restrained behavior even as its military capabilities grow—albeit unevenly, inconsistently, and not always strategically.

The rise to power of Modi, once a Hindu nationalist firebrand, might have undermined Nehruvianism. Instead, despite his energy, and despite the appointments of a realpolitiker, S. Jaishankar, as foreign secretary, and a Hindu nationalist, Ajit Doval, as national security adviser, Modi's rise seems to have only led to incremental change and minor modifications to an inherited strategy. This may illustrate the power and the flexibility of Nehruvianism as a strategic culture, balancing as it does idealist and realist approaches to policymaking and implementation.

---

[92] See BJP, "BJP Election Manifesto 2014," 1–3, 39–40.

EXECUTIVE SUMMARY

This chapter analyzes Indonesian strategic culture by examining its origin and underlying logic and assesses the impact on Indonesian foreign policy and civil-military relations.

MAIN ARGUMENT

Indonesia's strategic culture is influenced by a combination of three major elements. The first is a constructed past that provides a united identity for a diverse population. The second is the narrative of the struggle for independence, in which the military plays a central role. The third element is the idea of a "free and active" foreign policy that stresses nonalignment. This combination creates a strategic culture that abhors the idea of military pacts, viewing them as a threat to independence; emphasizes a defensive orientation; and fears interference by foreign countries, making the country wary of any outside power growing too strong or unchecked in the neighboring region. As a result, there is a tendency for Indonesia's foreign and military policies to underbalance against growing threats from China in Southeast Asia, especially in the South China Sea, which may detrimentally influence regional security, the unity of ASEAN, and Indonesia's own strategic interests.

POLICY IMPLICATIONS

- Although Indonesia does welcome defense cooperation, it does not want to be engaged in military alliances and pacts for fear of losing its independence.

- The inward orientation of Indonesia's military means that it does not have much power-projection ability, which undermines the country's strategic position in the region.

- While Indonesia is a key player in Southeast Asia, the U.S. may find it difficult to involve the country in broader regional efforts to counter Chinese assertiveness.

Indonesia's Strategic Culture: The Legacy of Independence

Yohanes Sulaiman

In the past several years, growing Chinese military assertiveness in the South China Sea has alarmed many of China's neighbors in the Association of Southeast Asian Nations (ASEAN), notably the Philippines and Vietnam. The Philippines, for example, given its lack of military power vis-à-vis China, has been increasing its military cooperation with the United States and Japan in response to China's threat.[1] Surprisingly, however, another ASEAN member has remain subdued in the face of Chinese assertiveness—Indonesia. Granted, under President Joko Widodo (popularly known as Jokowi) Indonesia has become much more active in both asserting and defending its claims in the South China Sea. On June 23, 2016, for instance, in light of a Chinese excursion into Indonesia's territorial waters, Jokowi held a cabinet meeting aboard the Indonesian warship KRI *Imam Bonjol*, signaling that the Natuna Islands and their seas are part of Indonesian sovereign territory.[2] Yet at the same time, considering the fact that Indonesia's military expenditure is much lower than China's, or even Singapore's, it is surprising that the idea of military alliances or pacts with other states to balance against China was

Yohanes Sulaiman is a Lecturer in the School of Government at the Universitas Jenderal Achmad Yani in Cimahi, Indonesia. He can be reached at <ysulaiman@gmail.com>.

---

[1] Ernest Bower, "The Emerging South China Sea Security Alliance and ASEAN-Centricity," ASEAN Strategic, April 23, 2016, http://www.aseanstrategic.com/2016/04/south-china-sea-security-asean.html.

[2] Anggi Kusumadewi, "Rapat di atas kapal perang di Natuna, Jokowi 'gertak' China" [Having a Meeting on a Warship in Natuna, Jokowi "Threatens" China], CNN Indonesia, June 23, 2016, http://www.cnnindonesia.com/nasional/20160623091859-20-140309/rapat-di-atas-kapal-perang-di-natuna-jokowi-gertak-china.

never broached. In fact, while the latest Indonesian defense white paper mentions regional instability resulting from heightened tension in the South China Sea, it never addresses China's nine-dash line as the main factor causing the disputes in the first place.[3]

This behavior can only be explained by Indonesia's strategic culture. The combination of Indonesia's sense that its archipelagic unity is constantly being undermined, its inward-looking military culture, and its desire to remain independent in foreign affairs cause Indonesia to underbalance against China's growing threat in the South China Sea.

This chapter explores the dominant narratives of Indonesian strategic culture and explains how they influence Indonesia's decision-making process in foreign and military policies. In order to do that, it considers three major elements that compose Indonesian strategic culture. The first element is how Indonesians look at themselves ideally as a nation that comprises hundreds of different ethnic groups and has a long and illustrious history as the successor state of the ancient kingdoms of Srivijaya and Majapahit. Yet at the same time, there is always a latent fear that the country's unity could be easily undermined through policies of divide and conquer. This chapter will first discuss the founding myth of Indonesia as the successor state of Majapahit and how this provides the country with an identity and a sense of pride as a nation, which in turn explains the preoccupation of Indonesian political elites with a united Indonesia.

The second defining element of Indonesia's strategic culture is the narrative of the struggle for independence, in which the Indonesian Army supposedly wrested victory from the jaws of defeat. The second part of this chapter will discuss civil-military relations, which were most importantly shaped by the military's experience during the war for independence. Even though it was outmatched by the Dutch, and despite the fact that the Dutch arrested the civilian government, the military managed to drive the Dutch forces to stalemate by its fighting spirit and effective guerilla warfare. The decentralized organization that the military built in turn became the nucleus of today's territorial command, which has many functions.

The third element, the "free and active" narrative, shapes Indonesian foreign policy by stressing that, in order to be completely free, Indonesia must have an independent foreign policy that is unrestricted by any military pacts or alignments with great powers. The third part of this chapter will discuss how this idea came into being, how it influences Indonesian foreign policy decision-making, and how this element of strategic culture makes it impossible for Indonesia to fully commit to strong international security arrangements.

---

[3] Ministry of Defense (Indonesia), *Buku putih pertahanan Indonesia 2015* [Indonesian Defense White Book 2015] (Jakarta, 2015), 11.

The fourth part of this chapter will assess how all three elements of strategic culture influence the Indonesian political and military elite's foreign and security priorities. In particular, it will explore how Indonesia has tried to ensure the freedom of Southeast Asia from outside powers' interference. Finally, the chapter will conclude with a discussion of the implications of Indonesian strategic culture for the relationships between Indonesia, its regional partners, and the United States. The logic underlying this idealized form of strategic culture is a function of Indonesia's geopolitical, military, and domestic political calculations. Thus, it is important for U.S. policymakers to understand this logic in dealing with their Indonesian counterparts.

The Origins of Indonesia and *Wawasan Nusantara*

This section will discuss how during Indonesia's formative years its leaders tried to craft a united identity for a heterogeneous, diverse population based on a belief in a "glorious past" under the kingdoms of Srivijaya and Majapahit. While this belief fostered national pride and a sense of purpose for the young nation, Indonesians also fear that this unity could be easily undermined by foreign interference and subversion. This, in turn, leads Indonesians to stress the principle of noninterference in other countries' internal affairs at international forums.

The Creation of a Unified Indonesia

It is a common belief in Indonesia that the modern nation is the successor state of the two maritime kingdoms of Srivijaya and Majapahit, which are believed to have ruled the entirety of modern Indonesia, as well as the Malay Peninsula, between the seventh and fourteenth centuries. The pomp and prestige of Majapahit was such that ever since its fall, various Javanese kingdoms have used Majapahit as their *raison d'être*: that they were the legitimate successor states despite the fact that these Javanese kingdoms were Islamic kingdoms unlike Majapahit, which was a Hindu-Buddhist kingdom.[4] In a historical anachronism (and syncretism), the *Usulbiyah*—one of the sacred books of the Mataram Kingdom, the last powerful Islamic kingdom in Java, which was written around 1729—stated that Muhammad wore the crown of Majapahit.[5]

---

[4] Merle C. Ricklefs, *A History of Modern Indonesia since c. 1200*, 3rd ed. (Stanford: Stanford University Press, 2001), 46, 50.

[5] Merle C. Ricklefs, *The Seen and Unseen Worlds in Java, 1726–1749* (Honolulu: University of Hawaii Press, 1998), 89.

This belief that modern Indonesia is the successor state of Majapahit still resonates deeply today, despite the fact that the current state is actually based on the territory formerly belonging to the Dutch East Indies Company. After the company went bankrupt, in 1799 the Dutch government took over its Indonesian possessions. Later, the government expanded this territory to encompass modern Indonesia, installed a bureaucracy to govern it from Batavia, and established an education system to create a class of intellectual natives that would serve the bureaucracy. As locals became used to "the mesh of differential schools, courts, clinics, police stations and immigration offices," this created "traffic habits": the feeling that Indonesians, notably the educated elite, shared a common identity as members of this one big nation that transcended the mishmash of various and often conflicting ethnic groups and small kingdoms living under the suzerainty of the Dutch governor general in Batavia.[6] This feeling culminated in a youth congress on October 28, 1928, with the declaration of the three ideals of "one fatherland, Indonesia; one nation, Indonesia; and one language, Bahasa Indonesia," reflecting the conviction of elite Indonesians that they belonged to a single entity.

Over time, nationalists established the idea that Indonesia had existed "for centuries past" and that it had a golden era under Majapahit.[7] This issue came to prominence in 1945 during the debates in the Investigating Committee for Preparatory Work for Indonesian Independence in the months preceding the proclamation of Indonesian independence. At the time, Mohammad Hatta was opposed to historian Muhammad Yamin's proposal to include what he regarded as the former territory of Majapahit, which would have also included British Malaya, Borneo, and Portuguese East Timor.[8] Even though Hatta in the end prevailed in preventing what he saw as "uncontrolled passion for expansion of the country," the idea of Indonesia as the successor state of Majapahit was embraced by political elites regardless of their ethnic background.[9]

This belief is also reflected in pancasila, Indonesia's official philosophical foundation. Sukarno, the country's first president and the originator of the doctrine, maintained that it is not a modern "invention" but that he

---

[6] Benedict Anderson, *Imagined Communities* (London: Verso Books, 1983), 169.

[7] R.E. Elson, *The Idea of Indonesia: A History* (Cambridge: Cambridge University Press, 2008), 70, 72.

[8] Delia Noer, "Yamin and Hamka: Two Routes to an Indonesian Identity," in *Perceptions of the Past in Southeast Asia*, ed. Anthony Reid and David Marr (Singapore: Heinemann Educational Books, 1979), 258; and Muhammad Yamin, "Unity of Our Country and Our People," in *Indonesian Political Thinking 1945–1965*, ed. Herbert Feith and Lance Castles (Ithaca: Cornell University Press, 1970).

[9] Mohammad Hatta, "Let Us Not Encourage the Spirit of Expansion," in Feith and Castles, *Indonesian Political Thinking 1945–1965*, 442. As a side note, Muhammad Yamin was a Sumatran born in Padang, not a Javanese.

merely "'dug' it up from the 'pearls' left by the forefathers" of Indonesia.[10] This native philosophy of the old Indonesia transcends modern Indonesia's gamut of ethnic, religious, and racial diversity and unites the country under the five principles of (1) belief in one God, (2) just and civilized humanity, (3) the unity of Indonesia, (4) democracy that is guided by inner wisdom in unanimity arising out of deliberations, and (5) social justice for all. Therefore, despite Indonesia comprising hundreds of ethnic groups and languages, Indonesians believe that they are all part of a natural country. This belief is further reinforced by the national motto, *bhinneka tunggal ika*, which is a quotation from the old Javanese poem "Sutasoma," written during the height of the Majapahit Kingdom, that roughly translates as "unity in diversity."

This Majapahit viewpoint would later manifest in the Indonesian concept of *wawasan nusantara* (archipelagic outlook), which was declared by then prime minister Djuanda Kartasasmita on December 13, 1957. This declaration stressed the idea of Indonesia as an archipelagic state, that "all waters around, between and connecting, the islands or parts of islands belonging to the Indonesian archipelago irrespective of their width or dimension are...subject to the absolute sovereignty of Indonesia."[11]

The declaration was originally triggered by the realization that the Indonesian Navy and Air Force were not large enough to protect Indonesia, and thus a longer territorial water limit would facilitate the interdiction of foreign forces.[12] In the decades after the declaration, however, the idea of wawasan nusantara has gained a much broader meaning, notably the idea that Indonesia has always been an archipelagic state. In fact, the word "nusantara" dates from the Majapahit period, though back then it referred to the other islands outside Majapahit's core area of Eastern Java and Madura but still within its sphere of influence.[13] In 1953, Mohammad Yamin, then the minister of education, argued that nusantara referred to the entirety of modern Indonesia—a country between two islands of Sumatra and Papua.[14]

---

[10] Ken Ward, "Soeharto's Javanese Pancasila," in *Soeharto's New Order and Its Legacy: Essays in Honour of Harold Crouch*, ed. Edward Aspinall and Greg Fealy (Canberra: Australian National University Press, 2010), 31.

[11] "Memorandum from the Deputy Assistant Secretary of State for Far Eastern Affairs (Jones) to the Secretary of State," *Foreign Relations of the United States, 1955–1957,* vol. 22, *Southeast Asia* (Washington, D.C., January 1, 1989).

[12] Audrey R. Kahin and George M. Kahin, *Subversion as Foreign Policy: The Secret Eisenhower and Dulles Debacle in Indonesia* (New York: New Press, 1995), 125.

[13] S. Supomo, "The Image of Majapahit in Later Javanese and Indonesian Writing," in *Perceptions of the Past in Southeast Asia*, ed. Anthony Reid and David Marr (Singapore: Heinemann Books, 1979), 173; and Mahandis Y. Thamrin, "Nusantara bukanlah wilayah Majapahit?" [Nusantara Is Not Majapahit's Territory?], *National Geographic Indonesia*, October 11, 2013, http://nationalgeographic. co.id/berita/2013/10/faktanya-nusantara-bukanlah-wilayah-majapahit.

[14] R. Moh. Ali, *Pengantar ilmu sejarah Indonesia* [Introduction to the History of Indonesia] (Yogyakarta: LKIS, 1989), 219.

In doing so, Yamin hoped to stress the idea that modern Indonesia is the successor of the old Indonesian kingdoms of Sriwijaya and Majapahit rather than the Dutch East Indies. Still today, many Indonesians believe that Indonesia used to be a strong maritime empire. This sentiment was reflected in Jokowi's inauguration speech on October 20, 2014, which called on Indonesia to be glorious again in the seas like in the past.[15] This sense of maritime pride has led Indonesia to believe that it has a major role to fulfill in the global arena, dictated by history "all the way back to Sriwijaya."[16]

Although this idea of modern Indonesia as a successor of Majapahit is not without its detractors—especially outside Java, where people are more wary about what they perceive as Javanese domination of the rest of the country[17]—in general the idea forms the underlying narrative basis of Indonesia's strategic culture: that Indonesia has a long and proud history as a strong, united country. In essence, this modern construct provides legitimacy to the current Indonesian state and is the source of its power, following the Javanese tradition of "oneness is power and multiplicity is diffusion and weakness."[18]

The Principle of Sovereignty and Noninterference

The Dutch managed to occupy and rule Indonesia thanks to their ability to play the Indonesians against each other and then conquer them (*divide et impera*), underscoring the fragility of the country's unity. Indonesian political discourse has thus stressed the responsibility of the government to maintain the unity of modern Indonesia and to defend against any attempt to split the country again, especially through foreign meddling in domestic affairs. This fear of foreign intervention leads Indonesia, in every international forum, to always stress the principle of sovereignty and noninterference, seeing this as a way to safeguard its unity and independence. This in turn leads to contradictions in foreign policy, as Indonesia also believes that due to its "highly developed sense of national identity" and strategic position that it

---

[15] "Ini pidato perdana Jokowi sebagai presiden ke-7 RI" [This Is Jokowi's First Speech as the 7th President of the Republic of Indonesia], *Kompas*, October 20, 2014, http://nasional.kompas.com/read/2014/10/20/1318031/Ini.Pidato.Perdana.Jokowi.sebagai.Presiden.ke-7.RI.

[16] Franklin B. Weinstein, *Indonesian Foreign Policy and the Dilemma of Dependence: From Sukarno to Soeharto* (Ithaca: Cornell University Press, 1976), 194.

[17] Kahar Muzakar, "Down with the New Madjapahitism!" in Feith and Castles, *Indonesian Political Thinking 1945–1965*, 334; and Joseph Chinyong Liow, *The Politics of Indonesia-Malaysia Relations: One Kin, Two Nations* (London: Routledge, 2004), 38.

[18] Anthony Reid, "Political 'Tradition' of Indonesia: The One and the Many," *Asian Studies Review* 22, no. 1 (1998): 27.

"cannot avoid its responsibilities as a great power in Asia" and thus has a "natural" leading role.[19]

This contradiction is especially evident in its leadership in ASEAN, where Indonesia also sees itself as a role model on human rights.[20] Indonesia's attempts to promote a human rights agenda in ASEAN have been constantly rebuffed by the other members, who invoke the principle of nonintervention as an integral ASEAN norm.[21] The example of how Indonesia handled the Rohingya refugee crisis in 2015, caused by Myanmar's repression of this minority ethnic population, was telling. Although Indonesia had criticized and pressured Myanmar to change its discriminatory policies and to halt human rights abuses toward the Rohingya as a result of massive domestic pressure demanding the government help fellow Muslims in need, Indonesia and ASEAN as a whole were unwilling to force Myanmar to take ownership of the problem or to intervene directly to stop human rights abuses. In fact, Indonesia and the rest of ASEAN kept reacting to the results of Myanmar's policies, notably on "intensifying search-and-rescue operations, strengthening information and intelligence sharing mechanisms, and protecting the safety of those lost at sea," without dealing forcefully with the origin of the problem itself: Myanmar's discriminatory policies toward its ethnic Rohingya population.[22] This led one analyst to remark derisively that one of Indonesia's key achievements in this area has been in reaching a regional arrangement on semantics.[23] Not surprisingly, the Rohingya issue remains unresolved.

While it could be argued that Indonesia was unwilling to pressure Myanmar too much, lest it endanger the unity of ASEAN, it is clear that Indonesia was simply unwilling to create a precedent to allow other countries to interfere, particularly given the active separatist movement in Indonesia's own province of West Papua. Thus, despite the fact that Indonesia proudly touted itself as a role model for democratization and offered to share its experience in transitioning from authoritarian rule to democracy, it refrained from supporting the democratization process during the Arab Spring. In reacting to civil war in Syria, for instance, despite the evidence that the Assad

---

[19] Weinstein, *Indonesian Foreign Policy*, 194, 196–97.

[20] Dylan Amirio, "RI 'Role Model' on Human Rights in ASEAN," *Jakarta Post*, August 7, 2015, http://www.thejakartapost.com/news/2015/08/07/ri-role-model-human-rights-asean.html.

[21] Lee Leviter, "The ASEAN Charter: ASEAN Failure or Member Failure?" *International Law and Politics* 43, no. 1 (2010): 159–210.

[22] Andreyka Natalegawa, "As ASEAN Stumbles, Indonesia Must Find New Path to Aid Rohingya Refugees," *Jakarta Globe*, June 5, 2015, http://jakartaglobe.beritasatu.com/news/asean-stumbles-indonesia-must-find-new-path-aid-rohingya-refugees.

[23] Olivia Cable, "Indonesia and the Rohingya: De-legitimising Democracy?" New Mandala, May 29, 2015, http://www.newmandala.org/indonesia-and-the-rohingya-de-legitimising-democracy.

regime had committed massive and flagrant violations of human rights, Indonesia abstained from voting on a UN resolution to condemn the Assad regime in May 2013. It also refused to recognize the National Coalition for Syrian Revolutionary and Opposition Forces as the interlocutor by asserting that such recognition "ran counter to international law," notably unwarranted intervention into Syria's internal affairs.[24] Therefore, Indonesia's wariness of foreign interference has ultimately worked against its ambitions to be seen as a leading state and a beacon of democracy and human rights.

Civil-Military Relations: The Struggle for Independence, Resilience, and Territorial Command

The civil-military relationship in Indonesia is strongly influenced by the defeat of the Dutch by the Japanese in 1942. Although Japanese rule in Indonesia only lasted three and a half years, it left several legacies that continue to shape Indonesian military and strategic culture to this day, especially the idea of resilience.[25] The notion of "strength of the spirit over the strength of the material"[26] was instilled in Indonesian soldiers, indoctrinating them to have the "courage to struggle."[27]

After Japan surrendered and Indonesia declared independence, the new government managed to build a mobile police brigade unit and arm an effective and loyal military division, the Siliwangi Division, commanded by the highly competent colonel Abdul Haris Nasution.[28] At the same time, the government remained unable to control the armed militias that Japan had formed during its brief rule. Therefore, when the British arrived in September 1945 to disarm the Japanese and restore order for the Dutch, whose military units would arrive much later, it faced opposition from these armed militias, culminating in military clashes.

The government's failure to control the army led to a major battle in Surabaya after army units and youth militias in Surabaya refused the government's order to leave the city after a British ultimatum. While the

---

[24] Bulent Aras and Sinan Ekim, "Indonesia and the Arab Spring," Project on the Middle East and the Arab Spring, Policy Paper, no. 6, May 2015, 3, http://research.sabanciuniv.edu/28348/1/Paper6_Aras_Ekim.pdf.

[25] Raden Gatot Mangkupradja, Harumi Wanasita Evans, and Ruth McVey, "The PETA and My Relations with the Japanese: A Correction of Sukarno's Autobiography," Indonesia, no. 5 (1968): 123.

[26] Albrecht Fürst von Urach, Das geheimnis Japanischer kraft [The Secret of Japan's Strength], trans. Randall Bythwerk (Berlin: Zentralverlag der NSDAP, 1943), http://research.calvin.edu/german-propaganda-archive/japan.htm.

[27] Benedict Anderson, Java in a Time of Revolution (Ithaca: Cornell University Press, 1972), 239.

[28] George M. Kahin, Nationalism and Revolution in Indonesia (Ithaca: Cornell University Press, 1952), 184–85.

battle was both strategically and tactically a disaster for the Indonesians, the Surabayans' fierce resistance spooked the British. Concerned about the possibility of a violent revolution, the British pressured the recalcitrant Dutch to start negotiating with the Indonesians.[29] On the other side, the battle convinced the military that the Indonesian youth had the spirit and resilience to fight the invaders. In fact, November 10 would later be called Heroes Day to commemorate the bravery and fighting spirit of the people of Surabaya against the heavily armed and well-trained British soldiers. This became one of the biggest revolutionary myths within the Indonesian military—that the cultivation of national spirit is important to create a strong society and achieve victory.

In contrast, the military looked askance at what it saw as the lack of fighting spirit in the new civilian government, which would eventually lead to further confrontation, notably on the question of civilian supremacy over the military. Realizing that the Indonesian Army was badly underequipped and undertrained, the republican government decided to make territorial and other concessions in order to receive de facto recognition from the Netherlands and especially from the United States. The army was furious, with General Sudirman declaring that the country should "never mind about [diplomatic] agreement, just keep on fighting for independence of Indonesia" and ordering the army to continue fighting and send as many troops, arms, and supplies as possible to the front lines.[30]

The military's displeasure with the civilian leadership was further reinforced in 1948, when the Dutch finally invaded and seized Yogyakarta, the capital of the nascent republic, and arrested members of the civilian government. The civilian government welcomed the Dutch invasion, seeing that it would finally force the United Nations—and more importantly, the United States—to intervene, and thus the government surrendered to the Dutch.[31] The army, however, perceived itself as the only institution willing to fight for the independence of the country, while the civilian officials surrendered, abandoning their responsibility.[32] The aftermath of the revolution appeared to vindicate the army's self-perception: that its resilience to keep fighting against all odds against the superior weaponry of the Dutch allowed it to snatch victory from the jaws of defeat. Yet, while the Dutch did

---

[29] David Wehl, *The Birth of Indonesia* (London: Allen and Unwin, 1948), 67.

[30] "Telegram from the Consul General at Batavia (Foote) to the Secretary of State, December 2, 1946," *Foreign Relations of the United States, 1946*, vol. 8, *The Far East* (Washington, D.C.: Government Printing Office, 1969), 857, 859–60.

[31] Mohammad Hatta, *Memoir* (Jakarta: P.T. Tintamas Indonesia, 1979), 539.

[32] Michael R.J. Vatikiotis, *Indonesian Politics under Suharto: The Rise and Fall of the New Order*, 3rd ed. (London: Routledge, 1999), 64.

experience much difficulty from the guerilla war that sapped its resources,[33] it was the United States' threats to suspend Marshall Plan aid to the Netherlands and prevent it from joining NATO "so long as they had not solved their colonial difficulties" that forced the Dutch to negotiate independence with the Indonesians.[34] Still, the fact that General Sudirman, who was stricken with tuberculosis, was willing to suffer the hardship of guerilla warfare while the civilian leaders simply surrendered strengthened the military's dismissive attitude that civilians were simply unfit to lead the military.[35]

Tension between the military and civilian government persisted during the tumultuous era of constitutional democracy, when the military's attempt to reform itself by reducing the number of soldiers was politicized by civilian leaders, intensifying the officer corps' dislike and distrust of the government.[36] As a result, the military then saw itself as the savior of the nation in moments of trouble—from fighting the Dutch to dealing with Muslim and regional rebellions in the 1950s and decimating the Communists, who twice rebelled in 1948 and 1965.[37]

This view led to the development and later the implementation of *dwifungsi* (dual function)—the belief that, in addition to its role in national defense, the military needs to have a positive sociopolitical role. The goal, however, was not to establish a military dictatorship but to pursue a "middle way" of "constant vigilance and prodding to achieve good government."[38] The objective was to maintain national resilience by combining ideology, politics, economy, society, culture, and military strength to face aggression from outside.[39] The idea of dwifungsi provided the rationale for the army to become involved in Indonesian politics during the Sukarno era (1945–67). The military perceived the country as under an existential threat from the Indonesian Communist Party, which was the most organized political party at the time and had been growing in popularity.[40] Yet the army could not

---

[33] "Telegram from the Ambassador in the Netherlands (Baruch) to the Secretary of State, June 17, 1949," *Foreign Relations of the United States, 1949*, vol. 7, part 1, *The Far East and Australasia* (Washington, D.C.: Government Printing Office, 1975), 444–45.

[34] Dirk Stikker, *Men of Responsibility: A Memoir* (New York: Harper and Row, 1966), 145–46.

[35] Ulf Sundhaussen, *The Road to Power: Indonesian Military Politics 1945-1967* (Kuala Lumpur: Oxford University Press, 1982), 41–42, 44–45.

[36] Guy J. Pauker, "The Indonesian Doctrine of Territorial Warfare and Territorial Management," RAND Corporation, RAND Memorandum, November 1963, 14.

[37] R. William Liddle, "Suharto's Indonesia: Personal Rule and Political Institutions," in *Leadership and Culture in Indonesian Politics*, ed. R. William Liddle (Sydney: Allen and Unwin, 1996), 29–30.

[38] Pauker, "The Indonesian Doctrine," 2.

[39] Leonard C. Sebastian and Irman G. Lanti, "Perceiving Indonesian Approaches to International Relations Theory," in *Non-Western International Relations Theory: Perspectives on and beyond Asia*, ed. Amitav Acharya and Barry Buzan (London: Routledge, 2010), 149.

[40] John Hughes, *Indonesian Upheaval* (New York: David McKay, 1967), 85–86.

seize political power directly given Sukarno's adamant opposition to any attempt to do so and distrust of the military. More importantly, he was the most popular politician of that period, and even many officers in the army were loyal to him.[41] At that time, Sukarno himself was worried about the growing popularity of the Communists, but needed them to counterbalance the military due to their organizational prowess. Thus, the "middle way" was the compromise that the military could not become involved in practical politics, including elections, but would participate in the government.

Even after the army finally crushed the Communists and Suharto rose to power in 1967, it still feared the latent threat of Communism. To keep this threat at bay, the military was determined to be involved in every aspect of government in order to strengthen the country both economically and ideologically, including foreign policy decision-making, especially toward Communist China in the 1970s.[42] Indonesia's only foreign adventure under Suharto—the invasion of East Timor in 1975—should be seen from this perspective, that Indonesia feared the creation of "a Southeast Asian Cuba" next door.[43]

More importantly, under dwifungsi, the army has a territorial function in which each of its thirteen divisions has the responsibility to maintain the resilience of the people in its territory. This includes cultivating popular support by engaging in social works, helping citizens in any way, and more importantly, building their spirit, nationalism, and bravery so they would participate in the defense of their country if needed. This is important because the Indonesian doctrine of warfare has three phases. The first phase is frontal attack, opposing the invader by using air and naval power before it reaches Indonesian territory. The second phase consists of containing and challenging the enemy on land and consolidating the position to at least create a stalemate. The third phase is a counteroffensive to force the enemy to withdraw or surrender.[44]

Territorial function is the integral part of the second and third phases of warfare, requiring the maintenance of national resilience and the morale of both the military and civilians working together to exhaust and expel invaders. As a result, territorial function is the most important part of Indonesian military doctrine. Not surprisingly, this doctrine unconsciously forces the military to adopt an inward-looking orientation that focuses on

---

[41] Daniel S. Lev, "The Political Role of the Army in Indonesia," *Pacific Affairs* 36, no. 4 (1963–64): 359.

[42] Evan A. Laksmana, "Regional Order by Other Means? Examining the Rise of Defense Diplomacy in Southeast Asia," *Asian Security* 8, no. 3 (2012): 251–70.

[43] Michael Richardson, "Ford and Kissinger Had Bigger Problems/'We Will Understand and Will Not Press You': How U.S. Averted Gaze When Indonesia Took East Timor," *New York Times*, May 20, 2002, http://www.nytimes.com/2002/05/20/news/20iht-timor2_ed3_.html.

[44] Pauker, "The Indonesian Doctrine," 12, 13, 161.

passive defense and to prioritize the army as its backbone. At the same time, to maintain this function effectively, as was especially the case during the Suharto era, the military must maintain peace and deal with political dissent that could interfere with people's will to defend the nation.

The military's fixation on resilience remains influential in how Indonesia treats its security arrangements, especially with ASEAN. This is evident in the role of ASEAN in Southeast Asian security. Without being explicitly labeled as "a regional security doctrine," the principle of ASEAN centrality stresses that a secure international environment requires "regional resilience, in which ideology, politics, the economy, society, culture, and the military strength are combined through socioeconomic and cultural cooperation."[45] Thus, even though ASEAN was not founded as a security organization, it was actually seen as part of a security mechanism, a bulwark against external threats and subversion, notably from the Communists.[46] When in 1971 Malaysia proposed the Zone of Peace, Freedom, and Neutrality—the creation of a neutral zone across all of the Southeast Asia region that would be guaranteed by the three major powers (the United States, the Soviet Union, and China)—Indonesia flatly rejected it, arguing that ASEAN states should develop their own inner strength and resilience rather than rely on others. Indonesia only accepted the concept after it was assured of the commitment to a Southeast Asia that is free from "external interference in any form or manifestation" and to security and stability as "primary responsibilities" of members of ASEAN itself.[47] In essence, "the only way to guarantee security in Southeast Asia was for each nation to strengthen itself internally, which essentially meant improving economic conditions."[48]

After the reformation of 1998 that ended the authoritarian rule of Suharto and ushered in the era of democracy, the military formally abandoned the concept of dwifungsi and thus no longer intervenes and dominates in both the political arena and foreign policymaking. However, the military staunchly maintains its territorial function—absent political interference—which it believes is still necessary to maintain national resilience. Thus, one of the biggest priorities of the Indonesian military remains passing the reserve military force bill, which would allow the establishment of a civilian military reserve and require every citizen to take part in compulsory training to

[45] Jorn Dosch, "Sovereignty Rules: Human Security, Civil Society, and the Limits of Liberal Reform," in *Hard Choices: Security, Democracy, and Regionalism in Southeast Asia*, ed. Donald K. Emmerson (Stanford: Walter H. Shorenstein Asia-Pacific Center, 2008), 76.

[46] Dewi Fortuna Anwar, *Indonesia in ASEAN: Foreign Policy and Regionalism* (Singapore: Institute of Southeast Asian Studies, 1994).

[47] Alice D. Ba, *[Re]Negotiating East and Southeast Asia: Region, Regionalism, and the Association of Southeast Asian Nations* (Stanford: Stanford University Press, 2009), 71, 74, 76.

[48] Weinstein, *Indonesian Foreign Policy*, 187.

maintain national morale and the spirit of nationalism.[49] At the same time, the military denied the accusation that the bill was a backdoor to return to power. The military pointed to regulation number 34/2004, which specifically forbids engagement in practical politics as evidence that it is no longer interested in taking an active part in practical politics.[50]

Yet even though the military has surrendered its political role, its social role remains an important part of its doctrine. Thus, the military continues to focus on guarding against harmful foreign cultures and ideas, seeing these as part of "a proxy war," an indirect attack on the country through "systematic asymmetric warfare," cyberwarfare, and media propaganda intended to create conflicts based on "social, culture, primordialism, ethnicity, race, and religion."[51] The most recent Indonesian Department of Defense white paper suggested that this proxy war is basically a 21st-century version of "divide and conquer" and stressed the need for the government to be aware of any attempt by foreign countries to split Indonesia. It lists the "Arab Spring, political and security upheaval in Egypt, [and] civil wars in Iraq, Afghanistan, Libya, and Syria" as examples of how states wage such proxy wars.[52]

As a result, during the debate over the lesbian, gay, bisexual, and transgender movement in Indonesia, Defense Minister Ryamizard Ryacudu declared that this movement was a dangerous invisible enemy that brainwashes people and unknowingly would conquer the nation.[53] Likewise, General Gatot Nurmantyo, the commander of the Indonesian National Armed Forces, declared that "the Indonesian Communist Party is dangerous, but neocapitalism and neoliberalism are more dangerous" because they could turn religious people into atheists, who will then embrace Communism and become fifth columnists.[54]

Thus, although the military no longer interferes in foreign policymaking, it still has some impacts. This can especially be seen in Indonesia's

---

[49] Markus Junianto Sihaloho, "Ministry Urges Approval of Reserve Military Force Bill," *Jakarta Globe*, January 13, 2009, http://jakartaglobe.beritasatu.com/archive/ministry-urges-approval-of-reserve-military-force-bill.

[50] Abraham Utama, "Dipercaya publik, TNI tidak boleh berkuasa seperti zaman orba" [Trusted by People, the Indonesian Military Could Not Hold Power Like during the New Order Era], CNN Indonesia, October 26, 2015, http://www.cnnindonesia.com/nasional/20151026164701-20-87469/dipercaya-publik-tni-tidak-boleh-berkuasa-seperti-zaman-orba.

[51] Ministry of Defense (Indonesia), *Buku putih pertahanan Indonesia 2015*.

[52] Ibid., 11.

[53] Syaiful Hakim, "Menhan: LGBT bagian 'proxy war'" [Minister of Defense: LGBT Is Part of Proxy War], Antara News, February 23, 2016, http://www.antaranews.com/berita/546668/menhan-lgbt-bagian-proxy-war.

[54] Bisma Alief, "Panglima TNI: Neo kapitalisme dan neo liberalisme lebih berbahaya dari PKI" [Commander of the TNI: Neocapitalism and Neoliberalism Are More Dangerous Than the Indonesian Communist Party], *Detik News*, June 2, 2016, http://news.detik.com/berita/3223776/panglima-tni-neo-kapitalisme-dan-neo-liberalisme-lebih-berbahaya-dari-pki.

power-projection capability. The military remains inward-looking, focusing more on dealing with invasions to Indonesia's inner islands and perceived internal or subversive threats than on trying to craft active outward-looking policies, notably in the South China Sea.

The principles of territorial function and resilience that underlie Indonesian military doctrine help shape Indonesian strategic culture by making it inward-looking. This preoccupation with internal threats in turn weakens Indonesia's ability to project military power abroad and challenge any strong external threats. Combined with the third element of Indonesian strategic culture, which is the idea of *bebas aktif* (a free and active foreign policy), this approach reinforces Indonesia's tendency to underbalance any threat militarily.

The Struggle for Independence and Indonesia's *Bebas Aktif* Foreign Policy

The war for independence was the formative period of Indonesian foreign policy. In the beginning, the new, Dutch-educated leaders expected the United States to support the new republic based on the principle of self-determination that "recognize[s] the right of all peoples to live under a government of their own choice."[55] Sutan Sjahrir, the first prime minister, further positioned Indonesia within the sphere of influence of the "capitalist-imperialist" United States and Great Britain. He argued that Indonesia should diplomatically align itself with U.S. interests in order to achieve independence since it did not have enough power to fight the domination of the United States.[56]

With that calculation in mind, the republic tried to gain as much goodwill as possible from the United States. First, President Sukarno, with whom the Dutch refused to negotiate due to his collaboration with the Japanese during World War II,[57] was relegated to the background as the head of state, while Sjahrir led the negotiations.[58] Many Indonesians were wary of the United States due to what they perceived as U.S. support for the Netherlands, first by the transfer of military surpluses to the Dutch troops in Indonesia and later

---

[55] Paul F. Gardner, *Shared Hopes, Separate Fears: Fifty Years of U.S.-Indonesian Relations* (Boulder: Westview Press, 1997), 3.

[56] Soetan Sjahrir, *Perjoeangan kita* [Our Struggle] (Bandung: Anjing Galak Penerbitan, 2010), 13–14.

[57] Alastair M. Taylor, *Indonesian Independence and the United Nations* (Ithaca: Cornell University Press, 1960), 10.

[58] Rudolf Mrázek, *Sjahrir: Politics and Exile in Indonesia* (Ithaca: Southeast Asia Program, 1994), 294.

by aid to the Dutch colonial government through the Marshall Plan.[59] Still, the new government regarded U.S. support as critical and worked to bring the United States to the bargaining table as a third party that would act as an honest broker during the negotiations. With the United States' guarantee that the Netherlands would hold up its end of the bargain, Indonesian independence would be secured.

This policy, however, was not especially popular, particularly among radical leftists, militants, and even the military, which did not trust the United States because the Dutch army wore U.S. uniforms and carried canteens marked "USA."[60] Moreover, as noted in the previous section, for many preserving an independent spirit mattered more. Tan Malaka, an influential militant and one of the biggest critics of the diplomatic course, declared that, "recognition of the Indonesian Republic by another state is not a condition for the existence of the Indonesian Republic." He argued instead that Indonesia should focus on armed struggle, utilizing the fighting spirit of the people, which was at its apex.[61]

Furthermore, Sjahrir's decision to make large concessions to the Dutch in exchange for de facto recognition—in the belief that, sooner or later, a completely independent Indonesia could regain all it had lost—proved to be very unpopular and led to the fall of his government. The next government under Amir Sjarifuddin faced high levels of military and economic deterioration. The shortages were such that the assistant chief of staff of the Indonesian Army, Colonel Simatupang, stated that while the republic could raise any size of volunteer army, it was severely limited by the lack of equipment and poor training for its officers.[62] In the end, Sjarifuddin signed the Renville Agreement "under perceptible American pressure" in 1948, and less than a week later, his cabinet fell as a result.[63]

Vice President Mohammad Hatta took over as the head of the government, becoming the prime minister and implementing the agreement. At this point, the pressure to invalidate the agreement was overwhelming. The Indonesian Communists demanded that Hatta align Indonesia with the Soviet Union, which they believed was far more sympathetic to their struggle and would assist Indonesia in its war for independence. Hatta refused, believing

---

[59] Kahin, *Nationalism and Revolution in Indonesia*, 402–3.

[60] Robert J. McMahon, *Colonialism and Cold War: The United States and the Struggle for Indonesian Independence, 1945–49* (Ithaca: Cornell University Press, 1981), 102.

[61] Mrázek, *Sjahrir*, 307, 310.

[62] "Telegram from the Consul General at Batavia (Livengood) to the Secretary of State, November 17, 1947," *Foreign Relations of the United States, 1947*, vol. 7, *The Far East* (Washington, D.C.: Government Printing Office 1972), 1,073.

[63] Kahin, *Nationalism and Revolution in Indonesia*, 228.

that the only way to guarantee that the Netherlands would stick to its side of the bargain was to have the United States as the guarantor of the agreement. By aligning itself with the Soviet Union, Indonesia would gain the enmity of the United States while receiving nothing in return, given that it would be very difficult for the Soviet Union to actually assist Indonesia in any way due to the sheer distance. At the same time, should Hatta dismiss the demand for Indonesia to align with the Soviet Union, he would risk domestic unrest, especially from the leftist, pro-Soviet parties.

In the end, Hatta declared that Indonesia would pick neither. Instead of aligning itself, Indonesia would pursue an independent foreign policy, commonly known as *kebijakan luar negeri bebas aktif* (free and active foreign policy), which he elaborated in a speech on September 2, 1948. In essence, Indonesia would not simply choose between being pro-Russian and being pro-American but rather be "an active agent entitled to decide its own standpoint....The policy of the Republic of Indonesia must be resolved in the light of its own interests and should be executed in consonance with the situations and facts it has to face."[64] By pushing Indonesia toward a free and active foreign policy, Hatta managed to quell the demands to align with the Soviet Union. By not committing itself to either side during the Cold War, the country could maintain its identity and safeguard its independence from both internal and external threats.[65]

Later, however, the political calculation that had motivated Hatta to take this course was forgotten. Instead, bebas aktif gained a mythical status—that Indonesia was pursuing a free and active foreign policy due to the country's fierce desire to be independent. This principle was reinforced by the beliefs that Indonesia will never be truly free without an independent foreign policy and that it has the potential for such a policy, given its strategic geopolitical position, abundance of natural resources, and huge Muslim population that would allow the country to project itself as a representative of the Muslim world. Moreover, the fact that the policy was created during the height of the revolution gave the necessary symbolism and political capital to its advocates. The mere existence of an active, assertive foreign policy was taken as a mark of independence, while participation in any military pact was seen as a renunciation of independence, not to mention as an act of involvement in unnecessary conflicts.[66]

In reality, however, the basic calculation of bebas aktif remained the same: it served as a political tool to delay taking any action that may seem

---

[64] Mohammad Hatta, "Indonesia's Foreign Policy," *Foreign Affairs*, April 1953, 446.

[65] Arnold C. Brackman, *Indonesian Communism: A History* (New York: Praeger, 1963), 141; and Russell H. Fifield, *The Diplomacy of Southeast Asia: 1945–1958* (New York: Harper, 1958), 121.

[66] Weinstein, *Indonesian Foreign Policy,* 186–87, 189.

politically inexpedient.[67] Overall, there has always been a conflict between the idealism of bebas aktif foreign policy and the realpolitik of international relations. Indonesian leaders must always affirm the independence of Indonesian foreign policy, even when it is to the detriment of their own foreign policy goals.

This conflict is evident when the concept is used by the government to avoid taking a strong position in international conflicts, such as the South China Sea dispute. Here, Indonesia positions itself as an honest impartial broker that pushes for diplomatic solutions as a way to increase national (and the government's own) prestige. In light of the Jokowi administration's interests in attracting much-needed Chinese investment in Indonesian infrastructure, this opaque position allows Indonesia to have its cake and eat it too, even though this may actually hurt the country's long-term interests, especially if the South China Sea problem were to erupt into an armed conflict with the potential to fragment ASEAN.

At the same time, the concept of bebas aktif has repeatedly been used by critics of the government and by the opposition as a way to score political points should the government be seen as either too friendly to foreign interests or as not sufficiently independent. The risk for not following the accepted common wisdom on bebas aktif is high. For example, in 1951, Prime Minister Sukiman allowed Foreign Minister Subarjo to sign a mutual security act with the United States, in which the United States would provide military equipment and weaponry in exchange for Indonesia supporting the Western bloc.[68] Reactions within Indonesia were so hostile that the agreement led to the collapse of the cabinet.[69]

In summary, bebas aktif has two main purposes: serving as an ideal, independent foreign policy that reflects the identity of Indonesia as an independent country and, at the same time, serving as a foreign policy tool that enables decision-makers to avoid making difficult choices that would not be popular domestically. Unfortunately, these two purposes have sometimes conflicted and resulted in policymaking contradictions that lead to idealistic foreign policies lacking in both impact and credibility. As S. Jayakumar, a former foreign minister of Singapore, argued, this principle puts more emphasis on symbolism than substance.[70] Bebas aktif prevents Indonesia

---

[67] Vibhanshu Shekhar, *Indonesia's Rise: Seeking Regional and Global Roles* (New Delhi: Pentagon Press, 2015), 192.

[68] Raymond Edward Stannard Jr., "The Role of American Aid in Indonesian-American Relations" (master's thesis, Cornell University, 1957), 40.

[69] Herbert Feith, *The Decline of Constitutional Democracy in Indonesia* (Ithaca: Cornell University Press, 1962), 63.

[70] Shunmugam Jayakumar, *Diplomacy: A Singapore Experience* (Singapore: Straits Times Press, 2011), 242.

from actually joining any kind of military alliance or taking any strong foreign policy posture, except on politically acceptable issues that have minimal impact on Indonesia's interests, such as the Israel-Palestine conflict.

Indonesia's Strategic Outlook

This chapter started by asking what causes Indonesia to underbalance against the growing threat from China, even though Indonesia's size, geostrategic location, and abundance of natural resources make it one of the most important countries in Southeast Asia and theoretically the natural leader of ASEAN. These factors should provide Jakarta a lot of leverage in its relationships with both Beijing and Washington. The answer is Indonesia's own strategic culture, which is based on three main elements: the need to protect national unity against the threat of foreign interventions, an inward focus that emphasizes maintaining an independent and resilient spirit, and finally the adoption of a completely free and active foreign policy that rejects any obligations to join military pacts or alliances.

The influence of these elements of Indonesian strategic culture on the country's security strategies can be seen in its role in ASEAN—notably in determining what kind of organization ASEAN is and shaping the security architecture of Southeast Asia. One of the main reasons that ASEAN, even today, is not a military alliance is that the Indonesian military and Indonesian decision-makers have been allergic to the idea of regional military pacts. The military leadership specifically rejected ASEAN as a joint defense pact due to the fear that this would end Indonesia's bebas aktif foreign policy.[71]

At the same time, however, in arguing that ASEAN should not be a military pact, Indonesia also refused to allow other countries to determine Southeast Asian security arrangements. This was evident in Indonesia's efforts to pressure the Philippines to remove the U.S. military from Clark Air Base and Subic Bay.[72] Later, as described above, Indonesia rejected Malaysia's proposal for a "complete neutralization" of the region, even though keeping foreign powers out of Southeast Asia was a goal of Indonesian foreign policy. While the concept guaranteed that there would not be any interventions from abroad, it also suggested that ASEAN had a "certain incapacity to cope with the regional environment."[73] Instead, Indonesia pushed for ASEAN countries to develop their own capabilities and resilience and not rely on others for regional security and defense.

---

[71] Anwar, *Indonesia in ASEAN*, 131–32.

[72] Ibid., 134.

[73] Ba, *[Re]Negotiating East and Southeast Asia*, 74.

Of course, other ASEAN countries did not see these actions as benign, with Malaysia complaining that Indonesia's "aspirations for regional dominance are as clear as ever."[74] The assertion had a ring of truth. On the one hand, Indonesia did see itself as the natural leader of Southeast Asia. On the other hand, its actions were based on a strategic culture that saw any stronger power in the region as a potential threat to national unity, and thus Indonesia aimed to prevent Southeast Asia from again becoming an arena for great-power politics. Therefore, it was much better for ASEAN countries to develop their own internal strength—meaning improving economic conditions and resilience rather than depending on unreliable foreign powers.[75]

This strain of thinking is still evident today, as these three elements continue to distort Indonesia's strategic calculations regarding its position and the potential threats to its interests. For example, the United States has deployed a small contingent of marines to Darwin, Australia. Both the United States and Australia see the deployment of those marines as a key component of the U.S. rebalance to Asia.[76] Despite both U.S. and Australian assurances to Indonesia, however, many Indonesians view this arrangement warily, believing that the real rationale is to threaten West Papua and to protect Freeport, a U.S.-based gold and copper mining company operating in that region.[77] In other words, the presence of a U.S. military base so close to Indonesia, regardless of its purpose, is seen as a security threat.[78]

That is also one of the main reasons that Indonesia has been underbalancing against China. It sees China as a power to balance against the United States to keep the United States from being the world's policeman. By not challenging China's expansionist policy too much, Indonesia hopes to play an influential mediating role in the region, juggling the competing interests of the United States, China, Japan, and also India.[79] In fact, Indonesia tried to leverage its position under the previous president Yudhoyono and his foreign minister Marty Natalegawa. Using the ideas of "dynamic equilibrium" and "a thousand friends, zero enemies," Indonesia tried to "involve all major relevant

---

[74] Ba, *[Re]Negotiating East and Southeast Asia*, 74.

[75] Weinstein, *Indonesian Foreign Policy*, 187.

[76] Stuart Rollo and Tess Lea, "As U.S. Marines Arrive in Darwin, Australia Must Consider Its Strategic Position," *Sydney Morning Herald*, April 24, 2016, http://www.smh.com.au/comment/as-us-marines-arrive-in-darwin-australia-must-consider-its-strategic-position-20160422-goco5s.html.

[77] "U.S. Military Presence in Darwin Arouses Suspicion in Many Quarters," Antara News, November 23, 2011, http://www.antaranews.com/en/news/77866/us-mily-presence-in-darwin-arouses-suspicion-in-many-quarters.

[78] David McRae, "Indonesian Press Response to U.S. Marines Deal," Lowy Interpreter, November 23, 2011, http://www.lowyinterpreter.org/post/2011/11/23/Indonesian-press-responds-to-US-Marines-deal.aspx.

[79] Daniel Novotsky, *Torn between the United States and China: Elite Perceptions and Indonesian Foreign Policy* (Singapore: Institute of Southeast Asian Studies, 2010), 223.

powers within a more cooperative framework as a basis for the development of an inclusive regional architecture."[80] On the issue of the South China Sea, for example, Indonesia has always maintained that it is not a claimant state and thus is able to fairly mediate the disputes.[81]

However, the other reason Indonesia has been underbalancing against China is that it simply does not possess much ability to threaten China militarily, given its lack of power-projection capabilities and military alliances. As a result, Indonesia's foreign policy lacks credibility, especially as China starts to flex its muscles in the South China Sea. For instance, Indonesia is deploying marines, air force special units, an army battalion, three frigates, a new radar system, and drones and is planning to add F-16 fighter jets and an Oerlikon Skyshield air defense system at the Natuna Islands, whose surrounding waters overlap with China's nine-dash line.[82] While significant, these forces are barely sufficient for defending the islands and are inadequate for projecting power, considering that China will soon possess the world's second-largest blue water navy and already owns the world's largest blue water coast guard and maritime militia.[83] (**Figures 1** and **2** compare Indonesia's military expenditure with that of China and other regional states.)

Finally, Indonesia's unwillingness to set a precedent for foreign interference has made it very difficult for Indonesia and other ASEAN states to pressure recalcitrant members to fall in line and create a united front (e.g., by threatening expulsion from ASEAN). This was evident during the ASEAN summit in Cambodia in July 2012. When ASEAN failed to issue a joint communiqué for the first time in its history after Cambodia, then chair of ASEAN, refused the Philippines' demands to mention its dispute with China at Scarborough Shoal in the joint communiqué, the heroic shuttle diplomacy efforts of Foreign Minister Natalegawa prevailed in maintaining at least the facade of unity by having ASEAN issue a face-saving "common position."[84] It was clear, however, that China, through sheer political, military,

---

[80] Dewi Fortuna Anwar, "Indonesia's Foreign Relations: Policy Shaped by the Ideal of 'Dynamic Equilibrium,'" East Asia Forum, February 4, 2014, http://www.eastasiaforum.org/2014/02/04/indonesias-foreign-relations-policy-shaped-by-the-ideal-of-dynamic-equilibrium.

[81] Ministry of Defense (Indonesia), *Buku putih pertahanan Indonesia 2015*, 4, 7.

[82] Vishakha Sonawane, "South China Sea Controversy: Indonesia to Deploy F-16 Fighter Jets to Natuna Islands," *International Business Times*, April 1, 2016, http://www.ibtimes.com/south-china-sea-controversy-indonesia-deploy-f-16-fighter-jets-natuna-islands-2346657; and Ridzwan Rahmat, "Indonesia to Deploy Skyshield Air Defence System in South China Sea," IHS Jane's 360, April 6, 2016, http://www.janes.com/article/59305/indonesia-to-deploy-skyshield-air-defence-system-in-south-china-sea.

[83] Andrew Erickson and Conor M. Kennedy, "China's Fishing Militia Is a Military Force in All but Name," War Is Boring, July 9, 2016, https://warisboring.com/chinas-fishing-militia-is-a-military-force-in-all-but-name-58265cbdd7d#.k65dbf96h.

[84] Vikram Nehru, "Shuttle Diplomacy in the South China Sea," *Jakarta Post*, August 30, 2012, http://www.thejakartapost.com/news/2012/08/30/shuttle-diplomacy-south-china-sea.html.

FIGURE 1   Military expenditure: Indonesia and China, 2003–15

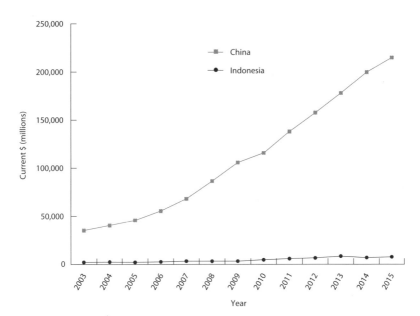

SOURCE: Stockholm International Peace Research Institute (SIPRI), SIPRI Military Expenditure Database, https://www.sipri.org/databases/milex.

and economic power, had influenced ASEAN's decision-making process.[85] Rather than pressuring Cambodia to conform to the expectations of other members, Indonesia and the rest of ASEAN acceded to Cambodian and Chinese demands.

Without any credible option left, ASEAN, especially Indonesia, has been pushing for a code of conduct with China that would have an enforcement mechanism to punish violations and would thus help limit China's intransigence in the South China Sea.[86] Yet despite China's delaying tactics and refusal to commit itself to a "code with teeth," most ASEAN countries, including Indonesia, do not push China too hard and instead are content to maintain the status quo. As Donald Emmerson asked, "Why not prolong the happy combination of American ships for deterrence and Chinese markets

[85] Carlyle A. Thayer, "Behind the Scenes of ASEAN's Breakdown," *Asia Times Online*, July 27, 2012, http://www.atimes.com/atimes/Southeast_Asia/NG27Ae03.html.

[86] Ministry of Defense (Indonesia), *Buku putih pertahanan Indonesia 2015*, 8.

FIGURE 2 Military expenditure: Indonesia and other Southeast Asian countries, 2003–15

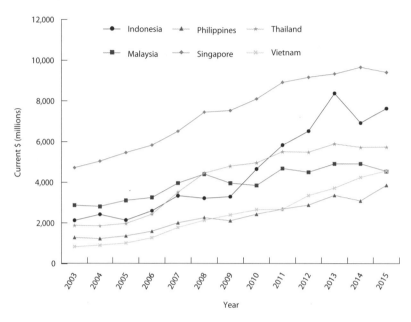

SOURCE: SIPRI, SIPRI Military Expenditure Database, https://www.sipri.org/databases/milex.

for profit?"[87] At the same time, however, this approach has the potential to leave Indonesia, as a powerless leader of ASEAN, with less and less credibility. By the time China is seen as a major threat in the South China Sea by ASEAN, Indonesia may not have many cards up its sleeve to deal with this problem.

Therefore, while President Jokowi seems to be taking a much harder stance against China's incursion in the South China Sea, Indonesia's foreign policy remains constrained by the country's own inability to project power. Indonesia is hamstrung by the defensive and inward-looking orientation of its armed forces, the fact that military pacts and alliances remain taboo and politically toxic, and the unwillingness to create a precedent by using international organizations, notably ASEAN, to interfere in other states' affairs. As a result, Indonesia has little room to maneuver in responding to China's threat.

---

[87] Donald K. Emmerson, "Sunnyland or Rancho Mirage? ASEAN and the South China Sea," *Yale Global*, February 23, 2016, http://yaleglobal.yale.edu/content/sunnylands-or-rancho-mirage-asean-and-south-china-sea.

Conclusion

In reacting to the rising threat from China to Indonesian interests in the form of the South China Sea disputes, Indonesia has mostly focused on diplomatic approaches. It sees itself as able to use China to balance against other potential threats, particularly the interference of the United States, in order to maintain a Southeast Asia that is free from the influence of outside powers. The logic is that if China is becoming too aggressive, then Indonesia will move closer to the United States, and vice versa. This approach is rooted in Indonesia's strategic culture of preventing the establishment of great-power competition so close to the archipelago, which could undermine its unity. More importantly, however, by focusing on diplomatic approaches, the government and military could actually bypass one of the most serious problems within the Indonesian military itself: the lack of a grand strategy on what the role of the military should be in addressing external threats.

The diplomatic approach itself is, by default, the only viable approach at this point to counter the rising threat from China. Indonesia simply does not have strong power-projection capabilities due to a military culture that puts more emphasis on defensive actions, resilience, and the spirit to wage incessant guerilla warfare until its enemy is forced to withdraw. The military's fixation on territorial doctrine has the impact of making it inward-looking, focused on internal problems rather than on possible threats from outside. It is still trying to determine its role in post-reformation Indonesia. On the one hand, the military believes that it is the ultimate defender of Indonesia as a nation and that, as a result, it needs to maintain its vigilance against both domestic and international threats. On the other hand, in light of the military's professionalization and separation from the police force, such a view hampers its ability and willingness to engage in painful reforms, such as strengthening the role of the navy at the expense of the army.

As a result, Indonesia faces the dilemma that it relies too much on its geostrategic situation to pursue its strategic interests, notably its location on a global trade route and abundant natural resources. Yet, when push comes to shove, Indonesian diplomacy is not backed by adequate military power, and thus the country may find itself in an awkward position with no other recourse but to keep negotiating.

Although Indonesia is still respected as one of the leading countries in ASEAN, not surprisingly in the past couple of years other ASEAN countries have been looking elsewhere for military cooperation in light of China's intransigence. Malaysia, Myanmar, the Philippines, Singapore, and Vietnam, for example, have been moving closer to the United States. While these countries are still paying lip service to ASEAN solidarity—as was evident during the ASEAN-China Special Kunming Meeting in June 2016—the facade of unity is starting to crack under Chinese pressure.[88]

Given the growing threat from China and the rising discontent of many Southeast Asian nations with China's intransigence, the United States has the opportunity to improve its position in Southeast Asia by stressing its interests and commitments to the region. The United States can do this not only by challenging China, especially in maintaining freedom of navigation in South China Sea, but also by pushing for more military cooperation among members of ASEAN. Considering that there is still quite a lack of trust among militaries, even between ASEAN members, the United States needs to put more emphasis on trust-building exercises, such as by becoming more involved in Indonesia's multilateral naval exercise Komodo and conducting more officer exchanges with members of ASEAN.

At the same time, however, it is important for Washington to understand the underlying logic of Indonesian strategic culture. Indonesia is deeply suspicious of not only the United States but also other countries that it perceives as having the ability to split the country apart. Washington must craft policies that will reassure Indonesia of the United States' benign intent toward the country. The United States needs to help secure Indonesia's position in Southeast Asia because it remains one of the most important countries in the region geostrategically and is a very useful partner in the U.S. pivot to Asia in addressing the challenge from China.

First, the United States needs to reassure Jakarta that it has Indonesia's best interests in mind by increasing military-to-military cooperation and especially by helping Indonesia modernize its military, both in educating its officers and in upgrading its outdated equipment, with the objective of improving the capabilities of the Indonesian Navy and Air Force. The United States also must stress the need for the Indonesian military to shift from an inward focus to a regional one and find a common ground from which to cooperate more fully with the United States and regional partners, such as Australia and other ASEAN countries.

Second, at least in the short term, the United States should stop needling Indonesia over its human rights record, particularly in West Papua. Granted that human rights are a U.S. foreign policy priority, but in the case of Indonesia pushing this agenda has done nothing but increase distrust among Indonesians, raising the fear that the United States is using

[88] Prashanth Parameswaran, "What Really Happened at the ASEAN-China Special Kunming Meeting," *Diplomat*, June 21, 2016, http://thediplomat.com/2016/06/what-really-happened-at-the-asean-china-special-kunming-meeting.

human rights issues as a cudgel to create disunity in Indonesia, or worse to split West Papua from Indonesia. Moreover, there are still raw feelings in Indonesia over the U.S. arms embargo in 1999 in response to human rights violations in East Timor, which led the Indonesian public to be mistrustful of U.S. intentions.

Finally, regardless of their differences, both Indonesia and the United States share a common interest in maintaining peace and security in Southeast Asia. The United States needs to emphasize that commonality while cultivating Indonesia as a valuable partner.

EXECUTIVE SUMMARY

This chapter analyzes the central components of U.S. strategic culture, considers the historical and contemporary sources of tension in that culture, and assesses their foreign policy implications.

MAIN ARGUMENT

U.S. strategic culture is informed by classically liberal assumptions dating back to the nation's founding. According to these assumptions, the U.S. has a special role to play in promoting a more open, democratic, and liberal international order, whether by expansion or example. Yet there has always been lively debate within the U.S. over how best to promote such an order. A strong emphasis on limited liability in strategic affairs exists alongside these liberal internationalist assumptions, modifying and constraining the country in significant ways. These dual emphases—a liberal world order pursued at a limited expense—often create tensions in U.S. foreign policy strategy, encouraging gaps between ends and means. Dissident strategic subcultures also exist, notably those of progressivism and nationalism, both of which surged to prominence during the 2016 presidential primaries. It remains unclear whether these dissident strains can be reconciled with continued U.S. support for a liberal international order.

POLICY IMPLICATIONS

- U.S. strategic culture tends to encourage gaps between declared liberal internationalist ends and limited forward means. These gaps have been observable even in relatively successful cases, such as the rebalancing of U.S. foreign policy to Asia.

- A central task of the next president will be to address these gaps—for example, by bolstering U.S. diplomatic, economic, and military presence in East Asia.

- The perceived failure to close the gaps between ends and means in U.S. policy toward China, in particular, will only increase the likely severity of a nationalist backlash within the U.S.

U.S. Strategic Culture:
Liberalism with Limited Liability

Colin Dueck

U.S. strategic culture and foreign policy behavior have long been influenced by a national civic creed that is classically liberal at heart. According to this system of beliefs, the United States has a special role to play in promoting a more open, democratic, and interdependent world order. However, there has always been lively debate among Americans regarding how to promote such a benign order. One school of thought suggests that the United States must expand the international sphere of democratic governance, even by force if necessary. The other school suggests that the United States can best promote liberal ideals overseas by example. These two schools of thought, expansionism and exemplarism, may seem like polar opposites, but they actually have a great deal in common—namely, the desire to see democratic values and systems of government spread globally. This classical liberal component operates in combination with another powerful element in U.S. strategic culture: a preference for limited liability. The United States often pursues very ambitious foreign policy goals through means that are disproportionately limited—not only relative to stated goals but to latent material power. This combination of ambitious classically liberal international goals with limited liability frequently creates contradictions or gaps between ends and means in U.S. national

Colin Dueck is a Professor in the Schar School of Policy and Government at George Mason University. He can be reached at <cdueck@gmu.edu>.

Sections of this chapter are adapted from the author's previous work in *The Obama Doctrine: American Grand Strategy Today* (New York: Oxford University Press, 2015); and *Reluctant Crusaders: Power, Culture, and Change in American Grand Strategy* (Princeton: Princeton University Press, 2006).

security strategy. President Barack Obama's foreign policy, like that of his predecessors, has illustrated some of the tensions between the promotion of liberal internationalist goals and the maintenance of limited liability.

If liberal internationalism combined with limited liability in one form or another has been the dominant strain within U.S. strategic culture over the past three-quarters of a century, there are nonetheless dissident strategic cultures or subcultures that have a significant ongoing impact—particularly given continuing frustration with the internationalist paradigm. U.S. nationalists favor hard-line counterterrorism policies and take limited liability seriously, but they oppose globalization and claim no special adherence to classically liberal goals overseas. Such nationalists proved to be a rising force within the Republican Party during the Obama era, eventually finding their champion in presidential candidate Donald Trump. U.S. progressives resemble liberal exemplarists in their resistance to military intervention abroad, but they have an even deeper commitment to what they describe as the demilitarization of U.S. foreign policy, combined with intense skepticism regarding traditional claims of American exceptionalism. Such progressives viewed U.S. foreign policy as overly militarized, even under Obama, and they rallied to presidential candidate Senator Bernie Sanders in 2016. Finally, U.S. foreign policy realists in both parties continued to emphasize international balances of power, the careful coordination of force and diplomacy, the limits of transformational visions, and the foreign policy actions rather than the domestic behavior of other states. Altogether, the liberal internationalist paradigm came under severe assault during the 2016 presidential election campaign, particularly within the Republican Party.

The United States' classically liberal strategic culture has great strengths, but it also encourages inevitable tensions in the creation of solvent security strategies. Popular debate over U.S. foreign policy tends to cycle through periods of support for international activism and periods of retrenchment. On balance, the Obama era was one of retrenchment. Yet it would be incorrect to suggest that the median U.S. voter favored isolationism. Rather, the popular mood regarding international commitments was mixed and ambivalent, even favoring continued engagement in multiple respects. It would furthermore be a mistake to suggest that U.S. strategic culture renders the conduct of effective international strategies impossible. Historically, the United States has often had considerable success in promoting its own position and interests abroad. The evidence suggests that the quality of political leadership, especially in the person of the president, is a crucial variable in the formation of steady, engaged, and prudent foreign policies.

This chapter begins with an examination of long-standing, distinctive traits in U.S. strategic culture, including its key qualities, sources, effects, and variations. Historically, the combination of ambitious liberal international goals with limited liability is a dominant theme in U.S. strategic culture. The Obama administration's policy of rebalancing toward Asia is then discussed in light of that theme. Next, the chapter continues with an analysis of three important yet "dissident" strategic subcultures: nationalist, progressive, and realist. Finally, the chapter analyzes the cyclical nature of foreign policy debates within the United States between these various cultural tendencies. Candidates in the 2016 presidential election campaign are described in terms of where they fit into these tendencies, and some predictions are offered as to their possible U.S. foreign policy priorities. The conclusion briefly summarizes the chapter's central findings, including implications for U.S. foreign policy.

Exceptional America

For realists, the international system is the single greatest overall cause of any nation's strategic behavior. When a given state becomes more powerful, for example, or faces greater threats from abroad, it tends to adopt a more costly and expansive foreign policy strategy. Conversely, when a state becomes less powerful, or faces fewer threats, then it tends to adopt a less costly and less expansive strategy. There is, however, normally some indeterminacy in international conditions, some range of strategic options that might plausibly serve the national interest, and within that limited range, a nation's culture can have a significant impact on strategic choice. Country-specific cultural variables can influence the preferences and prescriptions of a state's foreign policy leaders, predispose a state toward certain strategic choices over others, and delimit the range of acceptable choices in a given situation.

The United States is hardly exempt from the pressures and constraints of the international system. Historically, Americans have often been quite effective at promoting their country's relative power, influence, and interests overseas. Yet the United States also has distinctive cultural traits, and these traits have certainly shaped the precise manner in which it pursues interests. So in order to fully understand U.S. foreign policy behavior, it is necessary to understand the strategic culture of the United States.

U.S. strategic culture begins with a distinct national self-image of exceptionalism. For many foreign observers, and even for some Americans—especially within the academy—this conception seems awkward, insofar as it represents nothing more than a blunt assertion of U.S. national superiority. But in fact the term means something more than this, something quite different and specific. For nineteenth-century socialists such as Friedrich Engels, American exceptionalism referred to a bundle of national characteristics that made socialism difficult to promote within the United States.[1] These characteristics included a national creed that Engels recognized as classically liberal in its essence rather than socialist or reactionary. The fact that belief in this creed is still held with considerable intensity to this day, by a great majority of politically active Americans, is precisely what gives it such force.

The United States consequently has a very definite founding myth, not in the sense that it is untrue, but in the sense that it helps explain who Americans are. To an extent that is unusual compared with other countries, U.S. citizens define their national identity according to a classical liberal set of beliefs that emphasizes individual freedom, equality of rights, majority rule, progress, enterprise, the rule of law, and strict limits of the state.[2] No doubt the power of this creed within the United States over time has much to do with material conditions, such as plentiful land, a predominant middle class, and the recurrent need to integrate new immigrants from a variety of backgrounds. This creed was locked in, so to speak, by the justifications offered for rebellion against Great Britain, and it has persisted. That is not to say that this creed has been monolithic or unchanging. There has, in fact, been intense and sometimes violent conflict over its exact meaning and application. Nevertheless, the U.S. classical liberal tradition, broadly defined, is a big tent and has had remarkable success in integrating and defusing potential domestic-ideological opponents. Rather than really questioning the fundamental premises of this tradition, Americans tend to argue over its precise definition. So if there is such a thing as a distinctly U.S. approach to foreign policy—one due to cultural factors—then it ought to flow in part from this classical liberal creed, and the power it has over U.S. strategic culture.

Liberal Goals: Expansion versus Example

The classical liberal tradition assumes that progress in world affairs is possible—that the international system is not necessarily stuck in an endless cycle of conflict, war, and balance-of-power politics. According to classical liberals, democratic governments are inherently less warlike than authoritarian ones; democracy encourages trade, and trade, in turn, encourages peace.

---

[1] Karl Marx and Frederick Engels, *Selected Correspondence, 1846–1895*, trans. Donna Torr (New York: International Publishers, 1942), 449, 467, 501.

[2] Louis Hartz, *The Liberal Tradition in America* (New York: Harcourt, Brace, and World, 1955), 4–11; Samuel P. Huntington, *American Politics: The Promise of Disharmony* (Cambridge: Belknap Press of Harvard, 1981), chap. 2; and Seymour Martin Lipset, *American Exceptionalism: A Double-Edged Sword* (New York: W.W. Norton, 1997), 31–52.

The result is a virtuous cycle in which popular governments, commercial exchange, and peaceful international relations feed off one another.[3]

The United States, for its part, was founded in the hope of building a more liberal order in world affairs. This new order was to be characterized by peace, progress, republican forms of government, trade, freedom, and the rule of law.[4] It represented a self-conscious rejection of the eighteenth-century European order, supposedly characterized by militarism, autocracy, war, secret alliances, corruption, and balance-of-power politics. Many Americans thought of—and continue to think of—the United States as morally and politically distinct from the Old World. Beyond this belief, Americans have long taken it for granted that their experiment in republican government has implications for the rest of the world.[5]

The promotion of a more liberal international order, broadly speaking, has always been a central goal of U.S. foreign policy. It is of course only one of many such goals. But the United States is remarkable for the extent to which classical liberal assumptions have actually informed the nation's international behavior. A more liberal international system, characterized by democratic governments and open markets, is seen by many U.S. foreign policymakers as a worthy end in itself. More importantly, such an international system is seen as serving U.S. interests, given that it makes the United States more influential, prosperous, and secure. Consequently, there is fairly wide agreement, in the abstract, within the United States over the principle of promoting a more liberal world order. The real question has always been how to promote such a system. And on this question, two competing answers have traditionally been given.

One school of thought has argued that the United States must expand the global sphere of democracy and human rights, by force if necessary. This school is expansionist or interventionist, but toward classically liberal ends. The origins of U.S. expansionism are sometimes traced to Woodrow Wilson or sometimes even earlier to the war against Spain. In reality, however, the emphasis on creating what Thomas Jefferson called an "empire of liberty"—through physical expansion—dates back to the very founding of the United States. The nation's expansionist tradition certainly existed before Wilson and before the 1890s, as evidenced by periodic and popular support for U.S. expansion across the North American continent.

---

[3] Michael W. Doyle, *Ways of War and Peace* (New York: W.W. Norton, 1997), 205–311.

[4] Felix Gilbert, *To the Farewell Address* (Princeton: Princeton University Press, 1961), 16–17; and Gordon S. Wood, *The American Revolution: A History* (New York: Modern Library Chronicles, 2002), 106–8.

[5] Michael H. Hunt, *Ideology and U.S. Foreign Policy* (New Haven: Yale University Press, 1987), 17–18.

Expansionists believe that the United States should transform the international system to preserve the U.S. experiment at home. This school of thought had particular impact during the Cold War, as well as during both world wars, and it had a significant impact again under George W. Bush immediately following the terrorist attacks of September 11.

The alternative school of thought—comprising exemplarists—has argued that the United States best promotes liberal ideals overseas by example.[6] According to this tradition, the United States should remain somewhat detached from the messiness of international politics; it should provide a sanctuary for freedom but follow a strategy of nonintervention with regard to military conflict overseas. This school had special influence in the years prior to 1941 but has resurfaced from time to time, as it did during and after both the Vietnam and Iraq wars.

The debate between expansionists and exemplarists recurs again and again in U.S. history. The two sides seem like opposites, but they actually have much in common: namely, the desire to see democratic values and systems of government spread overseas. They differ on tactics, but both philosophies contain a strong element of idealism and reject older traditions of balance-of-power politics. Both expansionists and exemplarists, in other words, work from classical liberal assumptions. Americans can and often have been quite realistic in promoting their national interests abroad, but nineteenth-century European realism or realpolitik as a self-conscious school of thought has never had a very broad audience among the United States' opinion elites.

The Impact on U.S. Diplomacy and the Use of Force

One potential counter to the above assessment is to say that liberal ideas have little real impact on U.S. foreign policy behavior. And no doubt there is an important distinction between symbolic overarching idealism, on the one hand, and operational pragmatism, on the other. But in truth, public and presidential references to liberal foreign policy goals are not inconsequential. References to common ideals function as a form of communication between policymakers and the public so that foreign policy takes on a meaning intelligible in terms of the national creed. Classical liberal assumptions furthermore have a filtering effect on the process by which U.S. foreign policy officials formulate national goals and perceive international conditions. In this sense, U.S. liberal strategic culture really does help explain foreign policy outcomes. The better question is what sort of impact does this culture have.

---

[6] H.W. Brands, *What America Owes the World: The Struggle for the Soul of Foreign Policy* (New York: Cambridge University Press, 1998), 7–9.

The answer, it turns out, is mixed. The liberal tradition has many welcome and positive effects on the conduct of U.S. foreign policy, but it has unintended, negative outcomes as well. One obvious negative consequence is the implication that if the United States could only defeat or reform its overseas opponents once and for all, then it could achieve the definitive success of a liberal world order. The problem, of course, is that permanent victories in international relations are rare. When euphoric expectations are disappointed, frustration ensues, tempting Americans to retreat into an exemplarist or noninterventionist stance. These periods of disengagement typically leave the United States unprepared for the next challenge, and so the unfortunate cycle of under- and overreaction begins anew.[7]

In a sense, the classical liberal tradition sees the entire enterprise of national security strategy as rather suspect. Secret diplomacy, closeted elites, large standing militaries, security precautions, intelligence services, covert operations, powerful executives, and Machiavellian ethics—all of these are common features of national security policy, and all of them appear suspicious or even sinister from a classical liberal perspective. The liberal tendency is to want to keep a tight lid on these practices. At the same time, such practices are sometimes necessary to protect a liberal society from external dangers. Consequently, there is a natural and inevitable tension between the classical liberal worldview and the effective conduct of national security policy.[8] Can the United States play the role of a great power and still be true to its domestic libertarian traditions? This is a debate that recurs in U.S. history, reflecting a distinctly American set of concerns. It is hardly surprising that liberal ideas sometimes give way to national security. What is interesting, from both a historical and comparative perspective, is that this debate occurs at all.

Limited Liability

U.S. strategic culture is also informed by assumptions of limited liability, the strength of which varies over time. Limited liability may be defined as a preference for avoiding costs and commitments in grand strategy, to an extent that is actually inconsistent with stated goals.[9] This tradition has

---

[7] George F. Kennan, *American Diplomacy* (Chicago: University of Chicago Press, 1951), 65–90.

[8] Huntington, *American Politics*, 236–45.

[9] The concept of limited liability was developed by B.H. Liddell Hart during the 1930s. Liddell Hart argued that British interests would be well served—and had been well served in the past—by avoiding major ground commitments on the European continent. Subsequent commentators have countered this idea and shown that Britain frequently relied on substantial ground commitments abroad to achieve its foreign policy goals. See Brian Bond, *Liddell Hart: A Study of His Military Thought* (London: Cassell, 1977); Paul M. Kennedy, *The Rise and Fall of British Naval Mastery* (London: Ashfield Press, 1986); and John J. Mearsheimer, *Liddell Hart and the Weight of History* (Ithaca: Cornell University Press, 1989).

historically influenced U.S. foreign policy in two ways. First, it has meant that the United States often plays a smaller role in world affairs than one would expect given the country's considerable latent power. For example, by the beginning of the twentieth century the United States already had immense material capabilities, yet it was extremely reluctant to employ those resources to promote its economic and strategic interests in Europe and East Asia. It is perhaps surprising that such a powerful country failed to promote its own leading role in the world for as long as the United States did. One source of this refusal lies in a deeply rooted cultural preference for limited liability.

Second, assumptions of limited liability have encouraged the pursuit of foreign policy aims through disproportionately limited means. Indeed, the disjuncture between ends and means has been so common in U.S. diplomatic history that it appears to be culturally determined. This is not to deny that Americans have paid a heavy price over the years for sustaining a leading role in the world; obviously, they have. It is rather to state that the United States has generally been unwilling to pay the costs that would be fully commensurate with the goals and policies articulated by U.S. foreign policy officials. Historically, the United States has tended to prefer limited liability in strategic affairs relative both to the goals laid out by U.S. officials and to its actual material power. In this sense, a keen preference for limited liability is an important part of U.S. strategic culture. U.S. strategy in East Asia during the early twentieth century provides a leading example of this pattern. As Walter Lippmann pointed out in his classic work *U.S. Foreign Policy: Shield of the Republic*, the United States acquired control over the Philippines after a war with Spain in 1898, yet never really developed the capacity to defend it.[10] This gap between ends and means—the so-called Lippmann gap—had profound implications for U.S. policy in the region and reflected a long-standing desire to maintain limited liability in strategic affairs.

The inclination toward limited liability was especially powerful prior to World War II. This meant that the United States' preference was for a policy of strategic disengagement from other powers, not simply on utilitarian grounds but on the basis of deeply held cultural beliefs. George Washington best articulated these commonly held assumptions in his 1796 Farewell Address, in which he argued that "the great rule of conduct for us in regard to foreign nations is in extending our commercial relations, to have with them as little political connection as possible."[11] Of course, Americans never rejected trade and economic opportunities abroad—far from it. Nor did they reject U.S. expansion on the North American continent or within the

---

[10] Walter Lippmann, *U.S. Foreign Policy: Shield of the Republic* (Boston: Little, Brown, 1943), 24–46.

[11] Washington's address is available in Thomas G. Paterson, ed., *Major Problems in American Foreign Policy, Volume 1: To 1914* (Lexington: D.C. Heath, 1989), 74–77.

Western Hemisphere. They certainly hoped the example of their democracy would spread overseas. Outside Latin America and the Pacific, however, and well into the twentieth century, Americans were generally reluctant to make strategic commitments, to engage in alliance diplomacy with other major powers, or to make concrete material sacrifices in support of broad foreign policy goals. The 1941 attack on Pearl Harbor led to a new era in U.S. foreign policy, one in which strict non-entanglement would be laid aside for good. But assumptions of limited liability continued to inform U.S. foreign policy and still do to this day.

As to why this tradition of limited liability has been so strong within the United States, the answer seems to lie in a combination of historical, geopolitical, institutional, and cultural factors. Historically, Americans grew used to following a strategy of disengagement from European alliances; the country's prosperity seemed to justify that strategy, and it was only in the face of two world wars that this strategy was finally questioned and overturned. Geopolitically, the existence of two great oceans separating the United States from any other major military power has also encouraged a somewhat insular strategic mentality. The United States' relative distance and security from conventional military threats have frequently fostered a mindset that denies the need for costly, long-term commitments overseas.[12]

U.S. political institutions have reinforced the tendency toward limited liability in strategic affairs. The challenge of mobilizing public and congressional support for costly new foreign policy initiatives is considerable. Indeed, the U.S. government's foreign policy apparatus is fragmented, decentralized, and constrained to an unusual extent among advanced democracies. The most important constraint on executive power lies in the division of authority between the president and Congress—a division instituted deliberately so as to check the power of national leaders. Historical practice has not conclusively settled the issue of congressional authority in foreign affairs. Presidents are also constrained by public opinion and ultimately by the prospects for successful re-election. Public opinion within the United States grants considerable leeway to presidential activism in foreign affairs, but there are limits to this deference. The American public is usually unenthusiastic, for example, about military intervention overseas, and presidents are less likely to use force during election season than at other times in part for this reason.[13] While the evidence is mixed, on balance it suggests that within the United States domestic political considerations typically act as a constraint on costly strategic initiatives, rather than as a

---

[12] Colin S. Gray, *The Geopolitics of Super Power* (Lexington: University of Kentucky Press, 1988), 45.

[13] Kurt Taylor Gaubatz, *Elections and War: The Electoral Incentive in the Democratic Politics of War and Peace* (Stanford: Stanford University Press, 1999).

stimulus toward them.[14] In this way, the U.S. political system tends to pull its foreign policy back in the direction of limited liability.

Finally, in an important sense, assumptions of limited liability are implicit within the classical liberal tradition that informs U.S. strategic culture. Liberal ideas can certainly encourage a crusading approach to international affairs. Fundamentally, however, the liberal assumption is that such crusades are not typical—and neither, for that matter, is military competition between states. For liberals, the tendency of history is toward a peaceful, democratic international system. Military intervention may sometimes be necessary, temporarily, to stave off threats. But the baseline liberal assumption is that a more peaceful international order can and will evolve through economic exchange and social interaction without the need for regular military intervention on the part of any nation-state. Indeed, for much of U.S. history, assumptions of limited liability were seen as being entirely compatible with the most ambitious visions for a new and progressive world order. The U.S. liberal tradition has therefore played into long-term assumptions of limited liability, even when liberals are acting as crusaders.[15]

U.S. Strategic Culture and the Rebalance to Asia

President Obama's foreign policy illustrated some of the conflicting tendencies inherent in U.S. strategic culture, along with his own particular way of handling them. This was true even in relatively successful cases such as U.S. policy in the Asia-Pacific. During Obama's first term in office, his administration announced a new pivot or rebalance of U.S. policy toward Asia, building on the efforts of previous presidents. The administration's stated goal was to nurture the strength of an open, rules-based, interdependent, and cooperative democratic order within the Asia-Pacific—including with China. To that end, the Obama administration engaged Beijing diplomatically, militarily, and economically in hopes of pursuing common solutions on issues such as nonproliferation, climate change, human rights, trade, finance, and transnational crime. It built on the George W. Bush administration's extensive engagement with New Delhi, supporting India as a rising power in the Asia-Pacific. It negotiated and promoted the Trans-Pacific Partnership (TPP), a trade agreement with eleven

---

[14] This is not to say that the impact of these domestic political factors and institutions is, on balance, dysfunctional or irrational. For a spirited defense of congressional and popular influence on U.S. foreign policy, see Miroslav Nincic, *Democracy and Foreign Policy: The Fallacy of Political Realism* (New York: Columbia University Press, 1992).

[15] Frank Ninkovich, *The Wilsonian Century: U.S. Foreign Policy since 1900* (Chicago: University of Chicago Press, 1999), 17–47.

other countries, to promote U.S. exports along with a more fully liberalized regional order. The administration pursued "strategic patience" with North Korea, in an attempt to contain that regime without signing any new agreement that might legitimize Pyongyang's possession of nuclear weapons. It introduced new deployments of U.S. Marines to Australia and littoral combat ships to Singapore. The administration supported humanitarian assistance and disaster relief in the region, notably in 2011 in Japan. It reached out pragmatically to new and potential partners such as Vietnam and Myanmar, while simultaneously trying to nudge those governments in a liberal direction. Washington reiterated its support for traditional U.S. allies such as Japan, South Korea, and the Philippines—and for freedom of navigation in the South and East China Seas. At the same time, it urged all parties in local maritime disputes to reduce tensions and resolve their differences peacefully through the use of impartial multilateral mechanisms.

Conceptually, the rebalance was a sound initiative, as have been many of the specific components listed above. Yet there remain doubts as to whether the rebalance has received adequate follow-through. Words have not always been matched by concrete measures of support. In this sense, aspects of the rebalance, together with its detailed implementation, represent a recognizable case of ambitious liberal internationalist goals, matched and sometimes rendered less effective by the continuing desire for limited liability. For example, under the rebalance, the Obama administration implied a fresh need to provide counterweights against rising Chinese military power around the Asian littoral. Former secretary of defense Leon Panetta indicated that the U.S. Navy would henceforth shift toward the Asia-Pacific. Yet despite the assurance of a bolstered U.S. naval presence, the International Institute for Strategic Studies found the only addition to capacity in East Asia was four littoral combat ships deployed to Singapore, with three amphibious vessels rotated throughout the region and two expeditionary fast transport vessels deployed there.[16] Because of deep overall cuts to the U.S. Navy, a higher percentage of existing vessels deployed to East Asia did not amount to a great increase in actual numbers—only a dramatic decrease in the number of ships deployed to other regions, such as Europe and the Middle East. It seems unlikely that Beijing has not noticed this distinction. In absolute terms, the United States is militarily not much stronger in East Asia than it was a decade ago. Meanwhile, Chinese military expenditures—including naval expenditures—have grown dramatically.

The primary emphasis of President Obama's China policy was engagement. Still, pronouncements surrounding the rebalance need to

---

[16] International Institute for Strategic Studies, *The Military Balance 2016* (London: Routledge, 2016), 27–33, 38–52, 210–17.

be backed with credible material commitments, precisely to avoid any misunderstanding that might permit military escalation in a crisis situation. If the United States gives indications of profound ambivalence toward its own allies, this could, for example, lead to dangerous misperceptions whereby Beijing thinks that Washington will never act forcefully on behalf of those allies when in fact it will. Nor have repeated budgetary crises and threatened government shutdowns reassured friendly Asian powers of U.S. capacity to remain a stabilizing force within the region. To some extent, the consequent gap between forward capabilities and stated commitments has resulted from specific presidential decisions. But to be fair, this ends-means gap, as we have seen, is historically a bipartisan pattern with deep roots in U.S. strategic culture, and recent Congresses have certainly played a role in encouraging that gap as well.

Several of Obama's key foreign policy decisions in Europe and the Middle East have not gone unnoticed by both allies and competitors within the Asia-Pacific. The president repeatedly declared his goal of "ending wars," especially those in Iraq and Afghanistan, which were inherited from the previous administration. His stated view is as follows:

> There's a playbook in Washington that presidents are supposed to follow. It's a playbook that comes out of the foreign policy establishment. And the playbook prescribes responses to different events, and these responses tend to be militarized responses. Where America is directly threatened, the playbook works. But the playbook can also be a trap that leads to bad decisions.[17]

There is no doubt that Obama is committed to a liberal vision of world affairs. He did not scale back the U.S. military presence overseas to the extent that some of his supporters would have liked. But at heart he is an exemplarist who believes that the United States should focus on nation-building at home. So even when intervening in or speaking out on dangerous developments overseas, in cases such as Libya, Syria, or Ukraine, he took the principle of limited liability very seriously. Indeed, one of the most plausible criticisms of Obama's foreign policy was that he frequently combined liberal internationalist rhetoric with limited liability operationally in a way that undermined the credibility of his own statements. Still, Obama's critics were never able to agree on a single alternative to his preferred approach. Some argued for a more muscular reaffirmation of liberal foreign policy goals, with less emphasis on limited liability. Others argued for a stricter emphasis on the United States as a moral exemplar rather than an interventionist or a crusader. Still others drew on dissident strains in U.S. strategic culture to fashion new critiques and new appeals: nationalist, realist,

---

[17] Jeffrey Goldberg, "The Obama Doctrine," interview with Barack Obama, *Atlantic*, April 2016.

and progressive. At least in the case of progressives, one suspects that Obama himself had considerable sympathy for the critique.[18]

Dissident Strains: Nationalism, Progressivism, Realism

If classical liberal assumptions constrained by limited liability have informed the United States' dominant strategic culture, there have nevertheless been dissident strategic cultures or subcultures, operating sometimes in combination with the dominant one and sometimes against it. These strategic cultures can be classified into three types: nationalist, progressive, and realist.

Nationalists

Nationalists take for granted the superiority of the U.S. model but do not define their foreign policy goal as either the promotion or example of liberty. They do take the principle of limited liability very seriously. But for nationalists, an exceptional America is unusually great and unusually strong, rather than exceptional in terms of adherence to classical liberal ideals when it comes to foreign policy. Today's nationalists tend to be conservative rather than left of center. They are a part of what Walter Russell Mead calls the United States' Jacksonian tradition.[19] This tradition, dating back to President Andrew Jackson in the early nineteenth century, has its geographic and demographic base in the nation's heartland, especially in the south and interior west but also among rural white voters and working-class conservatives nationwide. After September 11, many conservative nationalists were entirely on board for the war on terrorism announced by President Bush. In the Obama era, they grew much more skeptical about the benefits of well-intended democracy-promotion efforts in the Middle East. Starting in 2009, the Tea Party's connection to conservative nationalism became especially noteworthy. Tea Party supporters were much more likely than either Democrats or mainstream Republicans to agree with the statement that the "best way to ensure peace is through military strength."[20] They were particularly likely to favor punishing China over international economic disputes. Although most Tea Party supporters actually expressed limited objections to the military component of the United States' presence

---

[18] For a fuller discussion, see Colin Dueck, *The Obama Doctrine: American Grand Strategy Today* (New York: Oxford University Press, 2015).

[19] Walter Russell Mead, *Special Providence: American Foreign Policy and How It Changed the World* (New York: Knopf, 2001), chap. 7.

[20] Pew Research Center, "Strong on Defense and Israel, Tough on China: Tea Party and Foreign Policy," October 7, 2011.

overseas, what they opposed was a liberal internationalist agenda, especially as executed by the Obama administration.[21]

Nationalists support a powerful U.S. military, have no trouble believing in concrete threats to U.S. security, and do not object to the use of force against such threats when convinced that it is appropriate. At the same time, nationalists view multiple aspects of the liberal foreign policy tradition—including foreign economic aid, nation-building, diplomatic accommodation, humanitarian intervention, and greater multilateral organization—as naive, wasteful, unlikely to earn foreign gratitude, and threatening to U.S. national sovereignty. Internationally, they favor sticks, not carrots. This sometimes creates the impression that conservative nationalists are purely isolationist at heart. They are not. Nationalists remain hawkish and hard line on a range of foreign policy and security issues, but they prefer international engagement on their own terms rather than on liberal ones. The United States saw the influence of this nationalist foreign policy strain in the force of Donald Trump's 2016 presidential campaign. As Trump demonstrated, nationalism can easily be combined with a foreign policy posture that is also protectionist on trade and nativist on immigration. Indeed, U.S. nationalists historically have sometimes defined their identity primarily in ethnic or religious terms rather than as a colorblind commitment to the U.S. creed. The late Samuel Huntington once pointed out that the classical liberal creed had its origins in a specific ethno-religious culture—Anglo-Saxon Protestants.[22] This has long created tensions between a civic definition of the nation and a cultural-ethnic one. The Trump campaign veered close to the latter type of ethno-nationalism in both the style and substance of its appeal.

Nationalists look to maintain the United States as a distinctive country. They do not aspire either to transform the world in a classical liberal direction or to see the United States transformed by globalization.[23] They tend to view the international arena as a dangerous place, characterized by genuine threats and resistant to progressive improvement. When they perceive the United States as threatened or under attack, they can be fiercely assertive and unyielding. What all of this means for U.S. foreign policy is that nationalists can move in multiple directions depending on the exact circumstance. The Tea Party's most dramatic symbol—the historic Gadsden flag from the American Revolution with its coiled snake on a yellow background declaring "Don't tread on me"—illustrates these differences quite vividly. The snake's

---

[21] Brian Rathbun, "Steeped in International Affairs? The Foreign Policy Views of the Tea Party," *Foreign Policy Analysis* 9, no. 1 (2013): 21–37.

[22] Samuel P. Huntington, *Who Are We? The Challenges to America's National Identity* (New York: Simon and Schuster, 2004), 37–62.

[23] Ibid., 362–66.

belligerent declaration can be taken as a preference for nonintervention, if possible. It can also be taken as a refusal to retreat or as a warning of combat if challenged. That is exactly the combination of foreign policy instincts embraced by U.S. nationalists to this day, and it continues to have a powerful impact on foreign policy regardless of the president.

Progressives

Progressives support the promotion of liberal goals overseas, such as democracy and human rights, but they generally oppose U.S. military intervention and are skeptical of traditional claims regarding exceptionalism. This strain of thinking has a long history, dating back at least as far as the early twentieth century. The progressive strain went into hibernation during the height of the Cold War but resurfaced strongly once U.S. support for South Vietnam turned sour. Reformulated by the New Left movement, 1960s progressives argued that U.S. foreign policy and the domestic socioeconomic order were both fundamentally unjust. In 1972, antiwar progressives were able to secure the nomination of their preferred candidate, Senator George McGovern, for president, highlighting the rise of a new post–Cold War foreign policy strain among Democrats. Progressives at that time argued for a reorientation of U.S. foreign policy away from anti-Soviet military programs, toward North-South issues, diplomatic accommodation of erstwhile adversaries, and humanitarian and environmental concerns.[24] Because the Cold War had not yet ended, the emergence of this progressive foreign policy subculture turned out to be premature. Even the disappearance of the Soviet Union in 1991 left Democrats torn between a demilitarized security strategy and a more muscular expansionist one. President Bill Clinton's foreign policies were informed by this ambivalence. But the 2003 war in Iraq under Bush eventually clarified a new foreign policy consensus in the Democratic Party. With the eventual collapse of support for that war, progressives argued that the moment had finally come for rearranging U.S. foreign policy under Obama.

A powerful suspicion of U.S. military intervention leaves foreign policy progressives arguing that the United States should be an example rather than a crusader overseas. Contemporary progressives also place tremendous emphasis on the importance of multilateral institutions and the need to work through them peacefully. What makes modern progressives distinct from traditional U.S. foreign policy exemplarists, however, is the former's deep unease over notions of American exceptionalism. Traditionally, exemplarists argued that the United States should stay out of military entanglement abroad

---

[24] Ole R. Holsti and James Rosenau, *American Leadership in World Affairs: Vietnam and the Breakdown of Consensus* (Boston: Allen and Unwin, 1982), 108–33.

because it might sully the United States' classical liberal experiment in limited government. Modern progressives, especially since the 1960s, have been at least as likely to argue that the United States should stay out of foreign military entanglements to avoid sullying other countries. There is indeed a left-liberal patriotic idealism at work in this tradition, but it is based on a social democratic vision of what the United States could be rather than on what it has been in the past.[25]

During the Obama years, Democrats, including the president, continued to wrestle with tensions between progressive foreign policy preferences and more traditional expansionist and internationalist ones. Public opinion polls revealed a Democratic Party with serious internal divisions over basic questions of defense spending, military intervention, free trade, drone strikes, counterterrorism, and diplomacy with Iran.[26] But because most Democrats supported Obama and his overall policy agenda, he tended to gather support from them for his handling of foreign policy. By 2016, there was clearly a constituency within the Democratic Party ready to push for more progressive foreign policy preferences, which was seen in the presidential campaign of Senator Sanders, a onetime independent and a democratic socialist.[27]

Realists

U.S. foreign policy officials are quite capable of flexibly promoting their country's interests within an overarching liberal conceptual framework. But inside the United States, realism as a self-conscious foreign policy tradition has usually been a secondary or dissident rather than dominant school of thought. Realist theories certainly help explain a considerable amount of U.S. foreign policy behavior, even though some academic versions of realism have a blind spot regarding the real-world importance of culture, ideology, regime type, and leadership personality. Still, explaining foreign policy is different from influencing it.

Realists emphasize the international balance of power, the careful coordination of force and diplomacy, and the foreign rather than domestic behavior of other nation-states. They caution against strategic overextension disconnected from geopolitical conditions. At the same time, prominent U.S. foreign policy realists such as Henry Kissinger have traditionally warned that diplomacy must be backed by force, that strategic competition between

---

[25] Martha Nussbaum, *For Love of Country: Debating the Limits of Patriotism* (Boston: Beacon Press, 1996).

[26] For more on these divisions, see Pew Research Center, "Public Uncertain, Divided over America's Place in the World," April 2016.

[27] Molly O'Toole, "Sanders May Have Lost the Primary, but He's Already Won Key Concessions on Foreign Policy," *Foreign Policy*, June 15, 2016.

major powers is historically normal and will continue, and that military instruments are by no means outmoded as a central tool of world politics. Realist foreign policy recommendations, therefore, tend to look different from classically liberal ones. Rather than relying heavily on the promotion of global governance, international law, multilateral institutions, economic interdependence, democracy, or human rights, realists usually focus on the workmanlike manipulation of perennial forces to promote achievable national interests, including a peaceful and favorable balance of power overseas. These perennial forces and techniques include concrete military and economic rewards as well as punishments—or sticks and carrots in more prosaic terms—to give diplomatic injunctions real bite.

The classical realist authors of the 1940s, such as George Kennan and Hans Morgenthau, understood that strategic culture can have a profound impact on the behavior of nations. Indeed, in the case of the United States, these same realists pointed to the impact of liberal idealism precisely in order to criticize its effect on U.S. foreign policy.[28] Contemporary realism, on the other hand—also known as structural realism because of its emphasis on the structure of the international system—tends to downplay, ignore, or even deny the influence of nationally distinctive strategic cultures. This sometimes leaves contemporary realists in the awkward position of decrying the impact of liberal idealism while at the same time denying its influence.[29]

As a matter of prescription, foreign policy realists are skeptical of classically liberal transformational visions of world politics. For classically liberal Americans, therefore, realism is at best a corrective, not a starting point. Moreover, realism is a mindset with which to approach international challenges, not a particular policy or strategy. Indeed, U.S. foreign policy realists often disagree over specifics. They even differ over basic questions such as whether to retain U.S. forward presence overseas or move offshore strategically.[30] It is worth noting that numerous U.S. foreign policy leaders commonly identified as realists, such as President George H.W. Bush, have typically shared a measured commitment to broad liberal goals in world politics—namely, the promotion of democracy and a more open international economic order. This is what makes them U.S. realists rather than unmitigated advocates of realpolitik.[31] One major weakness of pure foreign policy realism,

---

[28] Kennan, *American Diplomacy*, 65–90; and Hans J. Morgenthau, *Politics among Nations: The Struggle for Power and Peace* (New York: McGraw-Hill, 1993), 148, 155–64.

[29] John J. Mearsheimer, *The Tragedy of Great Power Politics* (New York: W.W. Norton, 2014), 22–27.

[30] For more on these differences, compare Stephen G. Brooks and William C. Wohlforth, *America Abroad: The United States' Global Role in the 21st Century* (New York: Oxford University Press, 2016), with John J. Mearsheimer, "Imperial by Design," *National Interest*, January/February 2011, 16–34.

[31] Mead, *Special Providence*, 127.

in political terms, is its uneasy fit with the United States' classical liberal political culture, especially at the elite level. This was certainly a problem for the Nixon-Ford-Kissinger approach by 1976. Yet there have been numerous articulate and influential foreign policy realists in U.S. diplomatic history, and realist-like assumptions have often produced more of an impact than one would think from the public pronouncements of U.S. leaders. Finally, the general public is closer to realism in its foreign policy assumptions than is commonly believed. Most Americans, for example, consistently rank the prevention of terrorism and nuclear proliferation as significantly higher priorities than the promotion of democracy overseas. The general U.S. public appreciates and rewards practical success in foreign affairs and is less messianic or moralistic in this regard than is often suggested.[32]

Cyclical Foreign Policy Debates

During the 2016 election season, the United States' post–World War II elite internationalist consensus came under unprecedented assault from populist presidential candidates on both the left and right. On the left, progressive Bernie Sanders challenged the more established, muscular form of Democratic internationalism represented by former secretary of state Hillary Clinton. Clinton's candidacy and her foreign policy platform held, but only after a strong tug in a progressive direction. On the right, nationalist Donald Trump challenged orthodox forms of Republican internationalism represented by candidates such as Marco Rubio, John Kasich, and Jeb Bush. Senator Ted Cruz attempted to navigate intra-Republican differences between the party's nationalists and internationalists. Trump's success in the Republican primaries shook the party to its foundations, shattering prior expectations and leaving the Republican commitment to traditional postwar internationalism very much in doubt.

There seems to be a historical pattern of cyclical upswings and downswings in the public's support for U.S. foreign policy activism. These shifts in opinion are usually based on real-world experiences and are not necessarily irrational. In the wake of World War I, for example, the general public had no interest in repeating that particular wartime experience. After World War II, the public was much more willing for the United States to remain engaged internationally, especially given the perceived looming threat from the Soviet Union. During the mid-1970s, after the U.S. exit from Vietnam, public opinion shied away from any similar interventions and

---

[32] Daniel Drezner, "The Realist Tradition in American Public Opinion," *Perspectives on Politics* 6, no. 1 (2008): 51–70.

indeed from foreign policy concerns altogether. By 1980, following the Soviet invasion of Afghanistan, the public was once again ready to countenance a tougher national security stance. After the fall of the Soviet Union, the general public viewed foreign policy as a low priority. Following the terrorist attacks of September 11, much of the public was ready to support military action overseas. By 2008, after several years of combat in Iraq and Afghanistan, the popular mood had shifted once again in an antiwar direction. None of these shifts in popular feeling were unreasonable per se. They did, however, create the domestic political context within which presidents might either resist or support more assertive foreign policy strategies.[33]

During the Obama era, popular opinion on foreign policy issues was mixed and largely downbeat: the public was tired of the recent war efforts, focused on domestic economic concerns, and generally averse to new military intervention overseas.[34] In other words, the United States was in the midst of a significant downswing within another cycle of public opinion against strategic activism. This downswing actually began during President Bush's second term, in response to frustrations in Iraq, then accelerated under President Obama. A 2014 Pew Research Center poll found that 60% of Americans wanted the United States to "concentrate on problems here at home" rather than "be active in world affairs."[35] Public awareness of budgetary constraints only reinforced such feelings. Overall, the popular preference was for a lighter international footprint than the United States had exercised a decade earlier.

Any inference, however, that the American public suddenly embraced isolationism during the Obama era needs to be sharply qualified. On a range of specific issues, majorities of the general public remained willing to support key components of international engagement, including militarily. For example, in 2015, some 58% of Americans supported the use of drone strikes against suspected terrorists, while only 35% opposed such actions.[36] An overwhelming majority also supported U.S. airstrikes against the Islamic State of Iraq and Syria (ISIS) by September 2014.[37] On defense spending, Gallup found in 2013 that only 36% felt that the United States spent too much

---

[33] For a cogent survey of cyclical U.S. foreign policy swings between activism and retrenchment since World War II, see Stephen Sestanovich, *Maximalist: America in the World from Truman to Obama* (New York: Vintage, 2014).

[34] For more on recent public perception on foreign policy, see Andrew Kohut, "American International Engagement on the Rocks," Pew Research Center, July 11, 2013.

[35] Pew Research Center, "Beyond Red vs. Blue: The Political Typology," June 2014, 61.

[36] The remainder said they had no opinion. See Pew Research Center, "Public Continues to Back U.S. Drone Attacks," May 2015.

[37] Dan Balz and Peyton Craighill, "Poll: Public Supports Strikes in Iraq, Syria," *Washington Post*, September 9, 2014.

on national defense.[38] On the issue of Sino-U.S. relations, the general public was, if anything, more worried about the rise of Chinese power—especially economically—than were most U.S. foreign policy elites.[39] Over 50% of Americans still agreed that it was important for the United States to remain the world's most influential country as well as its leading military power.[40] So it was not as though the public was demanding a systematic end to the United States' role in the world. Indeed, by the end of 2013, considerably more Americans felt that the Obama administration was too cautious in response to possible foreign threats.[41] Popular feeling regarding U.S. international commitments was therefore more mixed, ambivalent, and sometimes even hawkish, depending on the precise issue and how it was framed.

During her campaign, Hillary Clinton pledged to maintain broad continuities with the Obama legacy while making tactical adjustments in favor of military deterrence and international engagement. Clinton was a loyal secretary of state to Obama, but her own foreign policy instincts have generally been more interventionist than his. In many of the administration's internal debates between 2009 and 2013—over Afghanistan, Libya, Syria, the Osama bin Laden operation, and diplomacy with Iran—Clinton tended to look more favorably on U.S. military engagement than some in Obama's inner circle, for reasons both strategic and humanitarian.[42] She is a mainstream liberal internationalist who believes in the power of multilateral organizations to help solve global collective action problems. As secretary of state, Clinton championed the Obama administration's rebalance toward the Asia-Pacific, and her presidential campaign continued to stress the importance of strengthened ties with traditional allies, engagement with Beijing, and a bolstered U.S. deterrent posture. Clinton also emphasized the need to promote human rights and democracy, though the relative operational impact of these issues will be determined case by case.

At the same time, any radical overhaul of the Obama foreign policy legacy seems unlikely. For one thing, Clinton helped contribute to that legacy, and she states no disagreement with its essentials. Moreover, she represents roughly the same broad domestic coalition as Obama, including a progressive wing within the Democratic Party that is unenamored of military intervention

---

[38] Jeffrey M. Jones, "Americans Divided in Views of U.S. Defense Spending," Gallup, February 21, 2013.

[39] Pew Research Center, "U.S. Public, Experts Differ on China Policies: Public Deeply Concerned about China's Economic Power," September 18, 2012.

[40] "Survey on Foreign Policy and American Overseas Commitments," YouGov, April 26–May 2, 2012.

[41] Pew Research Center, "America's Place in the World 2013," December 2013.

[42] Mark Landler, *Alter Egos: Hillary Clinton, Barack Obama, and the Twilight Struggle over American Power* (New York: Random House, 2016). For Clinton's own perspective on several of these decisions, see Hillary Clinton, *Hard Choices* (New York: Simon and Schuster, 2014), chap. 7, 16, 18–19, and 24.

and resistant to new free trade agreements.[43] On this last point, as of summer 2016, the fate of the TPP remained a wild card. Clinton helped negotiate the agreement as secretary of state, but under pressure during the presidential primary, she declared that the TPP no longer met the "gold standard."[44]

To a greater extent than Obama, Clinton leans toward the expansionist strain within U.S. liberal foreign policy thinking rather than the exemplarist one. But she combines that leaning with an incrementalist decision-making style at the head of a coalition that includes antiwar progressives along with traditional internationalists.

Donald Trump's foreign policy priorities are considerably more difficult to predict, partly because of his unorthodox posture and partly because he favors unpredictability as a virtue. Many observers in Washington and abroad suggested, or at least hoped, that his presidential campaign would be greatly shaped and constrained by Republican Party leaders and advisers in making such decisions. But it is worth keeping in mind that individual presidents have remarkable leeway in setting foreign policy agendas according to their own specific preferences. Furthermore, Trump won his party's nomination in 2016 precisely by running against the Republican establishment, and there is little evidence from his behavior through summer 2016 to suggest that he would suddenly feel deferential to established Republican foreign policy traditions. During his campaign, Trump announced his support for the mass deportation of illegal immigrants, a temporary ban on all Muslims entering the United States, and the construction of a border security wall with Mexico. He also called for punitive tariffs against Chinese imports in the absence of unspecified concessions from Beijing. These proposals were extremely controversial yet central to his candidacy. Trump stated his belief that NATO is obsolete and that both Japan and South Korea should consider acquiring nuclear weapons.[45] He favored improved relations with Vladimir Putin's Russia, declared U.S. intervention in both Libya and Iraq to be mistaken, and announced his opposition to "the nation-building business."[46] Some of these policy positions were new departures for Trump, but others were not. Over a period going back several decades, he has reiterated his belief that U.S. allies do not pay nearly enough for their own defense, that the United States should avoid intervention in what Trump considers peripheral cases, that free trade

---

[43] For evidence of foreign policy differences between supporters of Clinton and supporters of Sanders, see Pew Research Center, "Public Uncertain, Divided over America's Place in the World."

[44] Jake Tapper, "45 Times Secretary Clinton Pushed the Trade Bill She Now Opposes," CNN, June 15, 2015.

[45] Philip Rucker and Robert Costa, "Trump Questions Need for NATO, Outlines Noninterventionist Foreign Policy," *Washington Post*, March 21, 2016.

[46] Donald J. Trump, "Trump on Foreign Policy" (speech delivered at an event hosted by the *National Interest*, Washington, D.C., April 27, 2016).

agreements such as the North American Free Trade Agreement (NAFTA) and the TPP are harmful to the U.S. economy, and that U.S. "generosity" leads to "very poor deal-making" internationally.[47]

These positions obviously have some appeal to sections of U.S. public opinion. Overall, Trump is very much an example of the nationalist strain of U.S. strategic culture rather than the internationalist one. He places great emphasis on limited liability and virtually none on the promotion of a liberal international order, or what he calls "the false song of globalism."[48] He even employs the catchphrase used by Charles Lindbergh and other noninterventionists in 1940: "America first."[49] At the same time, there is little doubt that Trump would favor increased U.S. defense spending together with some aggressive, high-risk actions against jihadist terrorists. No president ends up enacting precisely the foreign policy they initially expect; events intervene. Yet each president leaves a distinct stamp on U.S. international relations. Observers would therefore be wise to take seriously Trump's stated goal of implementing a dramatic overhaul of traditional U.S. foreign, defense, trade, and immigration policies.

Conclusion

U.S. foreign policy officials have never supported a liberal international order simply out of altruism. They have done so out of the belief that such an order would promote U.S. interests, by making the nation more prosperous, influential, and secure. The problem with the liberal approach has been that it tends to encourage highly ambitious goals and commitments abroad, while assuming that these goals can be met without commensurate cost or expenditure on the part of the United States. That is, liberal internationalists tend to define U.S. interests in broad, expansive, and idealistic terms without always admitting the necessary costs and risks of such an expansive vision. The result is that sweeping and ambitious goals are announced but then pursued by disproportionately limited means. Indeed, this disjuncture between ends and means has been so common in U.S. diplomacy that it seems to be a direct consequence of the nation's distinctly liberal approach to international affairs.[50] Americans have often been interventionists or crusaders in pursuit of a more liberal international order. But they have also frequently been reluctant to admit the full costs of promoting this liberal vision. These two strains

---

[47] Donald J. Trump, *The America We Deserve* (New York: Macmillan, 2000).

[48] Trump, "Trump on Foreign Policy."

[49] Ibid.

[50] Lippmann, *U.S. Foreign Policy*, 3–77.

in U.S. strategic culture—liberal goals and limited liability—have not only operated cyclically; they have operated simultaneously. In this sense, the history of U.S. foreign policy is truly a history of reluctant interventionists.[51]

These aspects of U.S. strategic culture hold significant implications both for security competition within the Asia-Pacific and for U.S. interests in the region. During his first term in the White House, Obama announced a pivot or rebalance of U.S. foreign policy toward Asia. Yet even as Washington declared a renewed interest in the region, it cut the size of the U.S. Navy, arguably the armed service most responsible for giving the pivot teeth in that part of the world. Serious questions have been raised regarding the constancy of U.S. regional commitments. There is an unmistakable impression overseas that the United States is to some extent disengaging from its traditional forward role.[52]

Today, orthodox liberal internationalism is under severe strain not only abroad but within the United States. Dissident strategic subcultures—including nationalism, progressivism, and realism—are gaining a new hearing in the United States partly because of these strains. During the 2016 presidential campaign, both progressives on the left and nationalists on the right questioned many of the premises of U.S. global leadership, including a measured commitment to free trade, globalization, and multiple strategic commitments abroad. In the case of the Democratic Party, Bernie Sanders made a remarkably strong showing and pulled the party in his direction on issues such as the TPP. In the case of the Republican Party, nationalist Donald Trump captured his party's nomination, leaving long-standing Republican traditions in doubt.

U.S. foreign policy is often more continuous than controversies during election years might indicate, especially in the Asia-Pacific. Still, individual presidents do make a significant difference, and in 2016 Republican Party nominee Trump stated clearly his desire for dramatic changes in long-standing U.S. policies. Overall, it is fair to say that traditional U.S. allies in the region are concerned by the prospect of a more detached U.S. presence overseas.[53] The governments of Russia and North Korea, by contrast, were intrigued by Trump perhaps for the same reason.[54] China, interestingly, also

---

[51] On this and previous paragraphs, see Colin Dueck, *Reluctant Crusaders: Power, Culture, and Change in American Grand Strategy* (Princeton: Princeton University Press, 2006).

[52] See, for example, Jakub J. Grygiel and A. Wess Mitchell, *The Unquiet Frontier: Rising Rivals, Vulnerable Allies, and the Crisis of American Power* (Princeton: Princeton University Press, 2016); Kenneth M. Pollack, "Fight or Flight: America's Choice in the Middle East," *Foreign Affairs*, March/April 2016, 62–75; and Leon Whyte, "Evolution of the U.S.-ROK Alliance: Abandonment Fears," *Diplomat*, June 22, 2015.

[53] Julie Makinen, "President Trump? Among U.S. Allies, Japan May Be One of the Most Anxious about That Idea," *Los Angeles Times*, June 26, 2016.

[54] J.H. Ahn, "North Korea Praises Trump and Urges U.S. Voters to Reject 'Dull Hillary,'" *Guardian*, June 1, 2016.

appeared interested in the Republican nominee's penchant for deal-making and tendency to play down issues of human rights. Yet it seems unlikely that Beijing would stand idly by if the United States were to implement protective tariffs against China.

Regional perceptions of a Hillary Clinton administration were almost exactly the reverse. Both allies and competitors within the Asia-Pacific viewed Clinton as far more of a known quantity—a conventional liberal internationalist, albeit a little more expansionist or hawkish than Obama. U.S. allies in the region found this reassuring, while U.S. competitors did not. The fate of the TPP remained a wild card, given that both candidates campaigned against it.

All things considered, the popular mood within the United States today is not so much isolationist as it is mixed and ambivalent regarding U.S. international commitments. Over the past decade, there has been a clear downswing in popular support for international engagement. This is entirely in keeping with similar periods in the past following U.S. military frustrations overseas. Looking forward, the United States will need to understand its relationship with China, in particular, as a long-term strategic competition that also includes cooperative elements. This understanding is not easy for a nation with a classically liberal political culture. China's rise will therefore pose a continuing challenge to U.S. statecraft, not only materially but also intellectually. As the United States enters 2017, a recalibration of its China policy in the direction of reassuring traditional allies, bolstering deterrence, and balancing more effectively is in order. The United States possesses a wide range of counterbalancing policy tools should it choose to use them.[55]

---

[55] Dennis Blair, "The United States: A Strong Foundation but Weak Blueprint for National Security," in *Strategic Asia 2015–16: Foundations of National Power in the Asia-Pacific*, ed. Ashley J. Tellis with Alison Szalwinski and Michael Wills (Seattle: National Bureau of Asian Research, 2015), 225–58; Aaron Friedberg, "The Debate over U.S. China Strategy," *Survival* 57, no. 3 (2015): 89–110; and Ashley J. Tellis, "Balancing without Containment: A U.S. Strategy for Confronting China's Rise," *Washington Quarterly* 36, no. 4 (2013): 109–24.

About the Contributors

Jiun Bang is a Postdoctoral Fellow at the University of Michigan. Her doctoral project examined the business of nationalism and explained how various actors within the nation-state (central government, subnational actors, commercial businesses, and entrepreneurs) package and sell nationalism. Dr. Bang's research interests include international relations theory, security, and Northeast Asia. She has published articles on Korea-related issues as well as on international relations and nationalism in East Asia. From 2008 to 2010, she was an associate at the Korea Institute for Defense Analyses, a government-affiliated research institute in Seoul. During that time, she was the assistant editor of the *Korean Journal of Defense Analysis*. She received her PhD from the University of Southern California, an MA in security studies from Georgetown University, and a BA in international relations from Ewha Womans University in Seoul, her hometown.

Alexis Dudden is a Professor of History at the University of Connecticut. Her work focuses on Northeast Asia's modern history through the legacies of the Japanese empire. Dr. Dudden's first book, *Japan's Colonization of Korea: Discourse and Power* (2005), examines Japanese efforts in the late nineteenth century to legitimate the nation's imperial project on the world stage through the takeover of Korea. *Troubled Apologies among Japan, Korea, and the United States* (2008) moves into the postcolonial and postwar era by interrogating mechanisms intended to settle imperial and wartime histories that instead created a political and social dynamic of coordinated remembering and intentional forgetting that defines the possibilities for regional interaction. Dr. Dudden is an editorial board member of the *Asia-Pacific Journal: Japan Focus* and is the recipient of Fulbright and ACLS fellowships. Her current work, *Islands, Empire, Nation: A History of Modern Japan* (forthcoming), analyzes Japan's contemporary territorial disputes through the changing meaning of islands broadly defined. Dr. Dudden received her PhD in history from the University of Chicago.

Colin Dueck is a Professor in the Schar School of Policy and Government at George Mason University. He studied politics at Princeton University and international relations at Oxford University under a Rhodes scholarship. Dr. Dueck has published three books on American foreign and national security policies: *The Obama Doctrine: American Grand Strategy Today* (2015), *Hard Line: The Republican Party and U.S. Foreign Policy since World War II* (2010), and *Reluctant Crusaders: Power, Culture, and Change in American Grand Strategy* (2006). He has also published articles on these subjects in *International Security, Orbis, Security Studies, Review of International Studies, Political Science Quarterly, Foreign Affairs*, the *National Interest*, and the *New York Times*. His current research focuses on the relationship between party politics, presidential leadership, American conservatism, and U.S. foreign policy strategies. He is the faculty adviser for the Alexander Hamilton Society at George Mason University and a member of the International Institute for Strategic Studies.

Richard J. Ellings is President and Co-founder of the National Bureau of Asian Research (NBR). He is also Affiliate Professor of International Studies in the Henry M. Jackson School of International Studies at the University of Washington. Dr. Ellings is the author of *Embargoes and World Power: Lessons from American Foreign Policy* (1985); co-author of *Private Property and National Security* (1991); co-editor (with Aaron Friedberg) of *Strategic Asia 2003–04: Fragility and Crisis* (2003), *Strategic Asia 2002–03: Asian Aftershocks* (2002), and *Strategic Asia 2001–02: Power and Purpose* (2001); co-editor of *Korea's Future and the Great Powers* (with Nicholas Eberstadt, 2001) and *Southeast Asian Security in the New Millennium* (with Sheldon Simon, 1996); founding editor of the *NBR Analysis* publication series; and co-chairman of the *Asia Policy* editorial board. Previously, Dr. Ellings served as legislative assistant in the U.S. Senate, office of Senator Slade Gorton. He earned his BA in political science from the University of California–Berkley and his MA and PhD in political science from the University of Washington.

Isabelle Facon is a Senior Research Fellow at the Paris-based think tank Fondation pour la recherche stratégique. She is a specialist on Russian security and defense policies and works extensively on Russian military affairs, the military reform process, and defense industry issues. She has also devoted research to the study of Russia's foreign policy. Dr. Facon spent her academic years at Université Paris IV-Sorbonne and was an associate member of Saint Antony's College (1993–94). Since 2008, she has been an Associate Professor at Ecole polytechnique, where she teaches the

Geopolitics of Eurasia seminar. She is a member of the editorial board of the French monthly *Revue de Défense Nationale* and of the scientific council of the online review *Journal of Power Institutions in Post-Soviet Societies.* Dr. Facon was awarded the cross of Chevalier de l'Ordre national du Mérite.

Christopher A. Ford is Chief Legislative Counsel for the U.S. Senate Foreign Relations Committee. He is a former senior fellow at Hudson Institute and previously served as U.S. special representative for nuclear nonproliferation and as a principal deputy assistant secretary of state. He has also served as the senior Republican lawyer on the Senate Appropriations Committee and the Senate Select Committee on Intelligence, chief investigative counsel for the Senate Banking Committee, and staff director for the Senate's Permanent Subcommittee on Investigations. A former reserve intelligence officer in the U.S. Navy, Dr. Ford has written extensively on China, including the books *The Mind of Empire: China's History and Modern Foreign Relations* (2010) and *China Looks at the West: Identity, Global Ambitions, and the Future of Sino-American Relations* (2015). Dr. Ford received his undergraduate degree *summa cum laude* from Harvard; holds a DPhil in international relations from Oxford University, where he was a Rhodes Scholar; and received his JD from Yale Law School, where he received the Sharps and Emerson prizes.

Ian Hall is a Professor of International Relations at Griffith University in Brisbane, Australia, and the Acting Director of the Griffith Asia Institute. He has authored and edited a number of books on Indian foreign policy and the history of international thought, including *The Engagement of India: Strategies and Responses* (2014) and *Dilemmas of Decline: British Intellectuals and World Politics, 1945–1975* (2012). Dr. Hall's articles have appeared in various journals, including *Asian Security, Asian Survey, European Journal of International Relations, International Affairs,* and the *Nonproliferation Review.* He is currently working on an Australian Research Council–funded project (2015–17) on the evolution of Indian thinking about world politics. He holds a PhD in international relations from the University of St. Andrews.

David C. Kang is Professor of International Relations and Business at the University of Southern California (USC), with appointments in both the School of International Relations and the Marshall School of Business. At USC, he is also Director of the Korean Studies Institute and the Center for International Studies. Dr. Kang's latest book is *East Asia Before the West: Five Centuries of Trade and Tribute* (2010). He is also the author of *China Rising: Peace, Power, and Order in East Asia* (2007), *Nuclear North Korea: A Debate on Engagement Strategies* (co-authored with Victor Cha, 2003), and *Crony Capitalism: Corruption and Development in South Korea and the Philippines* (2002). Dr. Kang has published numerous scholarly articles in journals such as *International Organization* and *International Security*. He has also written opinion pieces in the *New York Times*, the *Financial Times*, the *Washington Post*, and the *Los Angeles Times*, as well as writing a monthly column for the *Joongang Ilbo* in Korean. He received an AB with honors from Stanford University and his PhD from the University of California–Berkeley.

Yohanes Sulaiman is a Lecturer in the School of Government at the Universitas Jenderal Achmad Yani in Cimahi, Indonesia. He is also a Visiting Lecturer at the Indonesian Defense University, Indonesian Army Staff and Command School, Indonesian Air Force Staff and Command School, and Indonesian Military Staff and Command School. Dr. Sulaiman previously served as a consultant in the Coordinating Ministry for Political, Legal, and Security Affairs of Indonesia. His research interests include the diplomatic history, international security, and politics of East and Southeast Asia; terrorism; and civil-military relations. He earned his BA in international relations and political science from the University of Wisconsin–Madison and his MA and PhD in political science from the Ohio State University.

Alison Szalwinski is an Assistant Director for Political and Security Affairs at the National Bureau of Asian Research (NBR), where she manages and contributes to the Strategic Asia Program, the Pacific Trilateralism project, and the Space, Cyberspace, and Strategic Stability project. Prior to joining NBR, Ms. Szalwinski worked at the U.S. Department of State and the Center for Strategic and International Studies (CSIS). Her research interests include regional security dynamics in Northeast Asia and U.S.-China strategic relations. She is co-editor with Ashley J. Tellis and Michael Wills of *Strategic Asia 2015–16: Foundations of National Power*. Ms. Szalwinski has lived and worked as an English teacher in Shenzhen, China, where she also continued her language studies in Mandarin Chinese. She holds a BA in foreign affairs and history from the University of Virginia and an MA in Asian studies from Georgetown University's Edmund A. Walsh School of Foreign Service.

Ashley J. Tellis is a Senior Associate at the Carnegie Endowment for International Peace, specializing in international security, defense, and Asian strategic issues. He is also Research Director of the Strategic Asia Program at the National Bureau of Asian Research and co-editor of thirteen volumes in the annual series. While on assignment to the U.S. Department of State as senior adviser to the undersecretary of state for political affairs (2005–8), Dr. Tellis was intimately involved in negotiating the civil nuclear agreement with India. Previously, he was commissioned into the Foreign Service and served as senior adviser to the ambassador at the U.S. embassy in New Delhi. He also served on the National Security Council staff as special assistant to the president and senior director for strategic planning and Southwest Asia. Prior to his government service, Dr. Tellis was a senior policy analyst at the RAND Corporation and professor of policy analysis at the RAND Graduate School. He is the author of *India's Emerging Nuclear Posture* (2001) and co-author of *Interpreting China's Grand Strategy: Past, Present, and Future* (2000). His academic publications have also appeared in many edited volumes and journals. Dr. Tellis holds a PhD in political science from the University of Chicago.

Michael Wills is Senior Vice President of Strategy and Finance at the National Bureau of Asian Research (NBR). He coordinates all aspects of NBR's financial, business, and programmatic operations and serves as secretary to the Board of Directors. He also manages NBR's publications program, including the *Strategic Asia* series and the *Asia Policy* journal. Mr. Wills was formerly director of NBR's Strategic Asia Program (2001–7) and Southeast Asia Studies Program (2001–6). His research interests include international security and the international relations of Asia, particularly China's relations with Southeast Asia. He is co-editor with Robert M. Hathaway of *New Security Challenges in Asia* (2013) and has co-edited five previous *Strategic Asia* volumes with Ashley J. Tellis—including *Foundations of National Power* (2015), *Domestic Political Change and Grand Strategy* (2007), *Trade, Interdependence, and Security* (2006), *Military Modernization in an Era of Uncertainty* (2005), and *Confronting Terrorism in the Pursuit of Power* (2004). He is a contributing editor to three other *Strategic Asia* books and several other edited volumes. Before joining NBR, Mr. Wills worked at the Cambodia Development Resource Institute in Phnom Penh and with Control Risks Group, an international political and security risk management firm, in London. He holds a BA (Honors) in Chinese studies from the University of Oxford.

About Strategic Asia

The **Strategic Asia Program** at the National Bureau of Asian Research (NBR) is a major ongoing research initiative that draws together top Asia studies specialists and international relations experts to assess the changing strategic environment in the Asia-Pacific. The program combines the rigor of academic research with the practicality of contemporary policy analyses by incorporating economic, military, political, and demographic data and by focusing on the trends, strategies, and perceptions that drive geopolitical dynamics in the region. The program's integrated set of products and activities includes:

- an annual edited volume written by leading specialists
- an executive brief tailored for public- and private-sector decision-makers and strategic planners
- briefings and presentations for government, business, and academe that are designed to foster in-depth discussions revolving around major public-policy issues

Special briefings are held for key committees of Congress and the executive branch, other government agencies, and the intelligence community. The principal audiences for the program's research findings are the U.S. policymaking and research communities, the media, the business community, and academe.

To order a book, please visit the Strategic Asia website at http://www.nbr.org/strategicasia.

Previous Strategic Asia Volumes

Now in its sixteenth year, the *Strategic Asia* series has addressed how Asia functions as a zone of strategic interaction and contends with an uncertain balance of power.

Strategic Asia 2015–16: Foundations of National Power in the Asia-Pacific examined how the region's major powers are building their national power as geopolitical competition intensifies.

Strategic Asia 2014–15: U.S. Alliances and Partnerships at the Center of Global Power analyzed the trajectories of U.S. alliance and partner relationships in the Asia-Pacific in light of the region's shifting strategic landscape.

Strategic Asia 2013–14: Asia in the Second Nuclear Age examined the role of nuclear weapons in the grand strategies of key Asian states and assessed the impact of these capabilities—both established and latent—on regional and international stability.

Strategic Asia 2012–13: China's Military Challenge assessed China's growing military capabilities and explored their impact on the Asia-Pacific region.

Strategic Asia 2011–12: Asia Responds to Its Rising Powers—China and India explored how key Asian states and regions have responded to the rise of China and India, drawing implications for U.S. interests and leadership in the Asia-Pacific.

Strategic Asia 2010–11: Asia's Rising Power and America's Continued Purpose provided a continent-wide net assessment of the core trends and issues affecting the region by examining Asia's performance in nine key functional areas.

Strategic Asia 2009–10: Economic Meltdown and Geopolitical Stability analyzed the impact of the global economic crisis on key Asian states and explored the strategic implications for the United States.

Strategic Asia 2008–09: Challenges and Choices examined the impact of geopolitical developments on Asia's transformation over the previous eight years and assessed the major strategic choices on Asia facing the incoming U.S. administration.

Strategic Asia 2007–08: Domestic Political Change and Grand Strategy examined the impact of internal and external drivers of grand strategy on Asian foreign policymaking.

Strategic Asia 2006–07: Trade, Interdependence, and Security addressed how changing trade relationships affect the balance of power and security in the region.

Strategic Asia 2005–06: Military Modernization in an Era of Uncertainty appraised the progress of Asian military modernization programs.

Strategic Asia 2004–05: Confronting Terrorism in the Pursuit of Power explored the effects of the U.S.-led war on terrorism on the strategic transformations underway in Asia.

Strategic Asia 2003–04: Fragility and Crisis examined the fragile balance of power in Asia, drawing out the key domestic political and economic trends in Asian states supporting or undermining this tenuous equilibrium.

Strategic Asia 2002–03: Asian Aftershocks drew on the baseline established in the 2001–02 volume to analyze changes in Asian states' grand strategies and relationships in the aftermath of the September 11 terrorist attacks.

Strategic Asia 2001–02: Power and Purpose established a baseline assessment for understanding the strategies and interactions of the major states within the region.

Research and Management Team

The Strategic Asia research team consists of leading international relations and security specialists from universities and research institutions across the United States and around the world. A new research team is selected each year. The research team for 2016 is led by Ashley J. Tellis (Carnegie Endowment for International Peace). Aaron Friedberg (Princeton University, and Strategic Asia's founding research director) and Richard Ellings (NBR, and Strategic Asia's founding program director) serve as senior advisers.

The Strategic Asia Program has historically depended on a diverse base of funding from foundations, government, and corporations, supplemented by income from publication sales. Major support for the program in 2016 comes from the Lynde and Harry Bradley Foundation.

Attribution

Readers of *Strategic Asia* may use data, charts, graphs, and quotes from these sources without requesting permission from NBR on the condition that they cite NBR and the appropriate primary source in any published work. No report, chapter, separate study, extensive text, or any other substantial part of the Strategic Asia Program's products may be reproduced without the written permission of NBR. To request permission, please write to:

NBR Publications
The National Bureau of Asian Research
1414 NE 42nd Street, Suite 300
Seattle, Washington 98105
publications@nbr.org

Index